Reed Hundt

IN CHINA'S SHADOW

The Crisis of American Entrepreneurship

YALE UNIVERSITY PRESS / NEW HAVEN & LONDON

The Future of American Democracy series aims to examine, sustain, and renew the historic vision of American democracy in a series of books by some of America's foremost thinkers. The books in the series present a new, balanced, centrist approach to examining the challenges American democracy has faced in the past and must overcome in the years ahead.

Series editor: Norton Garfinkle.

Set in ITC Galliard by Integrated Publishing Solutions, Grand Rapids, Michigan.

Printed in the United States of America by Vail-Ballou Press, Binghamton, New York.

Library of Congress Cataloging-in-Publication Data
Hundt, Reed, E., 1948–
In China's shadow : the crisis of American entrepreneurship / Reed Hundt.
    p. cm.—(The future of American democracy)
Includes bibliographical references and index.
ISBN-13: 978-0-300-10852-1 (cloth : alk. paper)
ISBN-10: 0-300-10852-4 (cloth : alk. paper)
    1. United States—Foreign economic relations—China. 2. China—Foreign economic relations—United States. 3. China—Economic policy—2000– 4. United States—Economic policy—2001–
5. Entrepreneurship—United States. I. Title. II. Series.
HF1456.5.C6H86 2006
337.73051—dc22   2006009941

A catalogue record for this book is available from the British Library.

The paper in this book meets the guidelines for permanence and durability of the Committee on Production Guidelines for Book Longevity of the Council on Library Resources.

10 9 8 7 6 5 4 3 2 1

"Fall of Rome," copyright 1947 by W. H. Auden, from COLLECTED POEMS by W. H. Auden. Used by permission of Random House, Inc.

CONTENTS

Acknowledgments vii

Introduction 1

CHAPTER 1: LOOKING EAST TOWARD THE DAWN 11

Death of a Dream? The Challenge of China 11

    China Is Near 11
    Communist Mercantilism 15
    IT Is It 20

Response Time 24

    The Future Is Now 24
    Some Past Will Be Prologue 27

        America's Historic Culture of Entrepreneurship 27
        The Halcyon Era 34
        In an Uncertain Future 38

CHAPTER 2: THE UPROOTING OF AMERICAN BUSINESS 41

Only World Championships Matter 41

Flying Flags of Convenience 44

Reverse Immigration 47

Fading Friendship 50

CHAPTER 3: THE UP AND DOWN OF ENTREPRENEURIAL CULTURE IN AMERICA 57

Reform's End 57

The Golden Rules of the 1990s 61

Case in Point 61
Andreessen and the Browser 71
Leaders of the Net 76

Bringing Down the House 77
Change and Its Reactionaries 77
Enemies of Reform 80
Feckless Philosophers 83
Limitations of Capitalists 86

CHAPTER 4: HOME IMPROVEMENT: REBUILDING THE ARCHITECTURES OF CULTURE 89

The Laws of Entrepreneurial Encouragement 89
Spend Money to Make Money 90
Teaching Success 92
Antitrust for the Twenty-first Century 95
Growing the Market 98
Hand Up, Not Handout 101
Public Wealth and Private Gain 101
Worth What You Can Borrow 104

All Together Now 105

Principles of Technology Applied to Entrepreneurial Culture 108
Entrepreneurial Leadership 110
Risk-Taking and Risk-Reducing Leaders 110
Virtuous Cycles 114

CHAPTER 5: AMERICA THE HOPEFUL 117

The Power of Ideas 117
The Medium Is the Means 122

Notes 135
Index 187

ACKNOWLEDGMENTS

Although all errors of fact and judgment in this book are my sole responsibility, anything of value in it has antecedents in the questions, suggestions, inspirations, teaching, and friendship of many people over many years. I wish to acknowledge, among the many wise and learned professors in the Yale history department (where as an undergraduate I first became enamored of the pageant of Asian history), Harry Benda, Jonathan Spence, Robin Winks, and Arthur Wright. During my service in the Clinton administration (1993–97), I was privileged to learn about China from, among others, Vice President Al Gore, U.S. Trade Ambassador Charlene Barshefsky, and Peter Cowhey, the current dean of the Graduate School of International Relations and Pacific Studies at the University of California, San Diego, as we negotiated and promulgated—in Tokyo, Kyoto, Beijing, Hong Kong, New Delhi, Singapore, Manila, and Djakarta—the World Trade Organization Telecommunications Treaty of 1997. Of the many extraordinary Chinese business leaders and government officers I have had the pleasure of knowing, I wish to single out for special recognition former Minister of Information Industries Wu Jichuan. As a senior adviser on information industries to McKinsey & Company, I have benefited from the knowledge of many brilliant consultants around the world, but for this book I owe special gratitude to Gordon Orr and Richard Zhang. Dozens of people at Intel Corporation, of which I am a member of the board of directors, have taught me about entrepreneurship and globalization, but Andy Grove and Craig Barrett more than any others challenged me to do the thinking in this book—although I have no idea whether they would agree with my conclusions. Silicon Valley has warmly welcomed me into numerous ventures since I left government in 1997, and many people have contributed to my understanding of entrepreneurship. I particularly thank Benchmark Capital and Greylock Partners for their continued and substantial support of my start-up dreams. In the private equity world, the brilliant Stephen Schwarzman, founder and CEO of the Blackstone Group, has been the best of friends and tutors.

To all of the following I owe profuse thanks for their ideas, editorial advice, and in some cases (as these pages will show) their interview time: Marc Andreessen, Tom Boasberg, Kim Cameron, Steve Case, Tom Craft, Paul de Sa, John Doerr, Jim Fallows, Jeff Garten, Marty Kaplan, Eric Kim, Carlos Kirjner, Greg Lawler, Blair Levin, Stagg Newman, Andy Rachleff, Greg Rosston, Gretchen Rubin, Eric Schmidt, Richard Tedlow, George Vradenberg, Jon Wilkins, Tim Wu, and Bill Young.

I could not have completed this manuscript without the help, over time, of my assistants Katie Kerr, Jennifer Achieng, and Charissa Kersten. My two sons, Adam and Nathaniel, provided blunt and astute comments on the manuscript. The best agent in the book world, Andrew Wylie, was a constant source of encouragement and great advice. No one ever had a better editor than Jonathan Brent, and his colleagues Sarah Miller and Jessie Hunnicutt provided invaluable assistance as well.

From the first outlines of this book, my thought partner, research assistant, and local expert on logic, structure, and diction has been Elizabeth Cavanagh. Her patience, diligence, and astuteness are prodigious. This book could not have been written without her. My gratitude and respect are boundless.

This book is dedicated to my dear wife, Betsy, and written for our three children, Adam, Nathaniel, and Sara, and their generation.

Introduction

Or set upon a golden bough to sing
To lords and ladies of Byzantium
Of what is past, or passing, or to come.
          —WILLIAM BUTLER YEATS, "SAILING TO BYZANTIUM"

Men are we, and must grieve when even the Shade
Of that which once was great is passed away.
          —WILLIAM WORDSWORTH, "ON THE EXTINCTION
          OF THE VENETIAN REPUBLIC"

China challenges the American economy more than any other nation has ever done. Through a unique and oxymoronic combination of communism and capitalism, China is launching millions of firms into global competition with American firms. At the same time, it is putting hundreds of millions of low-paid, increasingly high-skilled people into competition with American workers. If Chinese firms win big shares of most markets and Chinese labor provides much of the goods and services produced by Americans today, then the American Dream of ever-increasing wealth for everyone who works hard will become a forgotten reverie.

Like the movement of tectonic plates, China's impact on the United States reveals itself in occasional business quakes and labor-market shudders, and over time it will realign the relationship of continents. A Chinese computer maker buys its American rival. A batch of Chinese software engineers takes work from an American team. A Chinese search company enjoys a Google-like rocket trip to an astral market capitalization. The Chinese government talks of creating unique standards for technology products and perhaps even a unique national Internet. Most Americans scarcely notice such events. The rest apply an anodyne "free market" philosophy to their discomfort. Nevertheless, the American Dream rests on a fault line created by the emergence of China's firms and citizens into the global economy. In one or two generations, the United States may find that China leads the world economy, and historians then will trace the pattern of causation to actions taken and not taken now, in the first decade of the twenty-first century.

China is becoming the world's center for enthusiastic business creation. It manufactures start-ups. It is fertile ground for entrepreneurship in virtually every market. Already, businesses in China number about 12 million, approximately twice as many as in the United States. Many are very small; perhaps only about three million own a personal computer. But China is one of the fastest growing computer markets in the world, and in less than a decade most of its businesses will do business online. From that point, the step toward participation in global markets is short and inevitable.

The possibility of Chinese global success is rooted in vigorous domestic competition among Chinese entrepreneurs. The Chinese winners bring well-honed efficiency and aggressiveness to competition in America and other foreign markets. Because the Chinese domestic market is so huge—the country is already first among nations in annual purchases of many technology products—winners in that market obtain economies of scale that permit them to offer products at very low prices in export markets.

Instead of organizing Chinese entrepreneurship, the government allies with it. Although the state still owns or controls many businesses, it has little capability to fashion a national business strategy. The Communist Party encourages some favorites and exercises control over such important sectors as media and communications. However, for the most part it has relinquished control over the business sector to regional governments and free-ranging capitalists. For their part, Chinese entrepreneurs neither disrupt nor operate outside governmental authority. They partner with the state, even when they are dismissive of its bureaucracy. They are creating a new hierarchy of wealth cemented with political power. By creating domestic markets in a country where only skimpy economic activity existed when Mao Zedong died in 1976, Chinese entrepreneurs are composing a new domestic order in China. At the same time, they are disrupting the existing global order. An important part of their wealth creation at home comes from their attempt to conquer American firms, take control of American markets, and wrest employment from American workers.

American firms in low-value added markets have long experienced Chinese rivalry, but American high-technology businesses know that Chinese firms are coming after them too. Chinese entrepreneurs are not nearly as well-equipped to compete in high-technology markets.[1] In those markets, the Chinese labor cost advantage is not as important as the sophisticated processes and proprietary techniques of American firms. Nevertheless, bolstered by large government support for technical education, a lawless disregard for intellectual property rights, and a favorable exchange rate, Chinese entrepreneurs are aiming at the single biggest piñata of wealth in the global economy, the American information sector. From 1998 to 2003, the United States captured 98 percent of all global economic growth, netting declining regions like Africa against gaining regions like Southeast Asia.[2] Even though the information sector of the American economy represented less than 10 percent of the whole, it accounted for about a third of the American economic success story in the Golden 90s. It continued to create much new wealth even after the market bust of the early 00s. Little wonder then that Chinese entrepreneurs intend to take a piece of the information sector pie, as well as going after share in the global markets for textiles and toys, cars and carbon. Chapter 1 maps the Chinese challenge to American businesses.

For societies, as for businesses and people, the response to an event determines its significance. Pearl Harbor, Tonkin Gulf, and the World Trade Center prove this point with respect to military matters. None of these attacks doomed the United States. It was in the response that Americans made their destiny. In terms of global trade, the pertinent example is Japan's massive economic assault on the United States in the 1970s and 1980s. In response, American businesspersons, academics, and political leaders of the "competitiveness" school prescribed changes in law and business strategy to meet Japanese competition. The new philosophy led to the balanced budgets of the Clinton administration. It caused many American firms to revise their inventory and supply-chain management. To sidestep Japanese rivalry, many firms shifted from manufacturing to information services. In general, the American business sector survived the Japanese challenge in fine style. While the American economy grew in the 1990s, Japan lapsed into a decade-long slump.

American workers did not cope with global competition as successfully as their employers. From 1968 to 2001, American workers in the bottom 80 percent of income classes saw their share of national income go down. In many of those thirty-three years, their real wages and income were flat or down. Since 2001, median household income has fallen in inflation-adjusted terms, while poverty and corporate profits have risen.

Slowly and steadily since 1968, however, individuals in the upper fifth of the United States have earned increasingly more income than the rest of the country. In terms of real wages and income, the other fifths have not only fallen further behind the top fifth but also spread away from each other. The rungs on the income ladder are becoming farther apart. As a result, people find it harder to climb up from wherever the accidents of birth or bad luck may put them.

As the ladder itself has reached higher, those on the top have an increasingly different relationship to America than those on the bottom. The top quintile can afford to purchase practical, personal solutions to societal problems. Members of the upper income class react to the deficiencies of public education by sending their children to private schools; the absence of universal health insurance by paying increasing sums for their families' care; the lack of public transportation by working from home offices. By contrast, those on the lower rungs need, and yet do not enjoy, large-scale public solutions to the same problems.

In the long New Deal era of 1932 to 1968, the middle rungs of the income ladder—the second, third, and fourth quintiles, totaling 60 percent of households—were sufficiently close together that they constituted a huge middle class. Their opinions, points of view, and needs defined the politics and culture of the nation. As the income quintiles have separated, that large middle has evaporated. By 2001, the United States was on the verge of losing its identity as a middle-class country. If the trends of 1968–2001 continue through 2035, by then China will be the largest middle-class country in the world, and the United States will have the greatest income inequality of any large nation.

In the sixteenth century, as Spanish conquistadores gilded a wealthy class in their home country with the plundered gold of the New World, Cervantes wrote of the eternal division between those who "have much" and those who "have little." For most of its history the United States did not fit this description. If in the twenty-first century America becomes two nations—one of cabernets and cabarets, and one of cable channels and retail clerking—then a common, consensual, countrywide response to China may be impossible.

Even those at the top of the American income classes, however, are exposed to the Chinese challenge. Chinese entrepreneurs and engineers compete for the work done by American software engineers, chip designers, and others in the top income class of the United States. American firms are sending not only low-paid manufacturing work but also high-paid, technologically sophisticated work to China and other Asian countries. Businesses will arbitrage Americans of every income level whose work can be done in China—meaning firms will give employees a choice between working at lower wages in the United States or watching their jobs go overseas.

Possibly, Chinese labor competition will reverse the trend toward increasing income inequality in America by sawing off the top end of the American income ladder and driving the high-paid part of the American workforce down toward the lower rungs. If America's ruling elite shared more intimately in the experiences of the lower 80 percent of the country's income classes, perhaps they would support a national response that served everyone's interest. In the oos, however, the top group supported changes in the rule of law that enhanced its own income and wealth creation. If that elite discovered that Chinese competition harmed their interests, perhaps they would intensify their efforts to benefit themselves at the expense of other Americans. Moreover, by the time the upper class suffered serious impact from Chinese rivalry, the opportunity for an effective national response probably would have passed.

The safe and sane course for Americans now is to respond collectively in the very short term to the serious long-term challenges from the far side of the earth. To date, Americans have scarcely grasped the dimensions of China's impact, yet already time is short. In the near future, the United States must reform and revitalize its historic commitment to a culture of entrepreneurship, as set forth in the second half of Chapter 1.

To encourage entrepreneurial firms and personal entrepreneurship, American citizens cannot depend on their existing big businesses for help as they did in the past. Chapter 2 explains that the firms that used to keep their best jobs in America must become global firms in order to survive. In so doing, they must and will relax their historic commitment to the best interests of the United States alone.

Chapter 3 recalls that in the Golden 90s Americans learned that entrepreneurship can create new, large, winning firms and income growth for every income class. Although Americans have long started new businesses at a greater rate than any other big society in the world, this entrepreneurial growth reached new heights in the 1990s, when not only the number of new businesses but the number of activities pursued seemed boundless.[3] People browsed and searched, decoded genes and encoded libraries, taught English as a second language and made PowerPoint presentations as an alternative to speaking. In the ten years between 1991 and 2000, new business births outnumbered business deaths by an average of 55,000 per year. In the best of the years, 1994–95, the positive beat the negative by almost 100,000.[4] The culture of entrepreneurship flourished: the 1990s was a firm-creation decade.[5] Because new firms abounded and a group of big, winning firms emerged from the competition, in the last half of the 1990s all income classes saw their real wages go up.

In that decade, the American culture, to the admiration of almost every other country, was perfectly reflected in the technology start-up, as illustrated in the stories of Steve Case and Marc Andreessen related in Chapter 3. In contrast to the vacuum-filling domestic activity of Chinese entrepreneurs, American entrepreneurs in the United States disrupted the status quo in a more Schumpeterian fashion: they were heroes of "creative destruction." They thrived in chaos, embraced adventure, and decentralized decision making. Disorder was their goal and method. Even when working within established firms, American entrepreneurs of the 1990s attacked the existing hierarchy of wealth and power. Their value creation stemmed from the freedom to think, invent, express, and act.

Entrepreneurial firms built the pieces of the Internet—chips for memory and processing, long-haul data networks, routers, data centers, and software systems. On that platform other entrepreneurial enterprises flourished—dot-coms, software applications, consulting, Internet service provision, portals, and e-commerce. Every new firm wanted to create its own space. Hundreds defined new categories. Many spawned new demand markets. Information technology became the emblem of the American growth story.

The information technology sector experiences the trends that will affect all other sectors. Information firms face competition at home from global rivals. They must hire and sell in foreign countries in order to survive competitively. They have major financial incentives to send jobs offshore. If they fail to defeat their global rivals, many American employees will suffer—by mid-2005 Yahoo! had 8,780 employees; eBay, 8,900; Google, more than 4,000.[6]

Big, winning firms of every sector are the engine of job creation in the United States.[7] About six million firms hire people, but almost four million have fewer than ten employees. About 100,000 firms employing more than 100 people each account for the jobs of more than 70 million Americans. Only 6,000 firms account for about 48 million of those 70 million.[8]

Of the six million employing firms in the United States, roughly about a tenth are born annually, and about a tenth die. Economic happiness results when births exceed deaths; economic misery when deaths exceed births.[9] In the future, the United States needs to create more firms in more new and old markets, accept the increasingly rapid demise of more firms in these markets, and produce not 6,000 big winners in global markets but 7,000 or 8,000 or more.

To this end, existing firms should enter or create new markets. Start-ups or expanding firms should produce new goods and services not only in information management but also in agriculture, health care, pharmacology, and carbon-free energy. The next Google should invent a greener Green Revolution. The next Yahoo! should persuade millions of individuals to consume pollution-free energy drawn from the sun, wind, and water. The next Intel should manufacture devices that enable the repair of all genetic defects.

The American elite should encourage expanded entrepreneurship, even though its disruptive force will threaten the status quo in government and business. American workers must support speedy turnover of employers and employees, even though that means everyone will move from job to job more quickly and face greater uncertainty in career progression. The national goal should be to make it easier for any worker to obtain the skills and the opportunities that are likely to produce a rising real income. Nothing in life can be certain, but everyone will be better off if everyone has a better risk-reward ratio in one's work life. Even if the top quintile grows richer faster than the rest, rising income and increasing mobility will create more social solidarity and generate wealth in which all can share.

For the past fifty years, Americans have made up about 5 percent of the world's workforce but produced about 20 percent of the world's output. If the world economy grows in the twenty-first century, Americans might make a smaller percentage of the world's goods and services, and still have greater income. But they would need to make and sell a disproportionately large share of global output in order to be better off in the future than in the present.[10] Enhanced entrepreneurship is the means to that end.

As described in the concluding section of Chapter 3, the 00s have witnessed a reaction to the 90s. Only by pushing back the forces of counter-reform can Americans renew the culture of entrepreneurship.[11] Any culture is a web of beliefs and action supported by three architectures: the systems or patterns of law, technology, and leadership. People spin the filaments of values and intention across those three architectures.[12] In postmodern terms, each of these architectures, or systems, is a discourse. Each reflects an exercise of power. Each defines, and thereby limits, the behavior of the country's people. Each creates identities for people in the culture's society. Postmodern critics might inveigh against the oppressive effects of these discourses. As architectures, however, each opens possibilities, sustains beliefs, and reifies values.[13] Law, technology, and innumerable acts of leadership have produced an American culture that choirs a grand hymn of individual risk and collective reward.

Chapter 4 describes how reform of the legal architecture of the United States can cause the culture to encourage increased breadth and intensity of entrepreneurship. Firms should be able to depend upon law to facilitate their creation of new markets or entry into established markets. Law should not favor the status quo, but instead support disruption in the marketplace. Individuals should be able to count on law to provide public goods—education, health care and other insurance—that will permit them to take more risks in business and careers. The law should reflect neither a leftist agenda of wealth redistribution to lower income classes nor a right-wing goal of wealth aggregation by the top income class. It ought not aim to produce equal outcomes or insist on absolutely identical opportunities. Instead, the law should encourage risk taking, produce more income mobility, and reduce the consequences of failure in business and career moves.

A technological architecture comprises science, design, and language. The great technology of the twentieth century, the computer, reflected widespread access to many basic sciences, an open and widely understandable design, and a binary language that can express unlimited information and reasoning. Wise reform of the American culture would extend the genius of that architecture to every field of endeavor, especially including the health care, education, and energy sectors of the economy.

Finally, in any society, the pattern of leadership creates an architecture. Leaders open the doors to some possibilities and close off other directions. Leaders are, by definition, individuals whose actions have effects; they are agents of causation. During the long-run crisis of responding to China, Americans need leaders who understand how to mitigate the dangers for the United States and maximize the chance for every American entrepreneur and citizen to succeed.

The necessary leaders may emerge from positions of power and authority, or from the ranks of the unknown and unprivileged. As described in Chapter 5, they will succeed if they can wield the power of ideas. Their natural means of acting will be the new medium of the Internet. Like all previous means of communication, the Internet is giving rise to a new form of culture. Belief and purpose in the Internet age may not be so very different than in the television, telephone, or telegraph eras, but the methods of weaving the strands of culture are already strikingly new. Whether the new culture encourages entrepreneurship, however, remains to be determined. No inhuman force dictates the outcome. Instead, people, acting alone and together, will decide the fate of the United States.

To be an American is to dream the American Dream: that oneiric contradiction of meritocracy and egalitarianism. The society is supposedly structured to guarantee that hard work, and a dash of luck, will produce both just deserts and a better life for all. The Dream does not make complete sense; after all, it is a dream. Nevertheless, it has long come true for enough people that it still inspires not only Americans but lovers of freedom all around the world.

The Dream is intrinsically about ethics as much as materialism. Hence, Americans saw a moral lesson in the British decline from world dominance in the nineteenth century to relative insignificance in the twenty-first century. Britain had a class system instead of a meritocracy, and decline, Americans thought, followed from that. Britain had a state religion. In the United States, each person chose his or her own religion, and freedom of thought stemmed from that. Yet despite their celebration of individuality, all Americans shared a faith in the virtues of both personal choice and personal success. Nothing embodied those conjoined values more than building a new business from scratch.[14] A song of freedom was long hammered into every American head, and its refrain was entrepreneurship. For Americans to select enhanced entrepreneurship as the principal response to the challenge of China ought to be as true to the national character as it is necessary for economic success.

Admittedly, even if the United States changed nothing in its culture, Chinese firms would be far from certain to defeat American firms. Nor is the addition of Chinese entrepreneurs to the ranks of global traders bad for the rest of the world. Increased global trade will produce higher standards of living for all consumers, as firms and workers pursue comparative advantage. The global population in 2005 included about one billion consumers who consumed most of the world's 32 trillion dollars of annual gross domestic product. Adding billions more people to a new global consuming class would guarantee tremendous growth of the global technology sector as well as reduction of global poverty.[15] The goal for Americans is not to resist the expansion of the global economy, but to start or work in firms that win in global competition.

No nation ever led the world in so many ways as the United States did in the late twentieth century. Most of the world wants to bring that era to a close. As the foremost nation of the new age, China inexorably obliges Americans to ask whether they will take the wise actions necessary to maintain their culture's values and purpose tomorrow. This book concerns the need to act, the difficulties of action, the possibilities for action, and the reasons for hope in the sweet land of America—the idea that for five centuries has heartened humanity, the dream that need never die.

I

Looking East Toward the Dawn

"Wherefore," [Kublai Khan] said, "should I become a Christian? You yourselves must perceive that the Christians of these countries are ignorant, inefficient persons, who do not possess the faculty of performing anything . . . whereas you see that the idolaters can do whatever they will."

—THE TRAVELS OF MARCO POLO, THE VENETIAN

I would build that dome in air
That sunny dome! Those caves of ice!
And all who heard should see them there,
And all should cry, Beware! Beware!

—SAMUEL TAYLOR COLERIDGE, "KUBLA KHAN,
OR, A VISION IN A DREAM: A FRAGMENT"

Death of a Dream? The Challenge of China

China Is Near

Westerners have discovered and rediscovered China many times since Marco Polo explained the Middle Kingdom to Europeans in a narrative dictated in a Genoese jail in the thirteenth century.[1] Polo may not even have been to China.[2] He certainly did not see all that he described. Nonetheless, although some scoffed at its "million lies," Europeans copied Polo's *Travels* for the next two centuries and passed them around like downloaded music files in the oos.[3] Christopher Columbus studied a copy in an effort to find his way to Asia.[4] Like Columbus, in the 700 years since Polo dictated his stories, many Westerners convinced themselves that they could grow rich from finding China. Traders, missionaries, soldiers of fortune, and diplomats believed that Westerners could impose their religions, manufacturing output, rule of law, and military power on a vast and impressionable population of Chinese who very much needed these interventions.[5] According to its ethical precepts, Western adventurism has always needed to justify itself.

The Chinese have rarely been empowered to explain themselves to the West. When Secretary of State Henry Kissinger "opened" China to the United States for President Richard Nixon in 1973, he told Chinese Premier Zhou Enlai that China was a "mysterious" country. Zhou responded that after several thousand years of history, the Chinese were not a mystery to themselves.[6] Because Westerners so successfully enriched themselves in the first and second industrial revolutions, they became ever more certain that the comparatively impecunious Chinese were passive, incurious, self-centered, pliable, weak, and serene.[7]

In truth, before the West grew rich, "in the year A.D. 1600, the empire of China was the largest and most sophisticated of all the unified realms on earth."[8] The Manchu conquest of China in the mid-seventeenth century exceeded in difficulty and scale the European conquest of the New World. In the eighteenth and nineteenth centuries, revolutions shook, and sometimes overturned, kingly rule in the West, but the Taiping Rebellion of 1850–64 dwarfed them all in violence: 20 million died in an anti-Confucian, anti-imperial revolt—an order of magnitude greater than the aggregate casualties of the American, French, and Russian Revolutions.[9] In the twentieth century only the German and Soviet histories compared to the misery and violence of China's experience.[10]

Ignoring the tumult and the horror, Western businesspeople repeatedly discovered gold mines of opportunity in China. In the eighteenth century, the British imagined the mills of Manchester going "forever" if they could only "add an inch of material to every Chinaman's shirt tail"—not that anyone knew why shirts might be too short on the other side of the world.[11] In the 1970s, and again in the early 1990s, New York financiers poured hundreds of millions of dollars into the Chinese economy. By and large, the glitter of fool's gold had lured them. China produced little wealth for itself or others in the nineteenth and twentieth centuries.

Twenty-first-century China, however, struck Westerners as a reincarnation of nineteenth-century America. To Western eyes, the Chinese apparently embraced capitalism rambunctiously, encouraging greed as good. Chinese consumers, now eager to buy not shirts but cell phones, composed the most populous market in the history of consumption. Innumerable Chinese laborers wanted to work prodigiously hard, at dirt-cheap wages, without the intervention of unions or annoying safety and health regulations. Everyone candidly wanted to be rich, and Westerners understood that urge.

Like Marco Polo's narrative, the new Western perception of China mixed fictions and facts, with the motive of encouraging Asian adventures. The Chinese political rulers think they are, as the proverb put it, riding the back of a tiger. Numbering somewhere between 5 and 500 people at the apex of the 65-million-member Communist Party, this group can barely rule their huge population, even when collaborating with the handful of super-rich Chinese who made their fortunes outside the People's Republic.[12] Centers of governmental and economic power are emerging in the various regions in rivalry against Beijing, as has repeatedly occurred in Chinese history. New influences threaten not only the existing order but anyone's ability to exercise order. Perhaps 30 million Chinese can taste the West's standard of living, and 500 million might hope to enjoy that life in one generation.[13] But a billion are still trapped in desperate poverty. Powerful forces rend the social fabric: international capital, the military strength of the West, an aging population and overwhelming population shifts, the Internet's disruptive spread of information, the devastating environmental impact of development, massive energy shortages, and the ever-present risk of political instability.

Nor do the Chinese elite believe they have adopted pure capitalism. After Deng Xiaoping cemented control in 1978, in the wake of Mao Zedong's death two years earlier, the ruling group, under his leadership, began to fuse a welfare state with an integrated business-government sector. The approach resembled the European experiments in statism of the 1930s. Indeed, with its emphasis on nationalism for the masses and wealth aggregation for an elite, it smacked of fascism.

Under Mao, the Chinese ruling group aspired to control labor from cradle to grave. They regulated travel, residence, schooling, and procreation.[14] Under Deng, however, the government eased, or lost the ability to impose, these controls. Millions of Chinese began to live outside the law. As millions began to seek money and communism's insistence on equality lost its adherents, the central government struggled to maintain control. After the Tiananmen Square massacre of 1989, the government did succeed in suppressing the growth of civil liberties. Deng and his successor

Jiang Zemin channeled the energies of the young into entrepreneurship, and away from political reform. Without a legitimizing political mission, however, the party elite under Jiang and, since 2004, his successor Hu Jintao have been unable to manage the growth of domestic capitalism. They have encouraged foreign direct investment, rigged the currency to expand exports, and pursued more diplomatic engagement with other developing countries, where they have focused on securing access to national resources. However, the elite have shown no significant signs of seeking legitimacy for government by obtaining the consent of the governed. As the historian Jonathan Spence wrote in 1990, "If China was to develop as a modern nation . . . those taking the chances would have to be given some role in the making of political decisions. . . . There would be no truly modern China until the people were given back their voices."[15]

Nonetheless, projecting its preferences as it had done on the less-developed world since the age of discovery, the West became mesmerized by China's booming consumerism and rush to capitalism.[16] In the late 1980s and 1990s the Chinese began buying the "Eight Bigs"—"a color television, a refrigerator, a stereo, a camera, a motorcycle, a suite of furniture, a washing machine, and an electric fan."[17] In the 00s, they added to the list of necessities personal computers and cell phones. Businesses seeking economies of scale identified China as the biggest growth market in the world. Everyone in information technology had to sell there. To do that, they had to put plants and people in China.

In the 1980s and early 1990s, Chinese capitalism was directed about one-third toward meeting domestic demand and two-thirds toward export. In that respect, the Chinese copied some parts of the Japanese challenge to the West of the 1970s and 1980s. Japanese export businesses had perfected new efficiencies in manufacturing. They intended to supplant less efficient American manufacturing facilities. The factories of the United States had produced a very large share of global goods in the time since the Second World War ended with the United States triumphant and the rest of the world in ruins, but from Japan's perspective that era had ended. Japan's government and businesses together decided to take market share from Western firms in all global markets, most prominently including the American automobile industry. Japanese manufacturers knew that their own small domestic market could not support economies of scale. They depended on the United States for consumption.

However, unlike China in the 00s, Japan in the 70s and 80s depended on the United States for military protection against the Chinese and Soviet communist threats on the other side of the Sea of Japan. As a result, the Japanese complied when the United States forced Japanese car companies to build facilities and create jobs in the United States. The Japanese government succumbed to the American insistence on revaluing the yen-to-dollar exchange rate so as to reduce Japan's ability to export. American firms meanwhile overhauled their facilities, broke their unions, fired employees, and became much more productive. In the end, Japan fell into a recession, at least partly induced by the success of the American competitive response to Japan.

The Chinese strategy of the late 90s and early 00s more seriously threatened American firms' success and American citizens' standard of living. For all their concerns about domestic order, the Chinese ruling elite had hundreds of millions of new capitalists from the erstwhile Third World to whom their firms could sell.[18] In the 1990s, the Chinese economy began shifting toward a domestic focus. Firms competed vigorously in every market. They used technology to build low-cost manufacturing facilities, and they put their inexhaustible supply of cheap labor to work with breathtaking rapidity. Eventually, the mass of Chinese consumers will define tastes, trends, and technological standards for much of global trade.[19] Meanwhile, unlike the Japanese, the Chinese have no need for a military alliance with the United States. Instead, by the 00s the United States looked for Chinese help in dealing with North Korea.

The table is turning between the West and the East. Westerners wish to manufacture and hire in China. Western firms no longer want to add length to Chinese peasants' shirts; now they want to increase the length of the Wal-Mart shelf space stocked with Chinese goods. The Chinese no longer struggle for ways to resist Western encroachments on their culture. Now they are bent on enriching themselves by importing Western investment and skills, while learning enough about Western tastes to succeed in exporting to Western markets.

Communist Mercantilism

The Chinese Communist Party apparently plans to craft a state corporatism that will manage the Chinese economic and political strategies for the next several generations. Entrepreneurs are to be part of political leadership. Political leaders, in their own names and through family members, will take a share of entrepreneurial wealth and portions of the state-owned firms as they slowly convert to private firms.[20] Meanwhile, the government will provide Chinese entrepreneurs with the trade policies, educational resources, transportation, and other public goods that let them take on Western rivals in the commercial battles of the century. The entrepreneurs may see the government as an unwanted partner, or even an agent of corruption. But as long as the country's economy grows at nearly 10 percent a year, everyone will make enough money for the new business leaders and old government elite both to obtain their shares of the country's wealth creation.

The Chinese leadership intends in the twenty-first century to create a host of champions not only in industrial sectors like textiles, oil, and chemicals but also in information technology. Edward Tian, in 2003 the president of one of the top four communications firms in China, had been inspired a decade earlier by a speech of Al Gore's about the information superhighway. He started a business with the plan to "wire China."[21] By the mid-00s, his vision was far on the way to reality. China was first or second among countries in the number of broadband users, PCs, TVs, and refrigerators.[22] China counted more than 300 million cell phone subscribers.[23] Because fewer than 30 percent of Chinese had cell phones, the industry anticipated adding more than half a billion additional users in the future.[24]

The Chinese leadership experienced the disasters of the Great Leap Forward and the Great Cultural Revolution. They understand that most Chinese are very poor in comparison to citizens of Japan, Korea, Taiwan and certainly the United States.[25] To all appearances, China's history has demonstrated David Ricardo's "Iron Law of Wages"—that wages will never exceed subsistence level.[26] The Chinese annual income per capita is only about $900, a mere one-thirtieth the American level.[27] However, while the whole country is poor, the current Chinese paradox is that a populous segment is becoming middle class in a hurry. About 100 million Chinese workers earn at least $5,000 a year. That Chinese middle class equals in size, if not wealth, two-thirds of the total American workforce. Their standard of living in some respects approximates the average for Americans. The Chinese in their own country can buy a great deal more with a dollar—when exchanged for "the people's currency" of the renmimbi yuan—than can Americans in the United States. Shanghai apartment dwellers pay five dollars a month for cable television, and in most cities people pay about the same for telephone service. Lenovo sells PCs for less than $200. The well-off in Beijing hire help to cook, wash, clean, and run errands for between $60 and $90 a month per employee. In addition, urban Chinese, about 30 percent of the population, obtain at very low cost some level of transportation, housing, health care, and education, although many of these public goods are inferior by most Western standards.[28] (The government provides these public goods on a much broader scale than do the U.S. national and local governments.)

Moreover, Deng's one-child policy concentrates parental and grandparental income behind a single member of the next generation. Partly for that reason, members of the youngest generation have a better education than their parents. In addition, where Chinese students in the 1960s lost much of their educational opportunities in the ravages of the Great Cultural Revolution, in the next generation the Communist Party embraced education as the path to increasing the national economy. The Chinese government continues in the 00s to encourage one child per family, especially in rural areas. Such governmental intrusion into conception in the United States would leave Americans on both sides of the abortion debate aghast. In China the policy, coupled with economic growth, has helped ensure that from 2004 to 2014 another 200 million will join the Chinese middle class—and in the decade that follows, another 300 million.

In the last quarter of the twentieth century more than 100 million Chinese moved from rural regions to the 100 cities that had a million or more in population. Indeed, the percentage of China's population in urban areas nearly doubled from 1990 to 2004.[29] The trend continues: About a half billion Chinese will move from farm to factory in the next twenty years.[30] In about 2025, 700 million Chinese in 100 or 200 cities will be consuming the same amount of goods and services as approximately 300 million urban Americans clustered in perhaps 50 cities. Measured by demand, the economies then will be about the same size. In terms of the number of consumers purchasing globally available products, by about 2025 China will rank higher than any other country.

Total Chinese consumption is already about one-third the size of American buying, measured in terms of what is bought as opposed to how much money is spent. According to this purchasing power comparison, the Chinese, Japanese, and Indians together buy about as much as Americans. These consumers, consequently, influence tastes, trends, and technology standards as much as do Americans. By 2025, Chinese consumers alone will have as much influence over supply as American consumers.[31]

Even though Americans increased their spending every year in the early 00s, in those same years China accounted for about 40 percent of the global economy's growth. Growing markets set trends and technology standards.[32] If Chinese purchasers sharpen the cutting edge of consumption, then the most creative makers, branders, marketers, and shapers of culture might more likely live and work in China than in the United States.[33]

The new middle class is appearing in many regional clusters, formed around industry leaders. The competition among regional governments and businesses has strengthened the diversity and creativity of Chinese businesses. Different regions specialize in different expertises. They create a broader portfolio of national assets than any Soviet centralized plan ever did.[34] China hosts the world's largest centers for making ties, shirts, and socks.[35] In nearby cities other firms aspire to create the global centers for making telecommunications equipment. Shanghai, 500 miles to the north, attracts foreign investment in finance, semiconductors, and media. Beijing intends to become the location for headquarters for multinational corporations.[36]

The new middle class exercises new freedoms to work, marry, move, choose clothes and music and even the number of children. However, it is not about to become an active electorate in a functioning democracy.[37] From China's perspective, the factionalism of Western democracy produces inconsistency from one election to the next. The Western system of judicial review, legislative process, and never-ending opinion polls leads to ineffectual and erratic execution of any strategy. China's leadership will tolerate some local elections to deal with some local matters. That sort of voting, like union hall elections in the United States, can help make small groups cohesive. Beyond that, a multiparty electoral system will serve no purpose sought by China's political or business leadership.[38] In both Hong Kong and Taiwan, distinctive democracies have developed, but Beijing regards these cases as warnings of what to avoid, not signposts toward the future.

Much elite thinking in America entertains the improbable hope that the path from capitalism to democracy is a slippery slope that China will inevitably slide down. As before in the history of Western assessment of

China, that perspective ignores the Chinese view. It projects onto the Chinese screen a vision, unreal as any motion picture, that the West prefers.[39] Chinese entrepreneurship is very different than anything recognized by that term in America.

Entrepreneurship, for that matter, has had different meanings in the West since the word was coined in eighteenth-century France by the Irishman Richard Cantillon. For him, the term meant someone who started a business. His own start-up activity was financial speculation. He sold out of the South Sea Bubble before it popped. Today he would be described as a founder of a hedge fund. In the next century, French revolutionary and laissez-faire economist Jean-Baptiste Say turned the word into a theory: an entrepreneur combined someone's land, someone else's money, and a third party's labor to make a product sold in the market. The difference between the sale price minus the rent on the land, interest on the money, and wages for labor equaled the entrepreneur's profit. In modern America, this sort of entrepreneur would be called a venture capitalist.

The Austrian economist Joseph Schumpeter went beyond this approach to label the entrepreneur's work "creative destruction." The entrepreneur's activity, Schumpeter believed, "interrupts the continuity of development . . . because [a phase of] development comes to a stop and a new one starts."[40] Schumpeter's disruption describes the battle of an entrepreneur to attack an existing hierarchy of power.[41]

Entrepreneurship in China is a different animal. It fills a vacuum once occupied by the Communist state's system of production.[42] Lip-Bu Tan, a prominent West Coast venture capitalist, says the principal traits of entrepreneurs in Asia are "humility, patience, willingness to learn, and total commitment to the business."[43] The picture contrasts with American brashness and pride. Chinese entrepreneurs are often famous risk takers, but for the most part, they are not financiers. They make things. They are the engine of the national growth strategy. They are acquisitive, but they believe their wealth will eliminate poverty in a trickle-down fashion. Their capitalism is "creative construction." They compete fiercely, but unlike American entrepreneurs, they do not seem to come from outside of society.

Like their American counterparts, entrepreneurs in China have contempt for government bureaucracy, corruption, and kleptocracy. Nevertheless they partner with the state. They accept joint ownership of assets and state presence in firms to a degree unimaginable to Americans. Nor do Chinese entrepreneurs advocate democracy. Some had been in the Tiananmen Square demonstrations as students and had learned to fight for money, not political change.[44] According to one survey, some 78 percent of entrepreneurs had joined the Communist Party; other estimates put membership at about 25 percent.[45] (It is inconceivable that 78 percent of American entrepreneurs regularly vote, and unlikely that even 25 percent consider themselves active members of a political party.)

The central and regional governments provide much support for entrepreneurs. The state built whole cities like Shenzhen or Pudong—replete with roads, electricity, housing, and communications networks—for business purposes. Government does not make firms clean up pollution.[46]

The state does not fund health care or pensions. Government pawns them off on business, as in the United States. Chinese employers pay for these safety-net protections, which amount to as much as 50 percent or 100 percent of wages. However, because Chinese workers make so little, foreign employers are scarcely burdened by the costs. Nor do these protections for workers inhibit Chinese employers from obtaining low-cost labor for production of virtually any good or service. Independent labor unions do not exist, because theoretically the Communist Party is the manifestation of the working class, and it has the power to set terms and conditions of employment.

Chinese entrepreneurs need natural resources to build their businesses, but their government intends to obtain those vital ingredients of economic growth from other countries. China's exports to the United States generate the dollars used by China to buy commodities from other countries. China accounts for most global growth in commodities.[47] It is bent on buying firms that own oil and natural gas resources.[48] The state intends to ensure that Chinese entrepreneurs will not lack the imports they need to compete with American firms.

IT Is It

To build a strong economy, the Chinese need not only Western dollars but also know-how. As with commodities, they will buy it. China and other developing countries offer substantial cash payments and other incentives to attract foreign technology firms into their domestic markets, so as to bring their skills into China. Here follows a report from one American technology company to the American government, written in early 2004. The alterations mask the source and the recipient, but not the meaning.

From: [CEO]

Sent: Wednesday, [month/date], 2004, 10:18 a.m.

To: [U.S. government official]

When we met last week I talked about the relative cost of one of our state of the art manufacturing plants, and the various constituent cost elements. Below I show some data for a 10 year net present cost for the same plant located in PRC, Malaysia, Singapore and the USA . . . using current labor costs, government grants that are likely, and tax holidays that are likely. As you can see by the data, the NPC [net present cost] differentials for an approximate $3B factory range from $1B to $1.5B less for the foreign sites than for the equivalent plant in the U.S. The NPC differentials are primarily driven by capital grants, tax holidays and lower labor rates.

Cost element	PRC	Malaysia	Singapore	US
Cash cost	$2.30B	$2.20B	$2.30B	$2.60B
Gross Capital	$3.10B	$3.10B	$3.10B	$3.10B
Taxes	—	—	$0.50	$0.90
Capital Grants	$(0.25B)	—	$(0.25B)	—
Total	$5.05B	$5.30B	$5.65B	$6.60B
Delta to US	$1.45B	$1.30B	$0.95B	N/A

The labor cost differential of approximately $300B is only a small part of the total. What is really difficult to compete with is the $500M to $1B in tax benefits and the big capital gains. These numbers suggest that it will be very difficult to justify building these sorts of factories in the US in the future. And, these are the highest end manufacturing plants known to mankind. . . . And, to reiterate, it is not a labor cost issue. We could live with the couple hundred million in labor cost. It is the $1B in other costs that drive the decision.

American firms can hardly refuse enormous cash payments in return for a commitment to manufacture in another country. In July 2005, for example, Israel announced it would pay Intel $525 million in cash in return for an investment in a chip-making facility of about $4 billion over a number of years. The factory will employ 2,000 people.[49] No Intel shareholder could want the firm to reject that offer. Intel employees in the United

States need their employer to use such deals to reduce costs, or else the firm will be less able to compete successfully against its rivals. But those new employees, nonetheless, will be in Israel, because the Israeli government is buying the jobs.

Developing countries might not obtain a good return on the money they spend to attract new businesses. They do not apply purely financial analysis to the topic. China wants to root its economy in high-end activities. Coal, oil, steel, and railroads produced a ferrous carbonate culture of big buildings, huge factories, heavy objects, pollution, and mass migration. China has all that and, as a result, has created enormous environmental and transportation problems for its society. By contrast, semiconductors, fiber optics, and software produce a culture based on silicon and electromagnetic radiation, as opposed to oil or print. The silicon and electrons make up goods and services that communicate, hold, and create information. These products satisfy and shape the intelligence, imagination, and values of the consumer.[50] The leaders of China and other developing economies believe that by hosting, and controlling, information technology firms they will be able to generate higher-paid jobs, reduce environmental damage, and direct development of their economy. Even if their investment in information technology does not produce returns equal to their coal or oil industries, they will not permit the brainpower of global development—information technology—to reside exclusively in the West. Just as they drove the United States and its Kuomintang allies off the mainland in 1949, they reject virtual colonization by Western information technology.[51]

By investing in information technology, China seeks not only to control its own development but also to dominate the leading high-value global industry. Because of economies of scale, increasing returns, and network effects, whoever makes the greatest number of information products—the most chips, DVDs, cell phones, copies of a software program—has a very good chance of winning the entire world market. Very large factories can make hardware components and systems at very low unit cost. The more chips, software packages, and cell phones a firm makes, the lower the average cost of each one. The more customers who adopt a firm's technical design, the more additional customers who pick that standard for ease of use with other interoperating information products. By entering the magic triangle of scale economies, increasing returns, and network effects, a firm has much lower costs and higher profits for its new products. Then it can keep a lead against rivals from its own or any other country.

By leading the boom of the Golden 90s, American information firms occupied that catbird seat. The six great virtual firms of the era—Intel, Microsoft, AOL, Yahoo!, eBay, and Google—established technology leadership
anew in America. In response, the Chinese leadership intend to induce
American information technology firms into their country as well as equip
Chinese information technology firms with the capacity to win in domestic and global markets.[52] They plan to lead the Asian boom of the twenty-
first century and thereby win information leadership for generations.

To fuel the growth of its entrepreneurial firms, the Chinese government
will provide legions of workers with manufacturing, management, and high-
technology skills. The U.S. government does very little to improve the skills
of low-paid workers. By contrast, the Chinese government aims to produce skilled workers in such numbers that their wages will stay down while
their skills enable their employers to turn out high-quality products.

The United States is ahead of China in educational capability. It annually graduates more engineers than China relative to population. By the
end of the 2004 academic year, American engineering schools had awarded
more than 70,000 bachelor's degrees, nearly at the record high reached
more than twenty years earlier. The number of bachelor's degrees awarded
in the computer and information sciences grew significantly between 1997
and 2003.[53] At a price, American entrepreneurial firms can acquire any
amount or type of skilled talent to design and build their products.

China's response, as in other respects, uses scale as a tactical weapon.
Overcoming Mao's attack on intellectuals during the Great Cultural Revolution, the country's leaders taught 85 percent of the population to read
and write.[54] The standard curriculum emphasizes technical topics, such as
engineering and, more recently, management. Chinese engineering schools
grant more than twice the number of degrees every year that American
schools issue. These graduates generally are not as prepared for global competition as their American (and even Indian) peers. However, their sheer
numerosity means that many Chinese entrepreneurs can hire new employees at low wages for the indefinite future.

China's entrepreneurs also import business skills from the United States.
Many Chinese employees, including founders of new firms, have studied
or worked in America. They return home to take much higher-ranking
jobs than they can find in the slower growing American market. Foreign
firms investing in China train their Chinese employees in modern business
practices. In a few years at most, their Chinese employees leave to start their

own firms, sometimes in competition with their Western mentors. Consulting, accounting, and investment banking firms opened offices in China in the 1980s and 1990s. Through those offices they transmitted Western management skills to Chinese entrepreneurs. Western business schools created partnerships with Chinese academies to create new training programs.[55]

The Chinese have created a macroenvironment ideal for entrepreneurship. It rivals the desirability of the American situation in the 1990s. Foreign investment pours into China, as it did in the United States.[56] In addition, Chinese workers save prodigiously, while Americans in their personal finances spend about as much as they earn.[57] Although state-owned banks have loaned much money they can never get repaid, the Chinese economy has plenty of savings that can start new businesses. In China a start-up can make it big overnight, just like in the United States.[58] In China entrepreneurs see the rising sun of opportunity, even as many Americans wonder if that sun is setting on the United States.[59]

Response Time
The Future Is Now

In response to rising China, some Americans prescribe laws the government should pass. They want, variously, to alter the currency exchange rate, adjust tariffs for affected industries, and establish common technology standards. Others want more education, communications networks, health care, and science research. Business and government leaders, however, do not agree on the theory of the case. No one seems to know whether, in response to China, the United States should have a more proactive government or a less interventionist government, more or less public spending, more or less dependence on big businesses for employment and economic growth.

Contradictions abound. The government favors free trade but protects the textile and sugar industries. Businesses ask for more educated engineers but reduce the number of jobs available for them. American firms have to increase exports, but some politicians stigmatize those American businesses that focus on foreign markets.

For three centuries, the West believed that it could teach China the secrets of progress, but it concluded that the pupil stubbornly refused to learn. In the twenty-first century, the United States should examine how China discovered, out of the darkness of Maoism, a new way to produce widespread, uncontrolled economic growth. The Communist Party did not order Chinese entrepreneurs to challenge American entrepreneurs for market share. Its rule of law is more an absence of law than an effective framework for seeking trust or justice. Its entrepreneurial practices stem not from its schools but, in large part, from the business experiences of Hong Kong, Taiwan, and other overseas Chinese communities. The Internet has not conferred unbeatable advantages on Chinese exporters, but it has lowered barriers to entry in the developed countries. Domestically, the spread of information technology has created a significant base of eager consumers. Chinese business and political leaders, meanwhile, rejected Maoism and celebrated the creation of wealth. They increased the opportunities for profit making, used technology to shape markets, and led the country into supporting the virtue of wealth creation. The combination of these radical changes in law, technology, and leadership has changed Chinese behavior. China has created a culture of entrepreneurship, where only a generation ago a very different culture prevailed.

These three sources of change—law, technology, and leadership—do not themselves constitute culture. Each is an architecture. Each creates some possibilities and limits others in the same way that a door creates an entrance or exit here and not there, a window provides a vantage point in this direction and not in that, a wall creates an inside space for activity and defines other spaces as outside. Individuals and groups choose among the opportunities presented by architectures.[60] The architectures of law, technology, and history support and invite some actions, and thwart others. Individuals act in light of architectures. By attaching meaning to their action, they create a culture.

Meaning lies in distinction. Architectures emphasize distinctions. Actions and meaning together compose culture. A culture is then described in terms of beliefs and values. The government and business elite in China, at least for now, believe in entrepreneurship. Individuals share those beliefs. As entrepreneurship is defined in China, it seems congruent with an amalgam of Confucian emphasis on family and order and Communist Party discipline. It is part of the new Chinese culture.[61]

China demonstrates that the architectures of culture do not remain the same over time. Hardly any big society has rebuilt its architectures as suddenly as China, but cultural change is ongoing everywhere. Every country has engines of change. Law changes when judges apply the law to hard cases. Law changes when factions of society persuade the politically powerful to make changes. In China, dissidents seek the freedom to choose whether to have more than one child. In the United States, the religious right asks the president to appoint Supreme Court justices who will constrain or reverse the constitutional protection of a woman's right to choose whether to bear a child. In both countries, the legal architecture itself admits of the possibility that it can be changed. In both cultures, scientific discoveries produced new technological architectures that expanded the potential for human action, just as the atomic bomb and the silicon microchip defined the last half of the twentieth century. Finally, in both cultures, individual leaders take actions that alter choices for others. They forge chains of causation that can strengthen or hobble their societies. Deng and Jiang extinguished Marxism and made entrepreneurship the engine of growth. The American administration fought a war of choice and jeopardized America's standing in the world. The acts of leaders have effects. These outcomes constitute an architecture of opportunities closed and opened.

Although the definition of culture is so broad as to create chronic ambiguity, everyone agrees on its importance. Culture accounts for the success or failure of careers, organizations, and governments. Law cannot mandate, technology cannot enable, and leaders cannot inspire the behavior of individuals to a fraction of the degree that culture does.[62] Culture is a "control mechanism" that shapes people like clay.[63]

As societies alter their architectures, they remake their culture. They reweave continuously the web of meaning that ties their members into a sense of belonging to a society. Anyone who seeks to change the behavior of a society must seek to change culture. In order to affect culture, reform must change some or all of the architecture of law, technology, and the conduct of leaders. Successful and enduring reform changes the web of meaning. It changes how members of a society act. If reform does not alter the actions and thinking of a society's members, it remains only an unpersuasive idea, or an unachieved program.

China has experienced reform. Its law, technology, and acts of leadership have reassembled ancient structures to create a new web of meaning. The new architectures of China have shaped both action and the meaning of action. They have given form and substance to a new culture. That culture breeds new firms that challenge the American Dream.

For the United States to respond effectively to the challenge from China, Americans need to change their culture. They need to recapture the spirit of the 1990s. They have to revitalize in their society a culture of entrepreneurship. That culture must expand in scale and scope. It has to alter the way people make choices for themselves and for the organizations in which they participate. If the United States witnessed half a million new businesses starting every year in the Golden 90s, that number needs to be much higher in the future. If its firms have always led in information technology, in the future they need also to become global winners in biological, chemical, and even manufacturing markets. If the economy registered 25 million new jobs in the 1990s, it needs to create many more in the next decade. If the top 20 percent enjoy rising incomes, in the future 100 percent need to be on the upswing.

China can provoke Americans to reform the legal, technological, and leadership architecture of the society. The reformed Chinese culture can stimulate Americans to believe in reform. Just a glance at China should persuade any American to fight fire with fire. The purpose of reform in the United States needs to be the renewal of the American cultural commitment to entrepreneurship.[64]

No single law, technology, or act of leadership can ordain that America renew its commitment to entrepreneurship. However, these architectures certainly will change. The nature of these changes will save or doom the American future. No one knows the outcome, but if Asia falls like night on the West's long summer day, it will look like this: Chinese and other Eastern firms will make almost everything for nearly everybody in the world, and nobody else will be able to say or do much about it. After that, the new rulers of the planet's productive capacity will decide whether to tolerate democracy, individual freedom, economic growth, or entrepreneurship in other societies. That will be up to them.[65]

Some Past Will Be Prologue
America's Historic Culture of Entrepreneurship

Since at least the eighteenth century, American culture supported entrepreneurship with a special passion. By the Second Industrial Revolution of the nineteenth century, the American culture surpassed every other nation in the depth and extent of its support for business creation.[66] When Europeans scorned Americans' lack of couth, the citizens of the United States had the last laugh that usually accrues to those with money and power.[67]

Culture is the crucial element of competitive survival for any individual business, for a national economy, and certainly for the slice of any market occupied by entrepreneurs. Americans did not have to pay much attention to the viability of their culture from the victory of the Second World War until the rise of China. In the twentieth century, the fact that Americans had a superior culture for business purposes was self-evident. In the twenty-first century, however, the American culture is no longer obviously the best possible culture for entrepreneurship. Not remembering well, or perhaps not having understood, the ingredients of the entrepreneurial culture of the 90s, in the 00s American business and political leaders do not share a comprehensive vision for renewing that culture on the terms necessary to compete with rising China. Particularly uncommon is the awareness that the essential traits of successful American competitiveness in the future include increased risk taking for firms, greater turnover of industry leaders in all markets, and more instability for individual firms.

These characteristics mark entrepreneurship in rich and broadly developed economies. They are less important in the relatively undeveloped Chinese economy, where both government and business leaders want to create new industry structures. In America, entrepreneurs are supposed to disrupt order; in China, they are supposed to perpetuate it. Tearing down is different from building; in that respect the American situation is more daunting for entrepreneurs than the opportunities presented in China. In the United States, most markets are led by longstanding, well-run, cash-flow rich, and politically powerful firms. These companies have the purpose and means to destroy new entrants, crush rivals, and maintain the status quo. The high rate of technological change, the rapidity of the growth of a new medium, and the easy access to risk capital made the 1990s an exceptional decade for American entrepreneurship. The more general paradigm is that entrepreneurs expect greater obstacles to creating successful new businesses in well-developed, existing markets such as those in the United States.

Of course, start-up and established American firms can count on the culture's longstanding commitment to entrepreneurship, access to sophisticated financial and skilled human capital, and widespread technological invention. Nevertheless, to respond to the Chinese challenge, Americans need to renew, on new terms, their culture of entrepreneurship.[68] If entrepreneurial activity intensifies in all markets, three results can be expected. First, more new, surprisingly successful firms will spring into global leadership. Second, even entrepreneurial failures will contribute through their competitive pressure to creating more productive microeconomies in all markets. Finally, more Americans will work in productivity-growing companies and so will enjoy rising wages.

Americans have to begin by changing the architectures of their culture. The first architecture, law, includes statutes and regulations that create rights and obligations, spend and tax, create incentives and punishments.[69] It creates choices, and makes some easier or more rewarding than others.[70]

As an example, in the 1990s, the American legal architecture made a great contribution to entrepreneurship by encouraging the cheap, broad, and rapid growth of the Internet. American government spending created a network of communications links among universities. However, the Internet escaped from a tiny academic community into the general populace in large part because American law freed it. The U.S. government precluded telephone companies from charging people extra to use their telephone lines to connect to the Internet. It required telephone companies to pay money to Internet access providers. It gave Internet access companies the right to buy high-speed connections to data centers at favorable prices. It declared that anyone could go into the business of selling Internet access without needing a license. It took billions of dollars from telephone users and gave that money to schools so that they could purchase Internet access for every teacher in every classroom. It refused to tax commerce done over the Internet.

The American cultural proclivity for sharing information found new expression in the Internet medium. By the end of the Golden 90s, more than 75 percent of all Americans used the Internet at home or at work and nearly 90 percent of all students had access to the Internet in elementary classrooms and computer rooms. Rapid adoption among a large number of users meant that the Internet became an American creation. Because Americans embraced the Internet in vast numbers before any other society did, English became the lingua franca of the Net. Rapid adoption of the Internet also caused the medium to become the language of entrepreneurship. To start a business in the 1990s, everyone began by acquiring a URL; in previous decades, entrepreneurship commenced with a phone line and a mailing address.

By contrast, in the 00s, Asian law did much more than American law to spread the new broadband Internet. Asian governments wanted higher-speed networks, sending pictures and sound as fast as narrowband sent text, to become a new medium and a new way to challenge the American cultural claim on the first generation of the Internet. They succeeded.

Meanwhile, the U.S. government abandoned its stimulus of the Net, and the country fell behind in high-speed connectivity. The United States ranked sixteenth in broadband penetration by April 2005.[71] Congress in 2005 agreed to spend nearly $290 billion over five years on roads and highways, but not a penny on broadband.[72] The preference for cars instead of computers will no doubt affect American entrepreneurship for years to come. An architecture of law opens up or closes off possibilities.[73]

Not just the legal architecture of the Net but also its technological architecture affected choices and opportunities in the 1990s. Specifically, the technological architecture was open, collaborative, flexible, and expansive. Therefore, it stimulated entrepreneurship.

A technological architecture includes scientific discovery, engineering design, and language. The most important technology of the late twentieth century is the computer. It combines many areas of scientific knowledge—electromagnetism, quantum mechanics, chemistry, and the logic of Boolean algebra. Computer design finds its origin in 1945, when John Von Neumann proposed to line up instructions in sequence, storing them in memory.[74] His design approach made computers reprogrammable, flexible in their purposes, and therefore very useful in practical terms. The design made the computer a valuable technology, as opposed to an interesting scientific discovery.

The language of computer architecture used two common states of electrical circuits, carrying electricity and not carrying it, on and off, to represent numbers and characters in binary form of 1's and 0's. Boolean logic employed the two choices—1's and 0's—to depict all information and express all logic. (By contrast, if the language used the three states of molecular structure—gas, liquid, and solid—then computers would have required a trinary system of logic.)

With Boolean algebra, any question can be broken down into a long series of questions that can be answered with a yes or a no. For example, what is two plus two? Is it five? No. Is it three? No. Is it four? Yes. So if every circuit can produce a pathway toward a yes or a no, then the electron's path can be mapped as a series of answers of yes or no to every question. Software code consists of instructions for the opening or closing of circuits so as to produce the right answer to the question of two plus two, and to every other imaginable question.

In general, everyone in the world can learn the science, design, and language of computers. That knowledge is open. Learning it can lead an entrepreneur to create great value. It makes those who embrace computer technology more wealthy than those who do not. The wealth stems from the technology's gift of the power to manage ever-increasing amounts of information reduced to the form of 1's and 0's. A culture that values the science, design, and language of computers will create a more wealthy and powerful society than one that shuns this technology.

The Internet's architecture could have been closed, unrevealed, secret, and proprietary. To a degree, the software of computers was not open. The famous Microsoft litigations of the 90s and 00s focused on whether Microsoft had to allow rival applications-software makers to use its operating-system software to compete against Microsoft. Microsoft licensed others to use its architecture, but the litigation concerned, among other things, the fairness of the conditions of the licenses. Similarly, telephone companies and consumer electronics companies did not create open technological architectures. Not surprisingly, hardly anyone introduces new goods or services that use telephone company networks or consumer electronics devices as integrated components of their systems. For example, consumers cannot easily plug a telephone line or a camera into a television set, even if they wanted to see who was calling.

Tim Berners-Lee, Marc Andreessen, and other early shapers of the Internet took the opposite approach. The academic origins of the Internet created a bias toward openness in its early architects. The Internet's founders designed their creation so that it would encourage an open architectural approach in related markets such as operating-system software. The open software called Linux, Microsoft's current rival, was therefore a natural descendant of the open design of the Internet.

Leadership, the third architecture, is the pattern of historical actions in a society—events that have consequences over time. People can change culture by persuading others to follow their advice, direction, behavior. Leaders are those who succeed in such persuasion. Leaders from above use the power of position to persuade; leaders from below depend more on the power of rhetoric and the association of many followers into like-minded groups. Some dictate outcomes; others mobilize to achieve outcomes. Both use the power of leadership to alter culture by opening some possibilities and closing others.

Myriad academic, professional, and lay writers churn out books and articles on leadership. Everyone looks for it, decries its absence, mistakes or finds it in actions famous and unnoticed. As with culture, few agree on its definition, but everyone acknowledges its criticality. The architecture of leadership for a society comprises the stream of events and beliefs that result from individual leaders in that society.[75]

Leaders' actions may include decisions to make war, to invest, to create and express ideas. By such deeds, leaders produce changes in the behavior and thinking of others. When leaders change the conduct and opinions of others, they change culture.[76]

Otto von Bismarck reportedly said that "political genius consists of hearing the distant hoofbeat of the horse of history and then leaping to catch the passing horseman by the coattails."[77] The flow of events, he meant in his Hegelian way, had a force of its own greater than any one person could overcome. In any culture, history, like a river, is more likely to follow existing channels than to carve out new directions. Yet rivers change course on occasion. Leaders can make those changes happen. Bismarck's own actions created the balance of power that, when disrupted, led to two world wars. He led; he had followers. His decisions had effects.[78] Similarly, no invisible horses pulled America into the Golden 90s. Instead, individuals made good laws, started great firms, invented great technologies, and talked others into the cultural changes that produced a golden age of entrepreneurship. Individuals are controlled by culture, but to greater or lesser extent cultures transmit freedom of action to individuals who are part of such cultures.

So, although culture shapes possibilities for everyone, people tinker constantly at the architectures of culture. They want the cultural machine to produce outcomes, measured by both action and belief.[79] Toward the goals of altering how others behave and think, individuals, acting alone and together, change law, invent technology, and exercise leadership.[80]

Perhaps leaders know, more than do lawmakers or technologists, that their principal achievements must lie in cultural change. Leaders make war, cut taxes, encourage oil refining, take a stance on global warming, and in each act they should know that in the long run their conduct will be judged for its effect on what people do and think. Leaders, technologists, and lawmakers usually have a view about the short-term effects of their actions. The long-term changes in culture that they cause are far less predictable.[81] Nevertheless, guessing about the future and searching for meaning, people in societies rebuild, support, renovate, and alter these three architectures, and hence change the culture of their societies.[82]

The three architectures do not much overlap, but they do have impact on each other. Former Intel CEO Andy Grove called "Grove's Law" his postulate that "technology will always win."[83] For example, the U.S. government cannot curtail stem cell research; even if others do the research, sooner or later it will be read and applied in the United States.[84] On the other hand, law, for example, can speed or slow the effects of technology.[85] Similarly, by its own terms law can thwart leadership, as the Jim Crow regime stifled and re-directed many African-American leaders for a century. Nevertheless, leaders can change a culture even against the force of law, as Rosa Parks did by refusing to give up her seat on a bus.[86]

The three architectures, like all discourses of power in a society, converse with each other. Technology creates issues and choices for law. No matter how law decides any particular matter, technology will continue to ask questions. Technology asks whether people want to alter purposefully their genes. It invents an atomic bomb and asks a president whether to use it. It creates thousands of nuclear weapons, but government leaders have to decide whether to corral them. Individuals make those choices, guided by culture and unable to depend on technology for their decisions.[87] Finally, leaders muster support for or opposition to changes in law, pursuits of technology. Collectively, leaders, technology, and law provide structures on which people spin the web of beliefs, values, motives, and objectives that govern the behavior and beliefs of people in society. That web is the culture of the society.[88]

The three architectures can each stimulate or suppress a cultural belief in entrepreneurship. In American culture, entrepreneurship stems directly from a belief in the virtue of individual liberty—including in particular freedom of expression and association.[89] When the culture favors disruption, American entrepreneurs are strengthened in their numbers, the range of their activities, and their likelihood of success.[90] Anyone in any country might open a shop. However, because the American culture values risk, challenge, competition, ambition, and independence, disruptive, Schumpeterian entrepreneurs have historically found more support and reward in the United States than in other countries.[91]

For centuries, the American culture—characterized by enthusiasm, crankiness, materialism, and belief in individual and societal progress—drew millions of immigrants who arrived with a hunger for work and a willingness to believe the culture.[92] The Americans who became the first Internet users re-created that American culture in a virtual world.[93] They made an Internet that emphasized individual action and expression, willingness to experiment, rejection of hierarchy, rambunctious pursuit of profit. America the physical country and America the Web country became the homeland of the start-up. That this occurred in the 1990s was no accident.[94]

The Halcyon Era

As the baby boom generation emerged from its collegiate chrysalis in the late 1960s, the American economy began a twenty-five-year decline. The belief that only big firms could achieve economies of scale led to the formation of huge conglomerates and a library of literature decrying the organization man that large firms seemed to require. Yet the large-scale firms failed to generate either productivity or wage gains. By 1970, the country was sliding on a downward slope of what looked like a Kondratiev wave.[95] At the nadir, in the late 1970s, investors focused on purchasing established businesses through leveraged buyouts that reaped fortunes for financiers but produced little for employees or the overall economy.

By the late 1980s many elite opinion shapers concluded that American firms could not compete in world markets, and that government had to remedy the situation. Bill Clinton based his 1992 presidential campaign's famous focus—"it's the economy, stupid"—on this imperative. His agenda aimed to enhance the competitiveness of American firms in globally traded markets. The actions included lowering interest rates by reducing "crowding out" from government debt, balancing the government budget, expanding research and development funding, and introducing competition in previously consolidated or regulated industries.[96]

Meanwhile, after a half century of cold war, the United States and its Western allies emerged victorious over the communist bloc. The Soviet Union dissolved. Led by the German reunification, Eastern European countries migrated into the European common market. All the world, in a flashback to nineteenth-century liberalism, suddenly and dazzlingly opened up to the export of Western goods and culture.

However, the most scintillating prospects turned out to exist in America itself. The world's money decided that it belonged in American equities and American debt. The country operated under a reliable, if complicated, rule of law. Its workers produced more per hour and dollar of capital investment than those of any other big country in the world, more than justifying their high wages. It had high employment and a constant stream of immigrants to fill both menial and sophisticated technical jobs. Particularly in information technologies, its firms led in all world markets. Its consumers spent prodigiously, saving little but always demanding more new products. Thanks to the convergence of communications and computing, technology showered those consumers with new goods and services.[97]

Interest rates dropped, so that investment in equities rather than bonds appealed to global money. Firms translated that investment into new productivity-gaining processes. Corporate income soared, especially in the technology sector. Even hysteria helped: the far-fetched possibility that old software would break when the clocks turned from the 1900s to the 2000s catalyzed a surge in corporate purchases of information technology.

At the macroeconomic level, the rule of law shifted favorably toward more wealth creation and income increases for middle and lower income classes, a strong dollar, and free trade. Purchases and sales of stock by American households during the bubble years resulted in a net gain of more than $2 trillion from equity markets. That cash went into real estate, increased consumption, and various investment vehicles. In the subsequent bust, long-term investors (such as pension fund managers) and those owning names that defrauded the market lost the most. However, even when the declining stock market hit bottom in 2002, the average household had much more money than it would have had but for the boom.[98]

At the microeconomic level, changes in the rule of law encouraged vigorous competition in communications markets, the expansion of the Internet, rapid replacement of old capital stock with new and more efficient assets, increased debt financing, and investment in start-up firms. In the 1990s, firms introduced innumerable goods and services into new and old markets. Michael Porter taught that the "home nation influences the ability of its firms to succeed in particular industries."[99] The "competitiveness" arguments of the 1980s had encouraged Americans to adopt a rule of law that promoted entrepreneurship. The architecture of the Net, however, stimulated a host of information technologies—operating systems and application software, microprocessor and memory chips, routers, servers, data centers, access and transport networks, radios, baseband and signaling processors. Start-ups invented components; incumbents raced to keep up. The component firms sold to start-up firms assembling systems; incumbents hurried to keep up. The systems firms sold to network start-ups; incumbents increased capital expenditures to match their new rivals. Networks spread across the land; everyone went online.

Each successful category created advantages for Americans in foreign markets. AOL entered the business of Internet access in Germany. Yahoo! led in broadband access in Japan. Qualcomm became a world leader in intellectual property embedded in handheld devices: hundreds of millions of cell phones generated royalty payments for a start-up founded by San Diego engineers.

During the 1990s American technology firms in general went from selling almost entirely to American end users to selling about 70 percent of their components and systems to users and assemblers outside the United States, and by the early oos the fastest growing markets for their products were in Southeast Asia. As Porter wrote in 1990, "A nation's firms are likely to gain competitive advantage in global segments that represent a large or highly visible share of home demand but account for a less significant share in other nations."[100] When the American culture created the information economy of the Golden 90s in its country, it also opened the door for American firms to export that culture and their goods and services to the rest of the world.

New communications networks generated and transmitted much more information at much lower cost. Almost everyone benefited as the cost of communications approached zero. With ever cheaper access to information and new competition from entrepreneurs, firms made goods and provided services at much lower cost. Productivity soared. Those productivity gains created new wealth. The direct winners included (1) the owners of the productive firms, because the increased return on investment made richer the shareholders and employees given shares in the form of options, and (2) the employees who negotiated higher pay per hour, because their skilled use of machines and information produced more output per hour. Capital and labor negotiated the division of the wealth, but productivity gains made the booty bigger. So in the 1990s employees reversed the negative trends of the previous quarter century, and for all income classes earnings went up.

As businesses made more goods and services per dollar invested, they provided more for consumers to purchase. Producers and consumers always negotiate the allocation of the "more"—what economists call "welfare gains." Producers of computer software and hardware got much of the welfare gains that their technologies created. That was one reason why Microsoft's margins were high and its stock went from a market capitalization of $37 billion in 1992 to almost $300 billion in 2004. By contrast, in long-distance service consumers won the greater share of the welfare gains, one reason why AT&T's market capitalization went from $34 billion in 1989 to $12 billion in 2004.[101]

That summery American decade of value creation had its epicenter in Sunnyvale, California, forty-two miles down Highway 101 from the central location of 1967's Summer of Love, the Haight neighborhood of San Francisco.[102] Sunnyvale, an eponymous name, was the municipality that contained the headquarters of Jupiter, AMD, Palm, Yahoo!, San Disk, and many other technology companies. By the late 1990s it and the hamlets composing Silicon Valley attracted legions of gifted, educable, and ambitious youths.[103] To bring people in from other countries, Silicon Valley employers persuaded Congress to expand the visa program known as H1-B. McKinsey & Company, the strategic management consulting company, explained to clients that there was a "global war for talent."[104] Technology firms scoured engineering graduate schools, business schools, and even law schools for new hires. Consultants, law firms, public relations firms, financial advisers, and other professional outfits serving information technology firms shoveled in new employees to keep up with demand. This demand helped cause workers' share of national income to increase from 64 percent to nearly 67 percent between 1997 and 2001.[105] Although academics do not credit the existence of Kondratiev waves, nevertheless after the quarter century of decline starting around 1968, an upswing began in the mid-1990s. In that era, investors looked for small, creative, disruptive firms. Small firms catalyzed the growth of the information economy.[106] In the 1990s most must have agreed with Marc Andreessen's explanation: "What is Silicon Valley really about? It's about a culture of risk taking, a culture of entrepreneurialism, a culture of new company formation."[107] To some, big firms appeared structurally incapable of advancing Schumpeter's creative destruction as quickly or extensively.[108] Moreover, the start-ups could return ten times an investment in a few years, or flame out in the effort. Netscape's initial public offering (IPO) in 1995 had magnetic and paradigmatic power: the firm invented a browser, and although almost no one had heard much if anything about it only months before, the stock was purchased with such eagerness that, in the first day of trading, its price went from $28 to $75 per share and John Doerr's venture capital firm's investment went from $5 million to $148 million.[109]

Whereas in the 1980s private equity expected to earn perhaps 30 percent return per year on virtually every investment, venture capital in the Golden 90s expected to create two or three big new goods or services out of ten investments and to earn ten to one hundred times their money on the winning investment. They called it "swinging for home runs." Never was so much money invested at so high a risk with so much reward. Total venture capital investment in the United States rose from just under $7 billion in early 1999 to more than $28 billion at the peak of the boom in the year 2000.[110]

Venture investing belied the psychological propensity of human beings to avoid risk. It undercut the hierarchies of professional advancement. It implied that creativity trumped station. It reaffirmed the American Dream. Anyone could be Bill Gates, Larry Ellison, Henry Ford, Andrew Carnegie, at least in the respect that none obtained a college degree before rolling the career dice. Indeed, the refusal to accept the natural order of advancement, the zeal to remake hierarchies according to one's personal vision, seemed crucial to success.[111] In the 1990s, the culture of disruptive entrepreneurship reached an apogee.

In an Uncertain Future

The Golden 90s ended with a stock market crash, and worsened into increasing income inequality and a loss of Americans' confidence in the future. The economy overall grew in the 00s, but most workers were worse off in the new century.[112] Members of households worked more hours in 2004 than the year before but for the fifth straight year could not increase household income (in real terms, meaning adjusting for inflation).[113] The government could not untangle the Gordian knot of inefficiencies in health care. As a result, virtually everyone paid more for health care, and more companies refused to pay those expenses for employees.

The slight recession of late 2000 and early 2001, along with the relative canniness of the Republican campaign and the failure to count all the votes in Florida, denied the presidency to Al Gore, one of the authors of the government policies that encouraged the entrepreneurial successes of the 1990s. In response to the recession, the Bush administration lowered interest rates and cut taxes. These stimuli lifted the stock market and caused a boom in housing prices. Because median and average wages did not rise, income inequality reached record levels. For those not in the ranks of property owners, the housing-price boom built a great wall between them and the traditional promise of a home of one's own. Meanwhile, more than a fifth of the population of New York, the global center of finance, lived in poverty in 2004.[114]

The probability that any family would suffer economic reversal rose. Immigration into the United States from 1870 to 1910 reduced wages by an amount ranging between 11 percent and 14 percent from what they would have been.[115] In the twenty-first century, instead of nearly 60 million workers coming from labor-abundant Europe to labor-scarce North and South America, jobs will head from the United States into Asia, and offshore employees will compete for work in America without moving across an ocean.[116] While massage parlors and restaurants will keep hiring in America, cheap real-time connections and computerized processes mean that any work embodied in words or pictures can be done offshore.[117]

In the 00s, all American engineers will face, sooner or later, the possibility of salary cuts or job loss because of global competition.[118] As many as half could see their jobs sent offshore within a decade. McKinsey Global Institute estimated in 2005 that by 2008, over one-tenth of service jobs globally could be offshored. As much as a third of accounting and financing jobs may be sent offshore by 2008.[119] Unless something changes, the result, as in the late nineteenth century, will be less labor scarcity in the United States, which will reduce wages from what American workers otherwise would earn. Unless America responds wisely, economic calamities will lead, in all likelihood, to more social problems such as divorce and personal problems such as depression.

Popular writers like Tom Friedman told their many American readers that the Chinese and other Asians wanted their jobs. Lou Dobbs used CNN as a platform for launching jeremiads against offshoring and outsourcing. Yet academic economists, business leaders, and business-friendly journalists asserted that free trade—including offshoring—benefited all Americans more than it hurt some. They proved with the precision of Euclidean geometry that buying cheap Chinese goods at Wal-Mart produced more gains for American consumers than the total of lost wages attributed to offshoring.[120]

Rising above this debate, economists Ralph Gomory and William Baumol explained in 2000 that American citizens would be better off if their American employers continued to make a disproportionately large share of the world's high-value goods and services.[121] That meant generally that Americans should want their information technology firms to have about 70 percent of global market share, as they had by the end of the Golden 90s. Americans will be best off if the rising Asian countries earn their economic growth from firms in lower-value markets like textiles or agriculture. Chinese information technologists can take up to about 30 percent global share in their high-value markets. That would benefit Americans as well as Chinese by expanding the size of the global consumption market. But if Chinese-hiring entrepreneurs take market share beyond that point from American-employing firms, Americans will be worse off.

Paul Samuelson made similar points in a controversial article in 2004.[122] Nevertheless, many academic economists prefer to avoid this all-important topic. They have a (well-grounded) despair that their government audience would not understand the complexity of the situation and might oppose free trade in a wrong-headed response to the competitive situation.

However, most Americans understand, if not the mathematics of the economic models, the home truths presented to them in their daily lives. Since the Second World War, they looked to their business employers and the government to create a system that produced income gains for everyone at all levels, save perhaps the very poor and the disabled. The culture worked to everyone's advantage in the 1950s and 1960s, not so much in the 1970s and 1980s, and well again in the 1990s. In the early oos it broke down. The overall economy grew, but somehow the big grew bigger, corporate profits increased, and the rich grew both more numerous and richer.[123] Everyone else had a harder time finding a path to success.

Americans looked for leadership in these years of uncertainty. In the Golden 90s, business executives embodied the idea of progress for all Americans. They captured imagination and justly became heroes, *Time* magazine Persons of the Year, inspirational figures for the next generation. In the oos, however, American business leaders have a very different focus. Whether they can lead Americans to an era of broader and deeper entrepreneurship—which aimed to disrupt market hierarchies—is far from clear. The problem, in part, is that the leaders of big American firms are no longer overwhelmingly concerned with the future of the United States.

CHAPTER

2

The Uprooting of American Business

What we're trying to do is outline an entire strategy of becoming a Chinese company.
— JOHN CHAMBERS, CEO OF CISCO SYSTEMS, INC.

Only World Championships Matter

American firms see that China's new culture is giving birth to entrepreneurs who will attack their markets.[1] In response, they could fight a competitive battle in China. Or, they could stay at home and negotiate joint ventures or other alliances that in practice amounted to a division of geographical markets. Alternatively, they could hollow out their activities, turning themselves into American retail stores for products invented, designed, and made in Asia.[2]

The first choice—competing in China's domestic market—is the path for most American information technology firms. To win in global competition, American technology businesses are replanting themselves far from their home ground. Firms are moving investment funds, jobs, and executive attention to China and other big new Asian markets. They realize that national boundaries have become as useless a defensive position as the Maginot Line had been for France. Technology products have a high value per ounce and can be shipped for a small percentage of their worth. Therefore, they are traded in a global market. Computers, for example, are assembled in a global supply chain. Moreover, to win sales in China, firms have to build plants and install equipment in China. They need to learn the territory. They have to be as adept in competing in China as any purely

Chinese-origin firm.[3] Ironically, this means that the American employees of a firm taking on Chinese rivals in China should want their country's businesses to invest in and move jobs to China. If some in their ranks lose their jobs to offshoring, the rest will benefit from working in a globally successful firm. If American firms compete successfully in China, they will deny their Chinese rivals the opportunity to obtain economies of scale in China. American firms succeeded with this tactic in the past and know better than to confer this advantage on their Asian rivals. By hiring in China, American firms can lower their average labor costs and more easily justify higher wages for their remaining American employees. Finally, American firms can earn new revenue in China, and at least some of their increased profits might go to their American employees. By choosing to participate in the Chinese market—as well as exporting into it—American firms expand their own prospects for survival.

Because American firms in the 00s focused more on high-value, traded products, and because the fall of the Soviet Union opened more markets to capitalism, the portion of the American economy involved in global trade increased from below 10 percent in 1990 to about 25 percent in 2003. The traded portion of the American economy grew at twice the rate of the entire global economy. Eventually, the percentage of American firms competing globally, measured by value of output, will rise to the levels of Britain (55 percent) or Korea (75 percent).[4] Therefore, the percentage of American firms entering the China market will increase.

As the global economy grows and the first phase of development in Asia comes to an end, the total demand for engineering skills might exceed supply. By 2015, every engineer in the world might enjoy wage gains. That prospect can cheer the hearts of American engineers only if they start, or find work at, an American firm that is more likely than not destined to succeed in global competition in the future. Working at a successful American technology firm means working for a firm that captures a handsome share of the growing Chinese market.

If Americans in Seattle write a software program, they can sell one copy or a billion copies without incurring significant additional costs. The more customers they have, the more products they can make at an average cost that continually drops. Therefore, if those Seattle software writers capture a share of the huge Chinese market, they will make increasing returns on their investment of time. They then will earn higher wages. If they are confined to the relatively slow-growing American market, they will have to watch Chinese software makers capture the increasing returns from China. In that case, their Chinese competitors will enjoy rising wages, while the Americans experience falling wages. Moreover, if the American software writers cannot generate enough sales to obtain increasing returns, then they cannot generate the cash to adopt new technologies that in turn will give them increasing returns.[5] Microsoft has to sell successfully in China if it is to pay higher wages in Seattle.

By selling into the big Chinese market, firms also create big network effects.[6] By selling chips in China, an American chip maker will gain hundreds or thousands of local developers who design other computer pieces and complementary software that use those chips.[7] Many Chinese firms will thrive, but the American chip maker will survive. It then can pay its American employees more money. In effect, the Chinese developers will create extra value for the American chip maker's American employees. The American firm also can more easily defend its domestic market share, if it battles successfully in China against its rivals.[8]

Because of increasing returns and network effects, winning firms in information technology tend to win almost completely.[9] Except insofar as rivals can obtain some market share by developing specialized products (like Apple's graphics and convenient interface), the winner will take most of the profit in the market. Winners are only as good as their next product, but they have more money and momentum with which to tackle the next product challenge than do their rivals.[10] For these reasons, if American employees do not support their firms' efforts to win competitive battles, their employers might totally abandon America or go out of business entirely.

American employees of Cisco, for example, need the firm to become, as its CEO said, a "Chinese" company. Only in that way can Cisco remain a big American employer.[11] At the apex of the boom Cisco's market capitalization made it one of the five most valuable companies in the world, and even after the market's fall it was valued at $150 billion. But in the 00s it faces a competitive battle with the secretive, fierce, and effective Chinese firm Huawhei. Private investors and the government own Huawhei. They keep its operations very secret. Although started in 1988, it began working on routers in 1994. It achieved very rough parity with Cisco in terms of product quality in about 2004. In that year, Cisco had about 50 percent of the Chinese router market and about 65 percent globally. However, Huawhei was attacking Cisco all over the world. It won a large router contract from Brazil Telecom in 2002, optical backbone contracts from Rostel-com in Russia and Berlikom in Germany in 2002, and an important equip-ment contract from British Telecom in 2005.[12]

Huawhei pays its engineers much more than the average in its southern region of China—but their starting salaries (as of 2005) of $7,000 a year are far below Cisco's $50,000. As hardworking as Silicon Valley thinks it-self, Huawhei employees average about 55 hours a week. Huawhei's total research and development cost on comparable products amounts to only 20 percent of Cisco's. Its cheap and high-quality workforce threatens to generate waves of new products that will challenge Cisco for years to come.

Flying Flags of Convenience

In the nineteenth and twentieth centuries, American firms be-came central parts of the American communities where they had plants, hired employees, and located their headquarters. The automobile industry was called simply "Detroit" because it had so much influence on the city. The culture of Intel became the culture of Silicon Valley. Microsoft shaped Seattle. Employees joined school boards, churches, synagogues. Their em-ployers paid taxes and became philanthropists. Between the local businesses and the local citizens the strands of culture thickened. The community's politics supported the firms by conferring tax advantages, providing real estate and utilities, enshrining executives as local heroes. At the same time, the community's culture constrained firms from driving too hard a bargain on the property tax base or firing too many employees in hard times. The big firm supported hundreds of vendors offering goods and services. The little firms spun more of the culture's webs. In time, political and business leadership overlapped. Firm executives became community leaders; may-ors advised firms. In this way the rule of law mirrored and strengthened the culture.

Since the Second World War, American firms generally have disrupted these local relationships by moving from the North and East to the South and West. They sought to escape unions, regulation, high real-estate prices, and the other trappings of developed societies in the middle of the last century. They found new governments that outbid older communities in offering tax breaks, cheaper land, bigger subsidies. The national govern-ment encouraged corporations to play off one state or community against another. Congress could have passed laws to encourage union organiza-tion everywhere, but it rarely did so. It could have made many regulations uniform across states, but it encouraged arbitrage in the choice of law by declining to do so. It could have used the powers of the Interstate Commerce Clause to bar states from wooing firms with tax breaks, land deals, roads, and airports, but it chose not to do so. Over the decades, firms' negotiating strategies, combined with the free labor market encouraged by Congress, led to a decline in unionism from 36 percent of private-sector workers in 1953 to less than 8 percent in 2005.[13] Over time, corporations succeeded in paying less in total taxes than do high-income individuals.[14] Migrating to new states was an important way to win these results, just as wealthy individuals benefited from moving to the low-tax, light-regulation states of Texas and Florida.

However, no one expected American firms would ever leave the country. After all, immigrants headed for, not away from, America. No nation had better transportation or communication networks, or a bigger consumption market. American graduate schools offered the world's highest level of education in all the basic science and mathematics fields. Every firm wanted to hire American graduates. No one with a choice wanted to raise a family anywhere but the United States of America, the land of country clubs and vacation homes, big roads and fast cars.

Moreover, as long as the Soviet Union existed, a facility or employees overseas might fall under the rule of a communist or socialist regime that might seize American assets or punish American firms depending on the tides of international politics. Firms did not want to leap into the front lines of cold war battles. While the American market rapidly grew, and firms obtained favorable treatment from the newly growing states at home, moving overseas posed unnecessary risks.

In the oos the reasons to stay American became much less compelling. On the other side of the world, China offered the advantages that in previous decades the South and West had presented in comparison to the Midwest and New England. Firms began to develop more internationalized cultures. They pulled away from their roots.

In business today, a firm's leading employees often follow a career path through more than one country. They connect mostly with the firm's culture, less with a state or even a nation. The firm's ethics trump those of any local culture. From the local perspective, the firm's employees, like colonial administrators, belong to a superimposed, transient culture.

These trends have accelerated in the oos as firm cultures reflect the borderlessness of internal communications networks. Firms' global networks,

like huge petri dishes, nurture an international culture. Employees working on a corporate network live in a separate reality from their friends and
family in the community where they live. Through their digital identities,
they live across boundaries. They work at different times, hear different
news, absorb distinctive values that their neighbors in their real world community do not share. In their digital personas, they negotiate the firm's
culture, do the firm's work, are rewarded according to the standards set by
the firm. The firm is more real than the imagined community of a nation.
In the medium of firm intranets, the internal rules, technology, and leadership actions of the firms shape the employees' culture more, while the
country in which the CEO places the headquarters has less influence on
that culture. For the stateless firm, no place feels like home. The firm exists everywhere that its network reaches. It marks time by iterative e-mail
chains, Web log (blog) threads, budget allocations, product introductions
or design wins, not by the rhythms of community life or the terms of a political leader. The firm's future follows the cycle of strategy and execution,
rather than the fortunes of a locality or nation. Cisco's John Chambers
does not have to move his office to Shanghai in order to make the firm
Chinese. He only has to extend the firm's network into China, then watch
the medium remake the firm's metier.[15]

The firm may even want some local cultures to fail or change, as the
United States government wanted the Soviet Union to collapse. Its relationship to local and national cultures is contingent on the gives and gets
of negotiation. Wal-Mart may leave an area where the employees vote for
a union: the global firm always balances local costs against local benefits.
In this measuring, even patriotic American business leaders cannot defer to
a claim that their firms owe a costly loyalty to America or its citizens. Indeed, ignoring such assertions is one of the purposes of the corporate form
of organization.

The American government in the mid-oos appears ignorant of the new
reality for its businesses.[16] In domestic markets it spreads a groaning board
of favors for business: reduced dividend taxation, reduced market competition, reduced regulation, incentives for automobile manufacturers, tax
breaks for oil and gas, no-bid contracts, record spending, and many others. In other countries, however, the American government emphasizes
support for American military activities. The war on terror has taken prece-
dence over the pursuit of business goals on behalf of American firms. In
response, erstwhile allies of the United States have concluded that they

should seek more independence from the United States on economic as well as security issues.

After the Second World War, American firms were in close, and beneficial, alignment with their government's efforts to stimulate economic growth among the world's poor nations. The World Bank, International Monetary Fund, Export-Import Bank, European Reconstruction Development Bank, and other global financing institutions supported by the United States probably did more to help American businesses enter foreign markets than to end world poverty. In the oos the U.S. government consciously played a lesser and more skeptical role in multilateral, treaty-based organizations championing global economic development.[17] Its attempts to thwart the United Nations' Millennium Goal of ending global poverty are emblematic of this new approach. Unintended victims are American businesses.[18]

The inattention of American government to the needs of American businesses has occurred at a particularly unpropitious time, when the American market is beginning to shrink in proportion to foreign markets. That trend will weaken the international influence of American firms. All else equal, firms in smaller markets have less negotiating power than firms in bigger markets, unless they obtain large export shares.[19] In addition, importers are less powerful than exporters, and the world has never seen an importer of the scale represented by the United States. Moreover, nations that borrow are more dependent on those who lend, and the U.S. government has never borrowed like it does in the oos. American businesses have many good reasons to fly many other flags and put the Stars and Stripes off to the side.

Reverse Immigration

New arrivals have fueled American entrepreneurship since before the American Revolution. Crossing the ocean, steel-driving the railroad across the Rockies, farming the homestead, raising a family in the noontime darkness of the mills: these images from scrapbooks and history books compose the national narrative. If Andrew Carnegie, the son of a poor Scottish weaver, could make it in America, so can anyone. In modern times millions of new arrivals obtain the lowest-paid jobs, live in crime-ridden neighborhoods, gain an inferior education, and cannot get health care or citizenship. Still, the rags-to-riches story, the American Dream, inspires the American entrepreneurial culture.

Selling their own cultures as reifications of the American Dream, American firms traditionally inculcated the values of hard work, loyalty, and patriotism.[20] In the 1990s, American technology firms marketed an updated, upscale version of the Carnegie culture. Technology firms wooed the best scientists from other countries, badgered the American government to grant them visas and citizenship, helped them buy houses, found them schools, and taught them to take for granted the luxuries of the ever-improving American standard of living.

American employers have also focused on training and educating the American employee pool, by sending employees to executive training courses at American business schools, helping pay for night school, recruiting from the science and mathematics departments of American universities, granting scholarships, and funding chairs at colleges and universities. American business leaders have spoken out for improving the quality of teaching. Executives like Jim Barksdale and Bill Gates have made huge charitable contributions to improve literacy, to make better use of technology, and to adopt more flexible teaching techniques. Craig Barrett caused Intel to take over the old Westinghouse science competition, through which Intel annually gave $2 million in scholarships in the 00s.

Globalizing firms, however, will shift their focus toward employees in other countries.[21] They have much to gain from helping to train teachers, set up endowments, and transfer learning to the education systems of other nations. Already, "return to home" is the new mantra for American technology firms. Globalizing firms entice foreign-born employees to move back to their countries of origin.[22] Native-born, American-trained employees have both American communication skills and local knowledge of languages and culture. Moreover, they accept perhaps half as much in pay. At that level they still earn much more than their counterparts in the home country.

American higher educational institutions also have gone international. The percentages of American students in mathematics and science decline steadily from freshman year of college through the level of post-doctoral programs. Foreigners fill the spots in such programs. As the saying goes, a graduate program in science in the United States is where a Russian professor teaches a Chinese student. In former years, neither professor nor student would return home; in the 00s, both do, often to start a new business. American firms can hire non-Americans trained in the United States, and send them, with their high skills, to fill important jobs outside America.

Changes in the architecture of international law ease the way for American firms to locate business units in other countries. Until the late 1990s, the legal architecture of international communications effectively taxed multinational corporations for communicating across national boundaries. Firms paid large sums for telephone calls from the United States to every country. Businesses and residential callers in the United States sent more than $5 billion a year to the foreign telephone companies, which were typically owned in whole or in part by their governments. Developing nations favored this approach because their state-owned or state-controlled telephone companies could easily collect revenue from incoming calls, whereas their internal revenue services were largely incapable of collecting income or sales taxes from their citizenry. In some developing nations, charges on inbound communications accounted for all the profits of the national telephone company. (Even so, foreign countries usually provided inferior communications capabilities, further discouraging firms from conducting their critical business activities outside the United States.)

In the Golden 90s, the U.S. government successfully advocated changing the law of international communications so as to lower prices and expand physical connections into all countries. Responding to both the change in law and new optical fiber technologies, global firms accelerated their use of high-speed data connections to transfer blueprints, drawings, spreadsheets, and databases in digital form throughout their organizations. They put much of their buying and selling online, thereby pulling vendors and customers into a global network of newly cheap and efficient communication. Developing countries licensed cellular telephony networks that made distant foreign employees accessible to their American employers anytime and anywhere. A firm's design team in Shanghai could see marketing plans for a product posted on a secure Web site, then discuss it in a conference call that included a team in California.

Firms prefer to concentrate ample research-and-development teams in geographic centers. They like to assemble top managers for in-person meetings. They are beginning, however, to create more centers and hold more critical meetings outside the United States. They are more likely than ever before to place business units in Shanghai, Beijing, and Hong Kong.

American firms are creating crucial intellectual property outside the United States. Ultimately, a firm exists wherever it creates and captures value. American firms fear theft of intellectual property in China.[23] Nonetheless, they routinely file for copyrights, trademarks, and patents in many countries. To make matters worse, the American patent system is breaking down. As of early 2006, the average waiting time for pending patent applications was more than two years.[24] Other countries have the opportunity to take the lead in protecting intellectual property away from the United States. If China does so, it will accelerate the creation and transfer of business ideas from the United States to China.[25]

If the United States offshores technology leadership along with jobs and investment capital, the firms left behind will not necessarily find big winners around which to cluster. They will become more tentative. They may not keep pace with Chinese technology development, or even obtain equally good service from Chinese technology sellers, as when California taught American business how to obtain the productivity gains of the 1990s.[26] The left-behind will struggle with the airline schedules to China and the language and mores of the Chinese. They may slow the pace of investment and lose competitive advantage in markets where foreigners can compete against them.

A more slowly expanding economy will not necessarily produce a government more inclined to increase spending on public goods, such as transportation, communications networks, education, and basic research. If the American economy grows more slowly, as fast-growing firms root themselves in other countries, then the claims of Medicare for the aged, Medicaid for the poor, and Social Security for the retired will take a greater share of the gross domestic product. Those who support those claims may not support spending more money, for example, on education. Indeed, school bond proposals often fail when parents with school-age children become a relatively small part of a city's population. Worries about pensions and health care may drive a graying nation to spend more on the welfare of seniors and less on preparing the future generation.

Fading Friendship

In the 00s optimistic commentators blithely opine that American entrepreneurs will invent generations of new goods and services, waves of new business models, encyclopedias of new ideas. Particularly the right-wing babblers and scribblers predict that the American economy will experience productivity gains that eventually lead to wage increases. Meanwhile, Americans will export goods, services, and ideas producing wealth for Americans and freedom of speech and religion for everyone. Yet no rosy dawn will produce a new morning for America, unless firms invest increasing amounts of cash in the United States.[27]

By 2000, for the first time in any nation, a majority of citizens in the United States owned shares of public corporations. Among likely voters, 70 percent owned stock directly or indirectly.[28] The shareholders of public corporations do not necessarily have the same goals as American employees. As shareholders in multinational corporations, they want their firms to invest in the fastest growing markets, even if in Asia.[29] They want their firms to hire cheaper labor, even if that means firing the guy next door or denying a salary increase to the lady across the street. They favor trade agreements that help their firms export, even if reciprocal terms drive their neighbor's company out of business. A shareholder cares about allocating capital and jobs where the most money can be made.[30] Shareholders know nothing of patriotism. The rational indifference of American shareholders toward American citizens will compound when, within a generation, foreigners own the majority of shares in most large American corporations, as will inevitably occur given the increasing foreign wealth and ownership of American assets.

Of course anyone can try to synthesize in one's personal life the points of view of a shareholder, homeowner, employee, Little League coach, parent with school-age children, child with parents in need of assisted living, and all the other points of view that life provides in due course to most people. If a corporate executive or a collection of shareholders could combine such different perspectives in determining firm conduct, perhaps those who direct firm strategy might reconcile the goals of American citizens with the profit-maximization purpose of the firm. However, the rule of law in America does not grant anyone the authority to balance different stakeholders' concerns in deciding what firms should do. Boards of public companies must maximize shareholder value, not balance the interests of capital, labor, community, and country. Even those elected to political office do not have much chance to reconcile competing interests, when they must depend utterly on the monetary support of well-heeled factions for their election campaigns. Circumstances preclude them from choosing the disinterested perspective advocated by the framers of the Constitution.[31]

In any case, even if an individual shareholder might wish to strike a balance between loyalties to American concerns and capital's value maximization, that individual usually delegates decision making to agents who, under the prevailing law, must focus unrelentingly on total return to shareholders.[32] Those agents pressure firms to put capital and jobs where revenue will be maximized and costs minimized. Perhaps unknowingly, the majority of Americans owning stock in American firms effectively push public firms to transfer American productive capability and American jobs at high and low income levels to other countries. A presidential candidate might call a job-exporting executive "Benedict Arnold," but the law of corporate governance makes turncoats out of all American shareholders.[33]

In addition, as a result of changes in immigration law in the 1970s and 1980s, by the turn of the century nearly 12 percent of American residents were foreign-born. Of these, more than a third came from Asian countries.[34] Both of the major American political parties woo the rapidly growing immigrant populations in order to seek long-term electoral advantage. Many of the new arrivals want the U.S. government to focus on the political relationship with their countries of origin. As a result, in the fast-growing states like Texas, Florida, and California where immigrants concentrate, political leaders tend to take more internationally oriented positions than in the slow-growing, more nativist states. These regional perspectives deepen the difference between those Americans who are the spearhead of globalization and those wounded by that process.

America's political system does not offer good ways for the losers in trade to redress their grievances. The mainstream media didactically informs Americans that free trade, including offshoring, benefits everyone. Academic commentators usually qualify their endorsement of globalization by noting that competition should be fair in all countries and that the United States should educate its citizens better.[35] However, Congress has not turned those qualifications into conditions of trade treaties.[36]

Many individual employees who have lost in global trade competition belonged to unions. Many manufacturers who have suffered from global competition had their facilities in the industrial Northeast and Midwest. The Republicans, however, draw their electoral strength principally from the nonunionized states of the old Confederacy and the Great Plains. A pure free-trade policy would harm textiles, sugar, and agricultural interests just as it has had serious impact on manufacturing, but the Bush administration has tended to protect the industries of its political base from global competition. Because the American voting system does not adhere to the principle of one person–one vote in either the Senate or the Electoral College, the less populous states exercise outsized influence over political outcomes than the more populous states. The agrarian interests of the emptier states therefore can thwart the interests of the majority of the people, in at least two respects. They obtain protection from trade for their products (raising prices to urban buyers) and deny redress for wage and job loss to the trade victims in the populous states.

In any event, the victims of globalization are strange bedfellows who hardly form a united front. They have no tradition of cooperation for political purposes. In particular, unions and entrepreneurs have much in common on global issues but see themselves as utterly dissimilar, or even antagonistic. The Democratic Party has made some efforts to unite these factions. But for the most part those who found small businesses remain a bastion of the Republican Party, even when it does not much advance their interests in global trade. Technology entrepreneurs typically espouse libertarian concepts, if they have any political views. Neither general nor technology entrepreneurs find unions and trial lawyers, two Democratic constituencies, to be comfortable company. Entrepreneurship clearly produces job creation and wage increases, but entrepreneurs and workers do not unite behind common political goals.

By the oos, global competition and American factionalism undermined the confidence of the American people.[37] Most people distrust the ability of political leaders to address the situation effectively.[38] They do not care for anti-trade gestures, such as tariffs on steel imports imposed by the Bush administration. Nor do they rally behind any pro-trade agenda.

A useful comparison is between the tumultuous years 1968 and 2001. The former was marked by the end of the New Deal consensus, the conclusion of the postwar boom, political tragedy and upheaval, and, with the founding of Intel, the commencement of the information age. The latter saw the end of the Clinton administration, the nadir of the stock market bust after the bubble, the worst single year in the history of the semiconductor industry, and the beginning of the war on terror. Throughout these thirty-three years (the summer of your author's life), almost all American households, in real, inflation-adjusted terms, saw their income go up. That was the great overall fact. In this era, however, the income and net worth of the rich grew much faster than anyone else's. Income inequality increased.[39] This large trend was reported in many different ways. At an accelerating rate, CEO pay rampaged upward, stock options minted millions of millionaires, tax cuts and tax breaks favored the upper-income fifth of the country, having higher education paid higher rewards and having less education exposed workers to more vigorous wage competition from immigrants and globalization.[40] Even if some headlines exaggerated the trend, its direction could not be denied. Except during the last half of the 1990s, America has been creating a hierarchy of income and gutting its middle-class character. Under these circumstances, the American people naturally did not believe business leaders would develop solutions for falling income and failing employment. Scandals at Enron, WorldCom, and other fallen firms surprised chiefly by their magnitude, not by the attitudes they revealed.

After the stock market fell in the oos, the income gaps continued to widen. It seemed that the rich had become immune to cyclical downturns. In 2004, while most Americans saw their income go down, the United States led the world in the creation of new millionaires.[41] Setting a new record for a nation with households of a net worth of more than $1 million, 7.5 million out of 105 million American households passed that mark.[42] The government's particular selection of economic stimuli caused the number of millionaire households to rise 21 percent in that year alone, even while nonmanagement employee wages fell.[43]

In the oos, American society is breaking apart like the Titanic, with a rich elite piling into the lifeboats of financial security and the rest left to hope for a raft. A fifth of the United States has the perspective on society previously reserved for only a few percent. So many have become rich that instead of the middle class defining the country, a large upper class runs it.[44] The new elite will be light on scientists and engineers. For computer programmers, 14 percent of jobs were lost between 2000 and 2002.[45] It will be packed with financiers, lawyers, consultants, business executives, and others comfortable in the globalized markets. This new big upper class is not likely to demand broader and deeper creative disruption as the response to the challenge of rising China or any other threat emerging from global trends. They will not even see the challenge as a threat, while the rest of Americans certainly will.

By possessing as of 2001 about half of all national income, the top fifth already has created among its members much short-term incentive and power to suppress the aspirations of the rest of the society. That topmost quintile of the society, acting through the agency of the Bush administration, has made many changes in the rule of law that further its economic interests much more than the interests of the other four-fifths of Americans. Indeed, if the trends of 1968 to 2001 extend for another thirty-three years, then by 2034 the top fifth will earn (in 2001 dollars) more than $275,000 per household, while the bottom fifth will earn $12,500 and the middle fifth $57,000. The United States will continue to have the largest group of rich people of any country in history. The average income in 2034 will be nearly $100,000, close to twice the median. However, approximately two-thirds of households will be below the average income. People do worry about keeping up with the Joneses, and if the Joneses are above the average, most people, under current trends, will fall way behind them over the next three decades. Under these circumstances most Americans are likely to feel that they are not doing well, even if in real terms they are earning more than they earned in the past. Moreover, the gaps between the rungs of the income ladder will be unsurpassably large. Individuals will have greater difficulty progressing upward through income quintiles, or classes, over the course of a work life. Class mobility will decline. People will lose the sense of a common American community, stop believing in an American purpose.

The 1990s created a fissure in American society by enriching 20 percent of the population far more than the rest. This created a generation of plutocrats. Within the top quintile itself, the wealth disparity broadened: more than 800,000 American families reported a net worth of more than $10 million by the end of the 1990s.[46]

As the winners of America's economic horse race have multiplied, a "winner take all" model of success has taken hold in the cultural value system. Those on the top control government and nongovernment institutions. They lower their own taxes, cut pensions, refuse universal health care, educate their children at private schools, and hire an army from the other half to wage war for their purposes.

Those on the other side of the income gap are suffering bouts of unemployment or underemployment.[47] Their tax burden is increasing on a relative basis, as sales and payroll taxes rise.[48] Their education, pension, health care, and other public benefits are diminishing in quality and quantity. They face competition more from immigrants than offshoring, yet have few ways to respond.

In the 00s all Americans on average are suffering harsher and more prolonged falls in personal income than in previous decades.[49] Participation in the workforce has dropped precipitously as people fail to find jobs.[50] The employed on the high side of the road are enjoying much faster income growth. Those on the other side have seen their income fall in real terms.[51]

As an increasing portion of American society experiences falling income, fewer in the society believe in the opportunity for success. Many have suffered catastrophe. Those who have avoided dire straits have come to believe that the American economy has lost the knack of wealth creation.

The American Dream has not yet lost all credibility. But the risk of that cultural erosion is increasing. If Americans no longer believe they can get from the low side to the high side of the street in their lifetimes, then possibly they will no longer support entrepreneurship. When people believe they are growing poorer, they tend to pull back from risk. They invest less in new goods and services. They do not join start-ups. They husband what they have. They cut back on consumption. The economy slows. Incomes grow even less quickly, or not at all.[52]

As societies lose confidence in future success, those in charge of money and politics want to protect their position in hierarchies of power. The nation's elite may not make commitments to others. If everything seems at risk, they may resist paying higher taxes, investing in broadband for everyone, lowering tuition at colleges, abandoning legacy preferences, and otherwise encouraging disruption of the status quo. Meanwhile, the non-wealthy may use the power of the vote to confiscate some of what the wealthy have stored away. They may impose higher income-tax rates on the wealthy. They may not stop at that measure. If misinformed or misled, they may vote against free trade. They may mulct entrepreneurs of the fruit of their success. They might expand entitlements like Social Security and health care but reduce the opportunity to create the wealth that funds those entitlements. In the 00s the United States seems to be too divided to make critical collective decisions.[53]

The twin national goals should be for total American income to rise at least as fast as total world income and for all income groups to go up at approximately the same rate. The United States should not relinquish its future income growth to other countries. Nor should it appropriate and redistribute the income growth of its top quintile. However, the country needs to reverse the thirty-three-year trend of increasing income inequality; if it does not, the society eventually will not be able to obtain a reasoned and uncoerced consensus on issues. The existing culture will dissolve, and another will take its place. Other values will define the meaning of America. The record of history suggests that the new version will be inferior to what today's Americans still can preserve for their progeny. A culture of creative destruction is not likely to be grounded in a society riven by income-class antagonism.

3

The Up and Down
of Entrepreneurial
Culture in America

One cannot bear to join the madness
But if he does not do so
He will not share in the spoils
And will starve as a result.
—TRADITIONAL BALINESE POEM, QUOTED IN CLIFFORD GEERTZ,
THE INTERPRETATION OF CULTURES

Private rites of magic send
The temple prostitutes to sleep;
All the literati keep
An imaginary friend.
—W. H. AUDEN, "THE FALL OF ROME"

Reform's End

Thinking about new jobs that will raise incomes for all Americans, everyone suffers a failure of imagination. Jobs, income growth, and economic health cannot come from arm-twisting big firms to "keep your best jobs here."[1] The better the high-paid jobs, the more transient they are. Many service jobs will stay in the United States, but that is no obvious cure to the American workers' plight. To gussy up the average income for this sector, the U.S. Trade Representative lumps tour operators and insurance adjusters in with doctors and bankers. This fit of egalitarianism cannot obscure the fact that in constant dollars the wages for most service jobs are falling.

Scientific breakthroughs can lead to new goods and services. Jobs in these new high-value markets should pay high wages. But what sciences? What breakthroughs will create new jobs? What firms will emerge to lead in world markets, hiring thousands of Americans as profits soar? Leaders quail at the prospect of picking the winners of the future. They should not be fainthearted. They should have the courage to give up this task. They need to stop trying to make too much sense out of the ferment of entrepreneurship.

No commissions or select group of leaders can or should invent the new jobs or select the new industries. The only adequate response to rising Asia lies in the cultural reform that will vastly increase entrepreneurship.[2] Leaders need to encourage broader (more markets) and deeper (more entrepreneurs) new initiatives without knowing what specific results will follow. They need to focus on architectural changes that support the culture of entrepreneurship. Then American society will see the creation of start-up technological companies in more numbers and in more markets—because increases in the scale (bigger efforts) and scope (more fields of endeavor) of entrepreneurship are required to meet the challenge of rising China. Entrepreneurial firms will stimulate, aggregate, and replicate the unpredictable creativity that lies in everyone. Acting formally or informally together, individuals will make new goods, services, markets, and jobs that are no more imaginable today than eBay or Amazon was before it started. While the Chinese ruling elite try to copy the American economy of the past, American citizens should change their economy, and export their "new new things" to China.[3]

In most underdeveloped countries, ruling elites can encourage national champions without challenging incumbents, because their economies have not produced powerful enterprises, outside of the state itself. In the United States, the serried ranks of highly productive capital stand as a massive barrier to entrepreneurial rivals. In the face of incumbent power, the United States should emphasize change, experimentation, high tolerance for failure, and rapidity of capital turnover as the key characteristics of its economy. This is entrepreneurship, American style. It is also the only viable choice for the American economy, because it already comprises too many markets, and each has too much complexity, for a top-down, centralized authority to implement a detailed plan for job creation. Well-funded special interests in any case would thwart or capture any government plan to favor national champions. The American culture has a long history of leading the world in change: building on that strength follows the sensible rule of doing what one does best.[4]

To meet the challenges of rising China, Americans need purposefully to expand the scale and increase the pace of productive change. The society needs both to lose and gain job classifications at a faster rate.[5] Individuals need to work at more, not fewer, firms during their careers, staying shorter times with each employer. Stability in a particular job at a single firm is not a goal for anyone, much less for the average person. Americans need to speed up the pace of evolution toward an ever more productive economy.

An entrepreneurial economy probably will create new, more challenging jobs and destroy old, easier jobs.[6] According to the Cato Institute, from 1993 to 2002 the private sector in the United States added 327.7 million new jobs and lost 309.9 million.[7] In effect, everyone in the workforce moved from an old job to a new job twice during that time, and the total number of jobs increased by about 20 million more than in the previous decade. The job classifications changed even more extensively.[8] Even jobs with the same title at the beginning and end of the decade had new and more complex duties. In successful firms the new jobs, with or without new titles, probably implied increasing income, opportunity for promotion, constant learning, and more interesting challenges.[9]

No one escapes risk in an entrepreneurial culture. Firms competing in high-value technology markets cannot count on long, useful lives.[10] In the decade from 1995 to 2004, 184 firms were added to (and of course 184 firms dropped from) the NASDAQ-100 list, which is generally reflective of the computer hardware and software and telecommunications sectors. On average, then, about 20 percent of the information technology list turned over annually.[11] The prevailing weather in that sector is stormy. The normal conditions are uncertain forecasts, unforeseen threats, and inevitable calamities. As the employees in information technology know well, entrepreneurial Americans must learn to survive like Odysseus, "the man of twists and turns driven time and again off course."[12]

Some advise the next generation of Americans to learn Mandarin.[13] Six months of an immersion course are said to open up a career avenue. In the United States population more than two million speak some Chinese language, a larger group of foreign-language speakers than any other, except of course the nearly 30 million Spanish speakers.[14] The country has more than enough Chinese speakers to meet any foreseeable business need for that facility. The United States hardly needs to create millions more Mandarin speakers. In any event, sending ambitious Americans to work overseas would ape Europe's unfortunate reaction to the rise of the United States in the late nineteenth century: shipping its would-be entrepreneurs abroad. Bad outcomes will occur for any country that keeps its timid or ill-equipped citizens at home, while shipping its ambitious and gifted people abroad.

Yet how should the young American select a career? One might become a canny sea captain or an adroit radio repairman yet never find a good employer for those skills. Those fields of work have gone fallow for a reason. No entrepreneur will create a start-up demanding those skills. No philanthropist will endow a research laboratory to discover better ways to sail the oceans or fix broken radios. The secret to personal business success as always lies in acquiring an ability to solve the complex problems of the era. There is no shortage of knots to untie; the unraveling, however, may take as long as Penelope's wait. That is the challenge of entrepreneurship.

The principal purpose of a nation's economic policy, stated Harvard Business School professor Michael Porter, is "to produce a high and rising standard of living for its citizens."[15] However, large-scale national success results from victories by individual firms and their employees. Americans cannot enjoy a high and rising standard of living on average, or at the median, unless many individuals obtain increasing income in ever-changing jobs provided by rapidly evolving firms that win new competitive battles in any and all country markets.[16] Americans, therefore, need to work at technology firms that invest in, compete in, and eventually hire in China.

Through the last half of the twentieth century, successful firms grew in scale and scope. Firms important to job growth started small but did not stay small. Britain, not the United States, deserved the label of "a nation of shopkeepers." Japan's economy, not America's, rested on mom-and-pop stores. Indeed, by the mid-00s half of Americans worked in firms that had 500 or more employees.[17] Firms of size suited the scale of the country.

To become meaningful employers, new business start-ups have to defeat big firms in domestic competition. If they cannot survive locally, they cannot challenge globally. To win, they need to build capable teams quickly, and to hire and fire rapidly until they have the right skills and firm culture. They have to attract individuals from other companies, universities, consulting firms, and even law firms.

The best way for Americans to respond to the emerging competition from China and other Asian countries is to intensify and expand the competitive process. Imagine that venture capital funded 1,000 firms in 20 markets, that 100 firms in 10 markets created value for venture investors, that 10 firms in 5 markets created more value for later stage investors, and that 2 firms in 2 markets survived for a decade, employed more than 5,000 people each, and became winners in global competition. That funnel of failure, with a few big companies squeezing through the aperture of success, resembles venture capital in Silicon Valley from the 1960s to the 00s. In the future, the United States should increase every number in the sequence: more start-ups in more markets, with more value creation at every stage, and ultimately more global winners in more markets. What can expand potentially infinitely is the number and size of markets, so that American start-ups become the world leaders in, say, solar power (of trivial size in the 00s) and quantum computing (not commercial in the 00s). American policy should be to intensify and amplify a culture of entrepreneurship to create and capture value in the future in ways scarcely imaginable in the present.

The government cannot order people to start new firms. No technology can send them through a production line. No leader can describe the thousands of new firms needed by Americans. The culture, however, can produce a great upsurge of entrepreneurship, as occurred in the 1990s. American citizens can depend on a brand new day of job creation if they can remember how law, technology, and leadership created an entrepreneurial culture in the last decade of the rapidly receding twentieth century.

The Golden Rules of the 1990s
Case in Point

America Online: the name itself had the force of destiny. Steve Case thought of it in 1987, half a decade before the birth of the commercial Internet. In the pre-Internet 1980s, America Online, Prodigy, and CompuServe went into business for the purpose of persuading Americans to write—that is, to type on computer keyboards—to each other through telephone lines. None of these firms contemplated the technology of the Internet. The history of communication inspired them. They proposed to fuse the telegraph and the mail. As the concept of electronic communication evolved in the 1980s and Golden 90s, Steve Case stuck with his vision. Others developed the Web protocols, but Case made e-mail a mass-market phenomenon. He changed the Internet more than it changed his business plan, but he needed the law to help him change American culture.

At the beginning, Case knew little about technology and less about law. He had, however, a deep connection to the narrative of American aspiration: start with nothing, learn the ropes, work hard, have a dream, change the world. Growing up in Hawaii in the 1960s, Steve Case and his older brother Dan were "always inventing little businesses," in Steve's words.[18] At distant, frozen Williams College, Case played guitar in a band patterned after the Cars and read Alvin Toffler. Just as young Congressman Newt Gingrich believed Toffler predicted a transformation in the methods of politics, Case believed that the popular visionary forecast a monumental change in the way people communicated with each other.

As a purposeful step toward this future, Case wanted to learn marketing. Graduating college in 1980, he landed a job at one of the icons of the second wave of industrialization—Procter and Gamble. The nineteenth-century Cincinnati soap manufacturer had become the leading graduate school for marketing consumer products. Looking back in 2004 Case said,

> I liked the idea of being in Cincinnati because that's where Time-Warner was trying Q, its first trial of interactive television. It spawned MTV. But I went there primarily because I thought P & G would be a stepping stone to learning how to market this vision. P & G tries to differentiate new products in a world where differentiation is hard. The lesson they taught is that you can create a new product if you can get people to try it. I worked on a hair conditioner on a dry towelette. This was an extension of the Bounce technology. You know, the cleanser on a dry towelette so you can dab it on a spot. The idea was you could apply hair conditioner just where you needed it, like on some particular spot of your hair. It flopped miserably. We got people to try it and it sucked.
>
> But that's just what we did at AOL to get people on the Internet. We put disks everywhere. Got people to try it.

Case did not have to add that people did not think e-mail "sucked" like hair conditioner on a towelette. E-mail was the greatest thing since— Ivory soap.

Case continued: "But P & G was too corporate and too bureaucratic. I went to Pizza Hut in Wichita. I liked Pizza because the franchisees really ran the company. They controlled their own destinies. They were more like guerilla street fighters. I never expected to be the CEO of Pepsi [the parent company of Pizza Hut]. Pizza was a stepping stone. I was always reading newsletters about interactivity. I became a self-proclaimed expert in a field no one knew anything about."

All entrepreneurial businesses, according to Silicon Valley's Randy Komisar, can be categorized as either "better, faster, cheaper" or "Brave New World."[19] Case wanted to pursue the latter. But Case could not create the brave new world until he learned how to sell products, and that proved very difficult: "I learned at Pizza Hut that it's easy to cook something in a test kitchen. You can make all kinds of interesting food. But it's a lot harder to have these products work in restaurants where the chef is a fifteen-year-old kid who's been there for twelve days. And you also find out that people want familiar things on pizza. Like pepperoni and cheese. People like to fit themselves in recognizable niches. These are business lessons that we applied at AOL. But it took us nine years to get one million customers. And another nine years to get 30 million."

AOL began as Control Video Corporation (CVC), founded and run by Bill Von Meister. "When I got to know Bill," said Case, "PC's were not popular and home PC's were less popular. The Mac was not yet launched. Atari video machines were in homes. Bill said, let's turn Atari's into interactive terminals not just for video games but for all kinds of communication. That was the basic idea. We could have waited for the PC but the Atari's were there."

Case accepted the CVC job in April 1983, wound up his work for Pizza Hut, and took off for a summer vacation in Europe, where he had never been before. When he returned to start work in September 1983, he discovered that CVC was "on the brink of collapse." The company soon laid off half the workforce. By that Christmas, Case realized that CVC's product did not work well, and that playing games with people's desire to communicate did not endear the company to its customers.

An entrepreneur reacts to being blown off course with optimism and an unrelenting desire to reach his or her Ithaca. Case's reaction to CVC's crisis was: "I felt I had no downside. Bill Von Meister was a P. T. Barnum–style entrepreneur. He had an idea a minute. He was always on the edge of collapse. My family and friends were concerned. I thought I learned a lot from Bill. I thought that this guy was a piece of work. I learned to take risks from him. He took too many. He didn't calculate them. But he taught me to be a risk-taker. I also learned that if you don't stick with something you may not be there when things get interesting. Bill moved on too quickly. I never felt like giving up. My parents and friends told me I should. The problems we had just strengthened my resolve to pursue the goal."[20]

In 1987 Von Meister left CVC. Case became executive vice president. Case focused on finding channel partners who would sell CVC's connectivity along with their appliance, whether game boxes or PCs. (Most information services are, like presents, better delivered when wrapped inside a box.) He changed the name to America Online, emphasizing the communications over the content. Apple, in search of an advantage in its losing battle with Microsoft, licensed its technology to AOL. On the strength of that license, Case raised venture money and hired new people. AOL planned to ride on top of the Macintosh into the interactive future.

However, culture matters. Information firms primarily consist of people sharing in a common culture that they hope to make productive. Apple's culture opposed licensing its technology, so by 1991 Apple blew up the partnership. Case said, "That brought AOL to the brink of collapse, again. We laid off a lot of people. We realized we couldn't sustain the strategy of partnering with PC companies to sell our product. Consumers weren't defining themselves by the names of their PC's."

Entrepreneurs find silver linings in clouds. Case continued, "If Apple hadn't blown up our partnership we would not have launched AOL. Crisis is a good thing for companies and for governments. People try to avoid crisis. Crisis forces you out of your comfort zone. It forces you to take risks. All institutions have antibodies that are designed to avoid risk. That leads to incrementalism. That can be a good thing, of course. Steadiness is a good feature. But the bigger the country or the company the more management has something big to protect. Only when things get bad does the culture of the company or the country have the potential to change."

After the Apple channel dried up, Case began selling AOL as an online connection directly to users. CompuServe and Prodigy led the industry, each with its own network. Neither would connect its customers to anyone but its other customers, thereby diminishing the value of each person's connectivity, in the doomed hope of capturing network effects for themselves. They tried to distinguish their business models to minimize competition. CompuServe primarily intended to provide business news to its customers. Prodigy aimed to sell things. Case focused on his fundamental vision: creating a new way for people to communicate.

When we found ourselves competing against those two firms we had to step up. Launching AOL against them came from a sense of having to do it. We were successful because we had no business to protect. We looked through the window instead of the rear view mirror. When Knight Ridder looked at interactivity they saw it through the prism of newspapers so they thought it was about distributing news. At Citibank they saw it through the prism of banking so they thought it was about banking. This technology was seen by everyone through their own historical prism. But at AOL we said we know nothing so we take the customer's viewpoint instead of the historical viewpoint. We didn't even view what we were doing through a technological prism. That was a problem Microsoft had. Silicon Valley tends to focus on technology for the sake of technology. In Northern Virginia we focused more on real people. We had more of a Main Street perspective. That was why MSN wasn't as good as AOL.

When AOL began to compete against CompuServe and Prodigy, the conventional wisdom assumed that the interactivity business belonged to huge firms that could sell PCs through thousands of stores and connect them with phone lines to packet data networks in part owned by the firms and in part leased by them from MCI or AT&T. However, the 1984 consent decree breaking up AT&T barred the local Bell companies from participating in those long-distance businesses, opening the online connection market to new entrants.

Steve Case, not the big firms, became the world's expert in bringing people online. Through AOL he changed culture by establishing a reason why tens of millions of people wanted to get on the Net. At first, they wanted to look at Web pages with Marc Andreessen's browser, but soon people dove deep into the Web not just to receive information, as from the television, radio, or newspaper. They wanted to *exchange* it. They wanted to write messages, initially on pages that looked like stationery, and later on tinier scraps of screens—dispatched instantly, like the famous *bleues* exchanged by fashionable Parisians a hundred years ago. Case, like most great entrepreneurs, discovered his firm's technology by trial and error, but he imposed his fundamental vision on the unknowing world through will, flexibility, and talent. He saw that the academic's Internet could become the fabric of popular culture.

The effect exceeded even Case's imagination. Like most entrepreneurial breakthroughs, users, not producers or sellers, thought of most of the applications. Congressman Ed Markey, for instance, saw e-mail as resurrecting the "ten-dollar bean supper." It put, he said, "politics back in the hands of the little guy."[21]

Intel's CEO Andy Grove identified another dimension, to paraphrase a statement he made in 1994: There are only two kinds of companies. Those that do their work on e-mail and those that don't. He alluded to a constellation of changes in business processes. The writer had to translate his or her thoughts to a higher order of clarity by typing them. Sent thoughts would be reviewed only when the reader had time, thereby optimizing efficiency and reflection. Unlike telephone calls or meetings, e-mail made time zones disappear, permitting much greater collaboration across geographical locations. E-mail's urgency extended conversations into long after normal working hours, giving the employer extra work for free.

E-mail served as a springboard for other entrepreneurs to invent a Web-based advertising business (Yahoo!), an auction business (eBay), and a bookseller (Amazon), as well as thousands of other businesses. Entrepreneurs launched all of these ideas on the strength of the browser, but none could have achieved success unless so many Americans so quickly used the Net to communicate. Entrepreneurship breeds more entrepreneurship. Internet entrepreneurship is, by and large, a commitment to create new mediums. Each medium is, in Marshall McLuhan's phrase, a "marriage," by which he meant "the change of scale or pace or pattern that it introduces into human affairs."[22] Tom Hanks and Meg Ryan met through a radio show in "Sleepless in Seattle" (1993), but by the time that they connected with e-mail in "You've Got Mail" (1998), AOL had changed the scale, pace, and pattern of (literally) affairs. In doing so, AOL had absorbed the character of the old media—it had become a movie star.

AOL opened up the Net's possibilities of meeting, matching, and mating. It marked the end of society as Americans knew it and the beginning of wholly new ways of seeking individual fulfillment. It even taught economists how to uncover the productivity gains of computers: when computers communicated, they produced efficiencies in design, manufacture, and distribution. Case did not just popularize e-mail. He generated productivity gains that made the 1990s golden. Within five years from the Net's invention in 1991, entrepreneurial success by AOL and other Internet service providers had created in the United States the world's largest

Internet community.[23] The American rule of law opened the door for AOL to change the country.

The AOL business model, the best of its breed, depended on a four-piece network. It consisted of (1) home computers, connected by (2) local telephone lines to a network of (3) city-to-city fiber-optic cables (originally built by long-distance companies) that in turn went to (4) other computers (or servers), displaying the pictures and text that were the visual manifestations of Yahoo!, eBay, and the rest of the dot-coms. The American rule of law made the second and third pieces available, at low cost, to entrepreneurs. The regulators and lawmakers did not foresee AOL, but they purposely created open access to the network's elements so that the network owners could not stop entrepreneurs like Case from launching their start-ups.

In 1913 the U.S. government and the national telephone company, AT&T, agreed in the Kingsbury Commitment that the government would bless a national monopoly that provided telephone service at an affordable price. State governments would set the local telephone service price, guaranteeing that AT&T obtained a good return on any investment it made in the network.

However, starting in the 1960s the federal government, through statute and regulations, ordered that other firms could attach any device to the AT&T network and that new competitors could connect their networks to its network. Eventually, this new rule of law permitted individuals to connect the personal computer to the telephone network. Intel had declared that the "PC is It," but when the Internet became the new "It," thanks to the government, the telephone companies could not prohibit, or charge extra for, connecting PCs to it. Although no one anticipated all the beneficial effects of this open network approach, its academic and government advocates intentionally created a legal architecture that encouraged the creation and distribution of new goods and services.

In the 1980s and again in the 1990s (when the stakes were much greater), the Federal Communications Commission told telephone companies they could not charge anything extra to consumers who used their telephone lines to connect computers to the Internet. In effect, the FCC ordered that telephone companies provide access to the Net as an extra and free use of the telephone line purchased for making a voice call. Because about 95 percent of households had phone service (due in part to state and federal price regulation), this decision opened to AOL the possibility of offering low-priced dial-up Internet access to virtually all Americans.

The local telephone companies argued, with some good logic, that eventually Net access would account for an increasingly large share of the use of the local telephone line, so they should be able to charge for it. In the 1990s, a prominent U.S. senator reminded the FCC chair that the long-distance companies paid a few cents per minute to the local phone companies for every long-distance call, because all such calls obviously originated from and terminated on a local line. Therefore, he said, AOL should pay the Bell companies something for every e-mail, like purchasing a stamp for a piece of "real" mail, given that e-mails, like long-distance calls, used local lines. However, the FCC wanted everyone to get on the Internet as fast as possible. The chair did not accede to the senator's wish. The FCC considered that AOL and its competitors would charge less for Internet connectivity (and e-mail) if neither they nor their customers had to pay the Bell companies for dialing up to the Internet. In addition, the FCC required that the Bell companies sell telephone lines to the Internet service providers (like AOL or Earthlink or one of several thousand other start-up Internet service providers [ISPs]), so that they could provide many dial-up numbers to their customers. The FCC also ordered the Bell companies to provide transport to the Internet at low prices.

In many other countries, governments allowed the telephone companies to charge extra for use of their lines to connect to the Internet. They also permitted telephone companies to discriminate against some access providers and in favor of their own Internet service providers. As a result of the pro-competitive laws in the United States and anti-competitive laws elsewhere, in the 1990s Internet service providers in the United States charged about one-tenth of the European rate and one-hundredth of the Asian rate. That low price, and the presence of computers in about 60 percent of households, meant that the American ISPs could achieve very rapid penetration rates. The United States raced online. The rest of the world scratched its collective head in wonder at this newest of the American culture's creations.

The Internet boom stemmed also from the American government's encouragement of long-distance competition in the 1970s and 1980s. By 1984, after much litigation, the government had broken up AT&T between local and long-distance entities so as to intensify competition in long distance. New entrants invested substantial sums in long-distance networks and deployed fiber-optic technology in the 1980s and early 1990s. When the Internet arrived, newer entrepreneurs carried billions of dollars into the easily entered market of long-haul competition. Many of these firms lost their investors' money, but they created the tremendous benefits of cheap communications services for American businesses and consumers.

In the 1980s, the FCC decided that anyone could communicate data—text and pictures—without being subject to state price regulation. In the 1990s, this decision enabled dot-coms to build their virtual businesses on national and international networks linking banks of computers in a few large buildings hundreds or thousands of miles apart. They did not have to obtain licenses or suffer state price regulation (which often raises prices above where competition will put them). These burdens slowed the Net's growth in other countries.

In other markets, the U.S. government did not always apply these principles. For example, for years government allowed Microsoft to extend its market power in operating-system software into the applications market by the same sort of actions that government prohibited the telephone companies from taking. However, in the case of the Internet, the government fairly consistently stuck to a policy of competition and open use of the telephone network from the 1970s to 2000.

Most Internet entrepreneurs never knew how the government helped them. Usually they scoffed at the idea that government had helped them. At most, they conceded only that a little research money had stimulated some data networking in the antediluvian past. By the 1990s the cult of Internet users convinced themselves that they lived outside the rule of law.[24] John Perry Barlow, former lyricist for the Grateful Dead, issued on the Web (the day after the signing of the Telecommunications Act of 1996) a "Declaration of the Independence of Cyberspace": "Governments of the Industrial World, you weary giants of flesh and steel, I come from Cyberspace, the new home of Mind. On behalf of the future, I ask you of the past to leave us alone. You are not welcome among us. You have no sovereignty where we gather."[25] A little less dramatically, in 1998 a White House adviser to President Clinton declared that the Internet should "be a market driven environment, not a regulated environment."[26] This ignored the reality. The FCC, state commissions, and Congress had already written many laws and regulations about the Internet. The "regulation" of the Internet had opened it to entrepreneurship. Indeed, the rule of law helped create in the culture a belief that "open"—meaning collaborative work and sharing of fundamental design features—was the most desirable way to design software. Openness of the network became an assumption in business plans. As a result, entrepreneurs of the 1990s considered closed networks to be abnormal.[27]

AOL was only one of more than 5,000 ISPs. The rule of law gave them all a chance to succeed in disrupting the economy and society. However, Case's energy, vision, and head start gave him advantages he did not waste. He let customers go through his portal to anywhere else on the Web and thereby enhanced the benefit of his service by effectively absorbing the browser into his value proposition. He created and captured new network effects by creating address books and offering widespread access to AOL through local dial-up numbers everywhere in the country, thereby avoiding long-distance charges.

As the 1990s closed, however, the law proved fickle for Case. Access technology advanced from narrowband to broadband. As a consequence of the change of administrations in 2000, the government made a series of decisions effectively denying AOL and other ISPs free (or "open") access to the broadband connections of cable and telephone companies. The new rule of law presupposed that firms building broadband should have the right to exercise market power over the content transmitted through broadband to users. Inevitably, speed thrills. Internet users switched steadily from narrowband to broadband access. As they did so, they largely dropped the use of AOL as their primary service provider. By the end of 2004, about one-third of Americans had a broadband connection, one-third used narrowband, and another third did not access the Internet from their homes and indeed did not have personal computers at home. Eventually, more than 80 percent would use broadband, and dial-up would wither away. The government meanwhile refused to adopt a policy for distributing broadband to everyone—a so-called universal service policy.[28] By contrast, the government had implemented various forms of such universal service policies for telephone, radio, broadcast television, cable, cellular phones, and of course narrowband access.

The change in the architectures of law and technology in time drove AOL down the alternative historical path followed by Yahoo!, eBay, and the other leading portals. Those firms reacted to broadband by making their destinations more valuable and persuading broadband access providers not to constrain users from going to their sites. When Case saw he could not obtain open access to broadband from the government, he realized his existing business model would not last. For that reason, among others, he decided to merge his company with Time Warner.[29] Not long after, the stock market bust occurred and the combined company's stock dropped. Neither Steve Case nor Time Warner's CEO Jerry Levin stayed with the merged firm.

Andreessen and the Browser

The Internet led to an explosion of entrepreneurship in large part because it had an open technological architecture. Marc Andreessen's browser set the direction toward openness. It established the technological philosophy. It built important pieces of the technological architecture of the Internet culture.

In the spring of 1992 cheerful Andreessen, six foot four, barefoot, missing only the Midwest straw in his sandy hair to complete the Norman Rockwell picture, arrived in gloomy Silicon Valley. He wanted to make a living, and he wanted to make something happen. He had gotten a kick out of the browser he and his friends had invented at the University of Illinois at Urbana-Champaign. He left because in his view the university discouraged entrepreneurship.[30] A stranger offered him a job on the coast. He went out to the Slough of Glumness, the Sand Hill Road venture community where the PC era had run its course, nothing had taken its place, and few could afford to build the really big Pebble Beach house. Like Persephone in bib overalls, he brought the springtime of the Internet to the Valley, and American entrepreneurship was reborn.

The National Science Foundation had richly funded the science labs at the University of Illinois at Urbana-Champaign. Andreessen, like other computer science students, headed to the cornfield-ensconced campus because it was a global center for particle physics and data networking. The funding created great equipment and a great faculty that taught students how to play with the toys. Born in 1970, Andreessen was of a generation that inherited computing as the way of the world. They did not see it as hieratic knowledge but as something anyone could enjoy. The Illinois group looked at the graphics on the Windows and Mac screens—tiny icons, such as pictures of printers and scissors and pieces of paper—and said to themselves, why must users type green letters on a black screen to send text across data networks? Why not make the Internet easy to use by pointing and clicking, just as Apple taught with respect to the computer? They wrote software that let everyone in the world create a page of pictures and words on his or her own computer. The software taught every computer to go take a look, over the Internet, at that page—Web site, it came to be called—and bring the image back for examination and storage. Tim Berners-Lee at CERN, the European particle physics laboratory in Geneva, had released in 1991 the software that permitted every computer to give itself an address, send a message to every other computer's address, and add links (in effect, footnotes) from those messages to any other computer. The software invented by Andreessen and his team retrieved whole Web pages from those addresses.[31] It permitted a computer user to flip through the pages of all other computers. One could "browse" the library of the Web, looking at pictures or words or even camera feeds. The browser, like the move from radio's mere aural content to television's visual material, transformed the experience of the Web. The Illinois team called the invention "Mosaic," because the experience of browsing in effect created a pattern of pictures.

Computer people saw that if the Net delivered the pages fast enough, then the sequence of pictures would constitute a "movie"—the Holy Grail of big media's information highway. Big media, however, paid little attention to the Net for as long as it could. Viacom CEO Sumner Redstone said, when asked how his Blockbuster Video would cope with the Internet, "When people say they want home delivery of movies, I will buy a fleet of trucks."[32] Nor did academe nurture Internet entrepreneurship. No one in the government-academy culture at Illinois offered Andreessen even a good job, much less the opportunity to start a tech company. He prepared his resume and used his own browser to post it on a Web page. In those early days of the Internet, only a few people noticed, but eventually Andreessen got a job offer from California. He decided to go where the weather fit his shoelessness. He had "no notion of starting a company."[33]

Jim Clark, who had built possibly the PC era's best screen of all when he invented a video chip for Silicon Graphics (SGI), used the Net to contact Andreessen.[34] He would not pay him, so Andreessen would have to find a day job. What Clark offered instead was wine, a kitchen table, and all-night brainstorming to the twenty-two-year-old. Clark, forty-five, had concluded from his earlier experiences, including co-founding SGI, that brains, creativity, and irritability constituted the key assets for a start-up. Andreessen had the requisite brains and creativity, of course, and he was, if not irritated, "a little bit mad" that Mosaic "had been taken over by the bureaucrats." Clark, in any case, had all these traits in abundance.

Enviously eyeing the growth rates (and accompanying high price-to-earnings ratios) of technology firms, in the late 1980s the large national and regional communications companies of America began to plan their expansions. Senator Al Gore had coined the phrase "information highway" after a conversation in the early 1980s with the head of Corning Glass. The Corning CEO explained to Gore the capabilities of fiber as a medium for carrying bits. The senator coupled this technological vision with the Interstate Highway Act of 1954, co-authored by his father, and came up with a plan for the federal government to pay for fiber links between every city in America. He said he wanted the "school girl in Carthage, Tennessee" to be able to "come home after school and plug into the Library of Congress."[35]

MCI in fact had borrowed billions, with the help of Michael Milken, in the 1980s in order to build fiber links for carrying long-distance calls more cheaply than its huge rival AT&T could on its older copper networks. The Bell companies envisioned that they could connect homes and businesses to rings of fiber. Their connections would be so robust and ample that they would happily sublet a portion of their capacity to the cable industry. The long-distance companies, on the other hand, imagined that they would build fiber not only between but also inside the cities that had long been the exclusive preserve of the Bells. Both agreed that fiber to the home would create an information highway. The government did not have to build or own it in order for Gore's vision to become true. This information highway would carry any amount of words, spoken or typed (or even hand-written if that ever proved to matter). More important, it would deliver what the big firms thought, in their failure to apprehend e-mail, would be the ne plus ultra of electronic communications: movies on demand.

At the time, Time Warner was installing in Orlando, Florida, a trial for a so-called switched video network—basically a ramped-up telephone network that enabled every customer to order a movie on demand. Time Warner CEO Jerry Levin, who had made his career on the strength of launching HBO, said that if each household ordered one or two movies a week Time Warner could break even on the network. He scoffed at Redstone's "fleet of trucks" approach to movie distribution. On the importance of movies, the telco executives agreed with Levin and John Malone of TCI. Malone saw the future of cable as the delivery of 500 cable channels. The telephone industry saw its future as the delivery of any movie to any customer in the instant after the customer called to place the order.

Malone was pushing all-you-can-eat smorgasbord; Ray Smith of Bell Atlantic and the other Bell CEOs, home-delivered pizzas.

Meanwhile the studio chiefs—Michael Eisner at Disney, Barry Diller at Fox, and lesser lights at Universal and Paramount—claimed that they would send their movies through the lines of cable and telephone firms. They wanted two pipes to every home. They hoped to play off telcos against cable in the new access networks. None of the big firms apprehended that the coming disruption would have nothing to do with movies for many a year.

One pipe versus two pipes, conduit versus content: these disputes occupied the communications and media sectors in 1991. Computing, on the other hand, meant staring into the world in a box. No studio or communications network was concerned with how the box was built (hardware) or what it displayed on its screen (software). However, computing, communications, and media had one thing in common: the big companies believed that they decided everything. Because small was ugly and little was doomed, venture capital was busted—until Andreessen and Clark changed the game.

Whereas the big company chiefs saw the future of media in terms of delivering the content of old mediums, Andreessen and Clark did not have a specific end goal. They just wanted to do something great. Their first idea involved building software for Time Warner's Orlando trial. Clark could not find a way into the big company's labyrinth of alliances with other big companies and its own divisions. The second idea was to build an online gaming network for Nintendo—that is, taking the game out of the box and putting it on the Net. Clark went to Japan and found out that Nintendo could not even ship its 64-bit software on schedule. It certainly could not alter its business model to selling on the Internet, given that hardly anyone used the Net and no one sold on it. Clark concluded that "the big companies were full of hot air." He became depressed.

Meanwhile Andreessen was insisting that Clark hire him as a paid employee, since his day job prevented him from working on new ideas. Clark, brainstorming on the possibilities for a new and profitable business, said, "The Internet keeps growing. Sooner or later it will be the information highway. That is the only thing that makes sense." Yet Clark had no answer to the venture capitalists who said that even though the Internet was growing, everything on it would be free.

Andreessen then said, "Let's just make a better version of Mosaic." In commercial terms, this meant build a great browser, sell it to businesses so they could build interesting Web sites, and give it away to consumers to create an audience for those Web sites. The end result, Netscape, at its core sold software, not online connectivity.

Not that its founders declined to speculate about the uses of the Net. Andreessen and Clark thought the Net could support buying and selling. MCI gave them a few million dollars to invent what firms later would call an e-commerce business model. But they focused on browser software. Someone else would have to invent eBay.

The Netscape founders also knew that one could modify the browser to search for information. That business required prioritizing among Web sites, and therefore would alienate Netscape's customers. Someone else would have to invent Google.

The Netscape guys thought some Web sites might become billboards that could sell advertising space. To that end Netscape offered two recent Stanford graduates $2 million to build an advertising business. But because the venture capital firm Sequoia took a chance on Jerry Yang and Dave Filo (now multibillionaires), Yahoo! invented the ad-supported business model. However, even if Andreessen and Clark did not invent e-commerce, electronic searches, and Net advertising, those and many other businesses all derived from Netscape in at least three senses. First, Netscape made the Web experience colorful, pictorial, easy, fun, cheap. Second, Netscape taught entrepreneurs to experiment with the Web both to do something "better, faster, cheaper" and to create a "Brave New World." Third, Netscape put the magnetism back in Silicon Valley by making its investors very rich in a hurry.

In the end, Microsoft invented a browser that it integrated with Windows and thereby effectively eliminated Netscape as a disruptive force. The famous antitrust litigation followed. However, Microsoft could not take fortune or fame from the Netscape team. Andreessen said in January 2004 that four possibilities attract people to start-ups: money, changing the world, fame, and solving interesting problems. He made all four come true for him and many others. He also killed the information highway in just the way cars killed passenger rail. Many open roads became the paradigm of the 1990s Internet. The moguls had it all wrong; big wins for entrepreneurs and their venture backers ensued.

Andreessen's tale demonstrated how American science can create new markets. When he was growing up, the American culture supported spending for national defense and very expensive research tools, such as the multi-million dollar supercollider dug into the plains of Illinois. The research might have had, in some remote conjecture, a security purpose, but it also filled a deep and open reservoir of knowledge. Andreessen's browser showed how a technology architecture can stimulate entrepreneurship. Programmers could review the browser's design. It was open to their scrutiny. Therefore, they could integrate it with other software and enhance the user's experience on the Internet. The architecture made the culture, and the culture made America richer.

Leaders of the Net

In the Golden 90s entrepreneurs seemed to wander from obscurity into the limelight of fame and fortune. Pierre Omidyar invented a way for his fiancée to pursue on the Internet her old hobby of collecting and trading Pez candy dispensers. Ultimately, by founding eBay he proved that the Internet could help any collector acquire a complete set of anything. His firm transformed the innate human desire to pay the lowest possible price for absolutely everything into an absolutely new way to make billions of dollars.[36] In early 1994 Jeff Bezos saw that Web usage was doubling every few weeks and reviewed the top twenty mail-order businesses to discover which could be done most efficiently on the Internet. He created Amazon because there were so many published books that no single catalog even existed.[37] These entrepreneurs became billionaires with different business models. They inspired thousands of others who passed on the long, slow climb up the hierarchical ladder of big, existing organizations to see if the Internet would let them change the ways of the world.

Most Internet stars had in common the fundamental American desire not to have a boss. Each of them had to become a leader in order to fulfill their dreams. The new American leaders, for the most part, lacked extensive management experience. Instead they had technical (Andreessen) or marketing (Case) backgrounds. Some came from law school or business school. However, the business challenges of the Internet involved so much technology and new growth economics that the academy was not yet geared to prepare students for them. The uncertainty of it all discouraged some from taking the entrepreneurial plunge. Yet no dearth of individuals hunted and pecked their PowerPoint slides, pitched in elevators and conference rooms, got the funding, and worked around the clock to succeed before the money ran out. From 1996 to 2000, American venture capitalists invested more than $200 billion in more than 22,000 deals, the largest splurge of entrepreneurship in history.[38] Each deal was an opportunity for new leadership.

In addition to the new start-up leaders, new leaders also appeared in investment banking and financial analysis. In the bust, some met disgrace. However, in no other national economy did the financial sector raise, and make, money at such a low cost and high speed.

Leaders appeared in technology circles. Erstwhile dull engineering conferences became Lollapalooza tours that drew overflowing audiences to expansive resorts. Every firm found an evangelist, sometimes called a chief technology officer (a job title that may not have existed before the 1990s), to preach its product roadmap as the one true path to universal perfection.

Leaders of the technology boom existed even in government. Elected officials invited Case, Andreessen, and other entrepreneurs to friendly hearings, private meetings, and affable soirees. President Clinton awarded the National Medal of Technology to two of the creators of Internet protocols.[39] Vice President Gore and venture capitalist John Doerr enjoyed the scuttlebutt that they would run as a Gore-Doerr ticket in 2000.

Anointment as a leader came when the Valley declared that one "got it." Not everyone had the right to make that declaration. Not everyone received that plaudit. But, in the nature of entrepreneurship, anyone could aspire to "get it," and any number might turn out to have "got it." In the Golden 90s the door of leadership opened to anyone. No academic, or business, or government hierarchy vetted the candidates. People competed to lead in old categories, and they created new categories of leadership. Leadership shaped the culture of entrepreneurship, but with the reciprocity built into the relationship between culture and its architecture, entrepreneurship came to describe the leadership style of the decade.

Bringing Down the House
Change and Its Reactionaries

The end of the stock market boom and government changes in the oos shattered the spirit of 90s leadership. Many of the new century's powerful figures in government and business show indifference or even animus toward entrepreneurship. The architectures of law, technology, and leadership itself are being reconstructed in ways inimical to entrepreneurship. The boom sparked a reaction to disruption that threatens the prospects for improving living standards for all Americans, save those at the top of the pyramid of power and wealth.

The reaction in part lies in the danger that the boom posed to the established incumbents in business, finance, and politics. Venture capitalists become richer than investment bankers. Kids without ties or suits flashed onto the front pages of newspapers and magazines, reciting like incantations the names of low-revenue firms whose market capitalization dwarfed old-line companies. Executives who had toiled for decades to reach the top of famous firms suddenly discovered they had no purchase on society's imagination. The political party of business was dismayed to see the workers' party woo technology libertarians to its ranks.

The boom stimulated new competition, also an unhappy event for incumbents. Start-ups spent capital freely to enter existing markets. Generous stock markets rewarded start-ups for their rapid growth. The financiers meanwhile punished incumbents for focusing on net income. As a result, incumbents entered new and adjacent markets in search of growth. Fixed-line telephone companies went cellular; AT&T bought cable companies; Microsoft invested in innumerable markets. The pursuit of growth expanded competition across the face of the American economy, much of it catalyzed by technology start-ups.

The boom's technological change disadvantaged incumbents. Moore's Law, which holds that processing power doubles every eighteen months relative to cost or size, applied not only to microprocessors but, in rough approximation, to fiber optics, storage, and any other technologies drawn from increasing mastery of quantum mechanics and electromagnetism. Therefore, equipment cost in the information economy went down precipitously. Economies of scale built on old technologies simply evaporated. Because their facilities were built years ago, their basic production cost exceeded that of upstart rivals.

Incumbents were not even able to maintain the advantage of scale in distribution channels. In earlier decades, booksellers, for example, had warehouses to hold inventory, trucking contracts for delivery, and well-located retail stores. Then, as if overnight, the Internet created new distribution chains, dependent in the case of Amazon on delivery services instead of physical stores. The incumbents' complex distribution system suddenly became another clumsy cost-generating disadvantage. Retailers had laboriously created buying clubs, coupon programs, and other discounts designed to nurture customer loyalty. Then e-mail, chat rooms, and social networking conferred network effects on virtual rivals like eBay and Yahoo! The Internet eclipsed years of direct-mail programs.[40]

In the upheaval, virtually every market experienced new entry from an unpredicted direction. Satellite video challenged cable. Satellite radio assaulted terrestrial radio. Internet portals attacked newspapers. The money centers of the East were rattled by the Silicon Valley venture capital firms.

The beneficiaries of the boom not only disturbed, they shattered many long-standing markets. For example, since the creation of the AT&T monopoly in 1913, AT&T engineers had created the largest integrated machine in history, the telephone network. Their design used centralized computers to record phone calls, report telephone numbers, and route telephone calls from person calling to person called. The network garnered high prices for conference calls, voice mail, and many other services, and it almost always produced very good sound quality and available dial tone, just as its designers wished. Just like big airline companies using a common set of computers to store flight and reservation information, even after the breakup of AT&T in 1984 the telephone companies shared much information in centralized computer banks. Like airplanes flying in and out of hub airports, the phone company networks sent traffic through central switches. The centralization of information made the network "intelligent." But the boom gave rise to rivals—data firms, soft-switch and router firms, open software designers, "voice over the Internet" start-ups, and many others—that had a very different vision. Their common idea was that customers with computers would store, control, and direct information over "dumb pipes." The network would become "stupid."[41] The customer, with the aid of a computer, would be king. This move of value creation to the edge of the network tracked the migration of product creation from centralized, integrated incumbent companies to a disintegrated system of collaborating start-ups. By the end of the 1990s, hundreds of firms specializing in piece parts had effectively assembled a data network coordinated by agreed-upon standards rather than common ownership of physical assets.[42]

The boom undermined hierarchies. Unknown start-ups lured brilliant young lawyers away from firms that expected them to toil for years before admission to partnership. Young consultants, the foundation stones of pyramidical organizations, chose to start new firms rather than advise old ones. Under the seniority systems of the pre-boom order, the older generation inculcated in the next generation a conservative culture inimical to the risk taking of entrepreneurship. During the boom, the old order lost the power to impose its discourse on the next generation. When Napster destroyed the hegemony of the commercial record business, the Internet revolution at last gained the expression in music that typically marks any significant change in culture.

The boom shook up the demographics of power in America. Immigrants discovered that start-ups gave them a much better way to obtain business success than that offered by the incumbents. At one point in the 1990s, perhaps half the CEOs in Silicon Valley came from India; the rest of corporate America differed quite starkly. In earlier decades these new arrivals would have worked for assimilation in their generation in the hope that their children could climb up America's ladder. In the boom, venture funding made everyone else accommodate the new arrivals' accents, culinary preferences, presence in schools and neighborhoods, social preferences.

In all these respects, the boom created enemies. Incumbents, Republicans, old companies, New York financiers, law firms, and consultants—all had reasons to want slower changes. When the bust arrived, perhaps none was thrilled at the new difficulties in making money, but all were at least a little happy to see "normalcy" return.

In the bust, entrepreneurs found themselves without voice. The boom's volcanic explosion of money had buried the social idealism of the Net's early champions. The bust embarrassed those who had predicted the great times would never end. Others had spent too much or exercised too few options. Instead of living like kings, they still had to work. They found their own rags-to-riches-to-merely-affluent stories too depressing to tell. In the bust, entrepreneurship lost its transcendent place in the American culture. Market consolidation, reduced investment, defense spending, tax breaks for the wealthy, and inflated housing prices took entrepreneurship's place as the means toward economic recovery.

Enemies of Reform

When the political winds shifted to the right with the Bush administration, the dynamism and entrepreneurial bent of the American economy did not appear to be on the mind of Washington's leaders. It is not as if no one in Washington knows what is coming from the other side of the world. Republicans and Democrats repeatedly hear from technologists, workers, business leaders, and even journalists that new laws are needed to support American competitiveness. But the parties cannot seem to find the time even to negotiate over such laws. They are otherwise occupied, to the general despair of the citizenry, as expressed in numerous polls.

The Bush administration bears no responsibility for making Chinese entrepreneurs a threat to American businesses. The trends behind this phenomenon developed in the Clinton administration or earlier. But in this matter, as in almost every aspect of life, the response is more important than the opening. The Bush administration showed little sign of delegating people or time to crafting an answer to the new China question. Meanwhile, the Democrats treated being out of power as an excuse for being out of ideas. The years 2001–05 should have been the political era in which America awoke to the brand new day of global competition. Instead they were when the sleep of reason produced nightmares.[43]

Even while all commentators identified educational reform as the source of new competitive energy to meet rising Asia, the administration selected religion and standardized testing as the two most important topics in education. Prayer in school had nothing to do with responding to global competition. Testing could diagnose performance problems but in no way could remedy them. Meanwhile, the administration failed to fund fully its own education law. It cut back public funds for college education. It discouraged American academies from recruiting the best students in other countries.

From its inception, the Bush administration rejected the use of treaties as a means to advance American interests. As a result, entrepreneurs could not count on trade diplomacy to create new large markets into which they could export. The trade agenda included the important reduction of agricultural subsidies, but by 2005 the administration assured special interests it would abandon that goal. To the least ambitious trade policy of any American government since before the Second World War, the government added the nurturing of the worst trade imbalance of any developed nation in modern history. When Americans bought more from foreign producers than they sold to foreign consumers, that meant American entrepreneurs had not succeeded enough in exporting from the United States, and that multinational American firms had moved to Asia in order to export back to the United States.

No one in government appears to have the duty of thinking about the totality of the American response to China. Some public intellectuals, like

Clyde Prestowitz, think planners and a plan should exist, and prescribe many parts of it. Some business leaders, especially from technology, advocate pieces of a plan. Yet scarcely anyone in Washington seriously discusses whether to have a plan, much less its authors, purposes, or techniques.

Although Prestowitz would disagree, a plan should concern not specific programs but the three structures or architectures—law, technology, and individual leadership. These are three categories of means or methods. They are mechanistic. They create a culture that in turn leads to behavior, and that behavior then can be described. Under this approach, leaders would focus on the cultural outcomes of, or changes in the machinery or architecture of, the society. This approach would be unlike the typical political plan in two key respects. It would not be government- or elite-dominated, as any plan always ends up being, because plans beget central planners. And it would be flexible and reactive, organized around goals and not around a plan itself, focused on change in thought, belief, and behavior and not on the execution of a program. The response to China should be an anti-plan, and much more robust and enduring for that reason. In any case, the Bush administration lacked either a traditional or a nontraditional political plan for responding to China. The government has not improved on the use of the legal architecture to encourage entrepreneurship. Instead, the three branches of government changed law to reduce entrepreneurial opportunity in the oos. The executive branch essentially abandoned enforcement of antitrust law. Such invisible and short-term chiefs ran the antitrust division that they scarcely seemed to exist. The chairman of the Federal Communications Commission openly encouraged consolidation in all industries—wireless, wire, and media. As a measure of the administration's extreme support of consolidation, even Congress balked at the FCC proposals to create larger media conglomerates.

The Bush administration did create a new public good in pharmaceutical benefits but then failed to pay for it. It repudiated citizens' assumption that decades of payroll taxes had been invested in Treasury bonds in order to fund retirement pensions. By injecting more financial risk into people's lives, the administration discouraged individual risk taking.

Government leaders changed tax and budget law so as to transfer wealth to high-income individuals. They intensified income inequality by reallocating tax burdens to the middle and lower income groups from the upper income class.

As important as any particular change in law, the national government's leaders communicated to their country's citizens that wealth could purchase changes in law. Big businesses and high-income individuals could change the legal architecture to perpetuate and even expand their privileges. Monied interests exercised great influence over decision making. Entrepreneurs could see that even if they might succeed in the marketplace, incumbents could use law as a weapon against disruptive start-ups.

Government operated less openly than at any time since the Second World War. Secrecy shrouded even such simple questions as who in the oil industry helped draft the energy law that, when finally passed, conferred benefits on the big companies. Routinely, government concealed the truth about climate change, employment statistics, the status of the violence in Iraq, the duration of the Social Security trust fund, spying on American citizens, and numerous other matters. The cultural effects included decreased confidence that from outside the circle of privilege anyone could disrupt the hierarchy of power.

The crucial commercial competition with rising China requires not centralized power and widespread secrecy but an open, honest, and common commitment to shared resources and collaborative decision making.[44] By empowering elites and expanding the scope of privilege, a government undermines the culture of entrepreneurship.

Feckless Philosophers

If, as Keynes famously said, every politician is the slave of some defunct economist, then today's academics must be waiting until death to exercise the power of their ideas.[45] That at least would explain their relative absence from debate over the fate of America. Tenured professors, deans, and university professors occasionally popped up as talking heads on television or popped off as opinion-page commentators. However, with the notable exception of Paul Krugman in the *New York Times* and a slowly increasing number of bloggers, for the most part academics did not press for political reform.

The academy's relative disinterest seemed to date from the 1980s. In the previous two decades, the utopian visions of the civil rights movement had benefited many individuals but failed to thwart rising class inequality. The freedom of Woodstock had been followed by the killings at Altamont and Kent State. Marches on the Pentagon had not stopped the invasion of

Cambodia or the growth of a right-wing conviction that the United States could have won the Vietnam War. Confronted with the Reagan Revolution, left-leaning faculty withdrew from the world.

The Clinton administration regathered old believers in the liberal way of thinking, but the decade brought them much disappointment. Their conviction in progress eroded in large part because America's successes in the 1990s seemed so fortuitous, politics seemed so artificial, and technology appeared uncontrollable. Progress was somehow accidental. The old school liberals were not in charge of anything, so they retreated to the academy and the law firms.

Conservative intellectuals asserted command of events. Right-leaners, however, tended to succumb to the blandishments of think-tank money and political power. Where liberal intellectuals made a point of pride out of their disapproval of Democratic politicians, traditional conservatives were all too silent when their chosen government leaders lost touch with logic and reality.

Postmodernism also had policy blood on its hands. Its stance distanced intellectuals from the architectures of law and technology. It made them skeptical of leaders and followers as well. Although postmodern thinking challenges hierarchies of power much as entrepreneurs do, it denies the possibility of reform. It has infiltrated much of the academy and sapped humanists of the confidence that they could build a fairer world. For postmodernists, entrepreneurship is not a way to build a better world. Instead, entrepreneurs are thought to be the subjects of capitalism. They differ from everyone else in business only in that technology chains them to an especially fast pace of work.

As the academy became less engaged with the outside world, academics professionalized their disciplines. Economics turned into mathematics; law into economics; history into historiography; psychology into chemistry. In these more abstract forms, the humanities speak less clearly on questions of government policy. Even law schools have a diminished role in preparing students to govern and to judge. Politics overwhelms the executive branch and infects the process of selecting judges. Much of the judiciary has become a bastion of right-wing ideology, leaving traditionally liberal law professors feeling as dumbfounded by the new judges' decisions as biologists confronting intelligent design.

Business schools burgeoned in the last half of the twentieth century. American business schools graduated nearly forty times as many people in

2000 as in 1950—an increase that signified (and contributed to) the global triumph of American firms and the American way of doing business. Business schools, however, have contributed relatively little to public policy discussion. The record-breaking ethical lapses and criminal behavior of the boom and bust hardly qualified business education as the source of reform. Business schools trained a generation of leaders but discouraged their pupils from considering social or cultural problems as part of their domain. Their pupils knew organization, strategy, and finance. They learned practical economics. However, at least until after the Enron and WorldCom scandals, business schools dedicated almost no attention to law, ethics, sociology, or any other discipline that would have created a supple understanding of culture. The students learned how to create business units and staff functions for capital allocation, recruiting, product development, sales, and marketing. The firms they staffed did not have a functional method for considering the legal, technological, and historical patterns of the United States. Culture existed outside the firm and the market.

The stewards of academe have not been the champions of reform. Like many others in inward-looking America, university administrations dedicated much effort toward building their institutions' wealth. They had good reasons. The oil shocks of the 1970s, and recession of the early 1980s, had left many universities in financial distress. Their buildings began to crumble. They discovered that they had no replacement budgets. Labor and energy costs rose. Their faculty salaries fell too far behind professional wages. Most of the great academic centers reacted by building huge endowments and administering universities in businesslike ways. However, the exigencies of fund raising and efficient business management left less room for academic leaders to pursue public policy goals.

In addition, American universities became less focused on the United States than in previous eras. They train students from many countries, grant tenure to faculty members from many countries, collaborate on research with universities in other countries. These trends expand the intellectual breadth of the universities and appeal to a vision of a unified world of knowledge. However, they do not necessarily benefit American citizens, or even the American donors who endow the universities.

A global perspective in the great American academies is not an unwelcome development. However, from the point of view of encouraging political reform in America, a passion resembling patriotism would be helpful. That zeal could be found in the conservative alliance of fundamentalist

Christians and corporate middle management that captured the federal and most state governments in the oos. In response, the academy is too quiet.

Limitations of Capitalists

From 2001 to 2004, American government granted more specific tax, spending, and regulatory benefits to American businesses than at any time since the Second World War. Congress gave direct grants to the airline and insurance industries. It issued sole source contracts with favored contractors. It reduced the taxation of dividends, increasing the attractiveness of dividend-paying equities. The Federal Communications Commission virtually exempted local telephone companies from competition by the long-distance firms—competition that had been imposed by the 1996 Telecommunications Act. Yet, although the government made its favored firms financially better off, by and large American business leaders are unhappy with the direction of the United States.

American business leaders despair over the education system of their country. Delegations of technology executives repeatedly complain to Washington that the United States does not adequately teach mathematics and science, from elementary school through graduate school. They blame teachers, teachers' unions, the monopoly of public school, the large size of schools, the lack of technology, and even the emphasis on technology at the expense of learning how to use it.

Their list of grievances is long. Immigration policies make business leaders unhappy. Health care policies distress business leaders. They worry about how to fund pension promises.

When a large number of American business leaders can agree on what to ask for, they usually can persuade any government, regardless of the party that is in power, to give it to them. For example, firms that had amassed profits overseas asked for a tax break on repatriating the money. They got it. In 2004 the president signed a law reducing taxes on foreign profits to a tiny 5.25 percent (an 85 percent discount off the normal level) as long as firms brought the cash home by the end of 2005. Firms repatriated almost a trillion dollars.

However, business leaders have not produced a comprehensive reform agenda for the United States. One explanation is that as global markets expand, top executives need to dedicate more time to foreign travel and more attention to foreign issues. That subtracts from the attention that they pay to Washington. In part, any reform will disfavor some business.

Universal federally funded health care, for example, will threaten the profits of insurers and health maintenance organizations. Energy efficiency and noncarbon energy may subtract from the bottom line of oil and gas companies. As long as the business lobby insists on near unanimity behind its agenda, business leaders will have a limited political agenda.

At least on an individual level, most American corporate leaders realize that their firms operate in society. They know their firms must thrive in a social context. They know they cannot be at war with the cultures of the nations in which they operate. The food industry has grasped that it had missed American consumers' increasing concern with diet and health. General Electric knows that energy efficiency will forever be important in a world in which oil will be increasingly scarce. American business can show its characteristic flexibility by developing new ways to understand social issues. The realization of the social dimension of business success will permit American businesses to become a more powerful force seeking a reform agenda. Business leaders and social activists may discover that they share many common goals, but they need to surprise themselves with this realization soon enough to change the American cultural response to China.

CHAPTER

Home Improvement

Rebuilding the Architectures of Culture

"It'll be a good fight, and I'll win," he said to himself, and his crossed arms tightened with a quick, savage contraction, as if the idea were something that could be pursued, tackled, and thrown headlong to the ground.
—OWEN JOHNSON, *STOVER AT YALE*

And some people arrived from the borders,
and said that there are no longer any barbarians.
And now what shall become of us without any barbarians?
Those people were some kind of solution.
—CONSTANTINE P. CAVAFY, "WAITING FOR THE BARBARIANS"

Notwithstanding the dearth of leadership, failure of institutions, and many other obstacles to reform, Americans must pursue changes in the architectures of law, technology, and leadership. The starting point is broad discussion of these changes. The details matter, but the general outline has to be agreed upon. Especially in the Internet age, the exchange of ideas itself changes culture.

The Laws of Entrepreneurial Encouragement

Change in the legal architecture means new laws, regulations, taxing, and spending. Technology changes include different directions in research and design. Leadership changes involve new thinking by those who hold institutional power but also new leadership from below, facilitated like all reform efforts by the most advanced media of the era, meaning

broadband in the instant decade. For political reform, however, the architecture most susceptible to change is law.[1]

Spend Money to Make Money

Spending money is one of the great powers of law. Everyone in
academe, business, or politics agrees on the happy sequence for an improved standard of living: researchers in academic laboratories make scientific discoveries, entrepreneurs translate those discoveries into new goods
and services, and their start-up firms create new high-paid jobs. But no one
knows how this process really works. Anecdotes control the discussion. So
in the 1980s Stanford computer scientists invented a new way to send particles of energy from one destination to another, and some left to start
Cisco. By mid-2005, that data networking company employed more than
37,000 in San Jose, California, and elsewhere.[2] At the most recent turn of
the century, Stanford graduate school students Serge Brin and Larry Page
worked out mathematical formulas for finding oft-visited information in
the vastness of the Internet's Web pages, and by mid-2005, the company
they founded, Google, employed more than 4,000 in Mountain View, California, and elsewhere.[3]

The American government and university endowments paid for almost
all the basic research behind Google, Cisco, and myriad other start-ups. Financial investors and firms paid for almost all development. Entrepreneurial ventures and big firms turned development into products sold in commercial markets, succeeding in making a profit on only a small percentage
of projects.

In the American system, commercial markets and investors make the
discriminations that turn some research projects into products and relegate
others to storage on a university server farm. The United States has perfected this process. The American government can readily tax its rich economy enough to fund innumerable projects and pay the tuition, room, and
board of legions of students.[4] Venture funds have more money to invest
than projects in which they want to invest, permitting them to exercise
judgment about the commercial potential of any particular research. Other
countries do not necessarily have these advantages: the American production line for high-income jobs works more smoothly and reliably than any
other country's system.

By the early 2000s, the United States dedicated more money to research than any other nation: as of 2004, the United States' public and pri-

vate sectors spent 2.7 percent of gross domestic product (GDP) on research and development, compared to 1.9 percent for the European Union.[5] The absolute level was double the amount in the next highest country, Japan.[6]

However, in the 00s the United States began to break its own system. Total spending on research and development adjusted for inflation fell slightly every year.[7] Federal spending on basic research in math and physical sciences has declined as a percentage of GDP since the 1980s, while federal spending on research and development for life sciences has gone up.[8] But did the United States decide that life sciences research would improve the standard of living, and other research would not? No one in government or industry would take responsibility for such an opinion. Somehow this large shift in spending priorities just happened. Research is the key to technology entrepreneurship, but no one with power in the U.S. government selects a research strategy. Even competence in defining research issues is hard to find in the executive branch.

According to a task force composed of technology companies, by 2005 the American lead in research and discovery was "eroding rapidly as other countries commit significant resources to enhance" the capability of their citizens and firms to compete with the United States.[9] The American share of scientific papers and patents is declining.[10] American citizens authored only about half the industrial patents sought in the United States by 2004, and less than a third of the articles in *Physical Review*, a physics journal.[11] Fewer Americans choose to study basic mathematics and science than in the past. In graduate science and mathematics American enrollment is dropping. The number of science and engineering doctorates granted to American citizens at American universities fell about 12 percent from 1998 to 2002. Federal research grants effectively buy students for such degrees. The government could pay doctoral and post-doctoral students more money. Now these students cannot expect to earn more than $20,000 to $30,000 a year during the five to ten years necessary to complete their studies. According to a National Research Council study in 2000, someone who spent five years earning a doctorate in computer science would need fifty years to catch up in total present value income with someone who went to work immediately after earning a bachelor's degree in the same subject.[12]

Even as the U.S. government fails to up the ante on scientific research and American students head away from vital fields of knowledge, the range of possible subjects is growing. Basic research needs to be done in quantum computing, data networking, genetic therapy, noncarbon energy creation, and many other topics.[13] No central planner can pick the best topics. A dispersed, decentralized ethic of well-funded curiosity would be ideal for American entrepreneurial culture. The guiding principle should be the sort of quasi-organized, semi-chaotic creativity facilitated by open, networked, decentralized collaboration. The government should close NASA, bring the era of Big Science to an end, celebrate the end of Bell Labs, and embrace modular approaches to research.

According to Robert Gordon at Northwestern University, the productivity growth of 1995 to 2000 was fragile—meaning that such felicitous events as the invention of the Internet might not naturally reoccur.[14] Therefore, to succeed in global competition a national culture should encourage entrepreneurship across a broad range of scientific topics.[15] Luck plays a part in determining which creek has the gold nuggets, so prospectors should look into every canyon. Instead of sending a few people to the moon, the United States needs to send hundreds of thousands into science labs.[16]

Teaching Success

For employees to win a larger share of new wealth created by gains in productivity, they need to know more, bring more information to bear on their work, and have greater skills than anyone else who could be hired in America, or Asia, or anywhere else. They have to make that case continually. In a static situation a worker might learn how to do a job once, and then perform it repeatedly for a career. In a dynamic market wrought by changing technology and riven by global competition, every worker has to be smarter, better, faster every year in order not to be valued more cheaply every year.

To this end, every employee has to become an on-the-job entrepreneur whether working in a big, old company or a brand new start-up. No government can require individual self-betterment by means of a law or regulation. No new technology can make every American become more productive (although professional athletes operating outside accepted norms aim to make exceptions to that principle). No leader can inspire everyone to go to night school while working a day job, to stay in school when a chance to make a little money beckons, to refuse the easy acceptance of the proverbial gentleman's C while in school. But law, technology, and leadership can support a culture of common belief in the value of education and a shared expectation of lifelong learning. That culture would not re-gard job retraining as a handout to the victims of global competition. It would see lifelong learning as an investment made in everyone in return for their agreement to participate wholeheartedly in the most dynamic, challenging, and productive economic system ever invented.[17]

For the most part American workers embrace change. They work hard. The American rule of law, however, does more to discourage workers from obtaining continual education than does any other developed nation's legal system. As the primary roadblock, Americans pay more for education than anyone in the world.[18]

In the 00s state universities raised tuitions and other fees, while Con-gress reduced federal aid for college education.[19] A bachelor's degree from a public college leaves an American student owing as much as $50,000. Debt presses American students to drop out without completing a degree program and get a job.[20] As tuitions rise, few of the students enrolled in the elite private colleges come from the bottom three-quarters of the coun-try measured by income.[21]

Meanwhile, other countries pay their best students to stay in school, and even to go to an American college. Foreign students get degrees in sci-ence or business in the United States, indirectly benefiting from American endowments that effectively provide tens of thousands of dollars of sub-sidy. Inexplicably, no one questions how American citizens benefit when the education system provides its highest-quality experience to non-Amer-icans while discouraging Americans from staying in school.

Even those Americans who do complete degree programs are aban-doning computer science and flocking to law school. They are passing on engineering and going to business school. Undergraduate enrollments in computer science and computer engineering dropped 23 percent in one year. In 2004 Bill Gates went on a speaking tour to elite universities to advocate enrollment in computer science. He said "people are way over-reacting" to job losses, and that "there doesn't seem to be the buzz, ex-citement and understanding of [the potential of computer science] so that the best young people are drawn into it."[22] But the "young people" knew that venture firms of the 00s had fewer successes, and won less when they did win, than in the Golden 90s. They calculated the high cost of study-ing computer science compared to working in an investment banking firm. They understood the zeitgeist. They did not need a computer genius to tell them which way the winds of change blew.

Americans should have to pay very little for education at any level. Lack of money and fear of debt should discourage no American citizen from college or graduate school. Science and mathematics students should be paid salaries to obtain advanced degrees. Reform needs to start at the elementary and secondary level. The critical relationships between teacher and students last a year or less. For that reason, and because of the balkanized jurisdictions of education, historically lessons of reform learned at one school rarely reach the ears of any other school. Hard-won truths of experience simply disappear from one year to another. However, the Internet defeats time and distance. In the information age, education reform can be transformed and replicated in thousands of schools, all over the world, as fast as an eBay auction moves merchandise.[23] The possibility for positive change has not been so high since Sputnik galvanized a rethinking of the role of science and mathematics in early grades.

The cause of change has not been advanced under the Bush administration. Appealing to some conservatives, the Department of Education attacked teachers' unions. The religious right battles to introduce more religion into schools. The administration failed to fund fully the law known as No Child Left Behind.[24] Meanwhile, the education system has been slow to apply new learning theory in order to reform teaching methodology. Sophisticated testing and rigorous study of brain function have revealed the failures of traditional ways of teaching mathematics and science. Bias against women and minorities has been discovered. Education has produced an undereducated workforce in large part because of unsound methods, not because of teachers' unions or Charles Darwin. Although teachers and courses use new technology to ever-greater effect, hardly any schooling at any level employs individualized testing and large databases in order to develop specialized teaching.[25] Americans can order a Starbucks coffee or a new car just the way they want, but education typically comes in one-size-fits-all.

In the mid-oos, only some Americans hold to the conservative shibboleth that salaries do not matter to teachers (while income apparently matters to everyone else). The many millionaires of America buy education for their children at a price vastly exceeding the average cost of public school for everyone else. Some catch enough of a glimpse at a mirror of their behavior to realize that every student would be better off if the society committed more resources to education. If the United States doubled its total spending on teachers' salaries, with some attention paid to merit and efficiency, the society and economy would benefit.[26]

If government spent money amply and focused on applying new discoveries in learning theory, the society would have a much higher level of literacy. Every student should be tested for learning style. Every learning disability should be diagnosed. Each student should be taught in the unique manner best suited to that student. Businesses seek individualized marketing. Communications firms track individual locations. Politicians appeal to individual tastes and biases. Using one method to teach all students is archaic, cruel, and contrary to the best economic interests of the society.

Antitrust for the Twenty-first Century

In the 1990s, antitrust law enforcement tended to side with entrepreneurs. The Department of Justice sued Microsoft in an attempt to give rival applications-software firms easy access to Microsoft's monopoly operating system. The Federal Trade Commission ordered that various Internet service providers share Time Warner's broadband connections. The Federal Communications Commission ordered the Bell telephone companies to share their networks with rivals. All these efforts supported start-ups seeking to enter monopolized or intensely consolidated industries. The purpose of the new antitrust policy was to encourage new entry into established markets and robust competition in new markets.

Under the Bush administration, antitrust policy has withered away. Businesses assume all mergers will be approved, and they are generally right in this speculation. In the 00s, government leaders encourage not competition but consolidation as a way to bolster corporate profits. The government has not been so strongly in favor of consolidation since Franklin Roosevelt's misbegotten experiment with the National Recovery Administration in the first New Deal.[27]

It is true that antitrust policy for networked industries must recognize the merits of the rule of winner-take-all. Netscape won, for a time, a very high share of the browser market. AOL had about 40 percent of the narrowband-access market, Microsoft more than 90 percent share in operating systems. Total victory stemmed from economies of scale, increasing returns, and network effects. Antitrust law plainly should not limit the incentives for competition, and competition inevitably produces a winner. The law should not punish victories by new firms and new technologies. Nevertheless, government antitrust policy makers should worry about whether rivals can reasonably compete in any and every market. They should be concerned with lock-in—the possibility that winning firms can use network effects and increasing returns to deter more efficient rivals from challenging their dominance.

In the Microsoft case, the government aspired to articulate a modern antitrust policy for networked industries. The Department of Justice argued that Microsoft used its monopoly in operating software to obtain competitive advantage in adjacent applications-software markets.[28] That harmed competition in the markets for e-mail, word processing, data storage, and other adjacent, linked, but discrete markets. Unfortunately for the entrepreneurs who might have benefited from a practical compromise of a result, the government blundered by seeking to break up Microsoft into different companies.[29] The conservative appellate court choked on that extreme remedy and reversed the trial court's ruling against Microsoft on various grounds.[30] Political support for the case waned, partly because Microsoft successfully wooed the Republican Congress and partly because the Department of Justice had, like the Confederacy, found its Gettysburg by reaching too far on the issue of remedy. After the presidential election of 2000, the government effectively abandoned the litigation.[31] Not only did Microsoft's rivals suffer, but the national search for a good antitrust policy lost steam.

Antitrust has always been rooted in a political view about business activities, notwithstanding the use of economic analysis. For stimulating entrepreneurship, the best antitrust policy should state its goals in terms of their impact on firms and people. The principal purposes should be encouraging entrepreneurs to introduce goods and services in existing and new markets, increasing the ability of existing and new firms to generate productivity, and expanding the chances of American firms to compete effectively in foreign markets.[32] The right policy should assume economics can predict ways to achieve these goals. The policy can be flexible in application but explicit in statement of purpose. The Department of Justice should take the lead in defining the law by pursuing litigations in important industries and by passing on proposed mergers.

In reviewing mergers, the Department of Justice should focus on encouraging multiple firms to compete in new product development in every market. To that end, antitrust law should insist that standard-setting bodies be open and public. It ought to reduce barriers to entry that do not result from marketplace success. For example, cellular telephone firms can merge without deterring new entrants as long as start-ups have a right to

obtain new spectrum licenses and connect their customers to existing networks at a fair price. Established software firms can merge if entrepreneurial firms still have practical access to customers. The government can
safely allow a winning technology firm to become very large in scale and
market share, as long as technical leadership in the field is divided among
various firms. Mergers can do little harm if old or new firms can reasonably
generate what Andy Grove called "10x change"—an order of magnitude
advance in cost reduction or performance enhancement.[33] If a telephone
and cable company wanted to merge to create a combined broadband system that could multiply bandwidth ten times, the deal should not be un-
thinkable. On the other hand, the government might want to impose as a
condition on such a merger the obligation to connect with their rivals' networks or the necessity of keeping the merged networks open to the content of challengers.

Moreover, the government should encourage existing firms to create
new markets or to compete in existing markets adjacent to those in which
they already compete. The Antitrust Division of the Department of Justice ought to have the power to preempt state price regulation or other
constraints that stop electric utilities from competing in communications.
At the same time it should proactively encourage firms to use power lines,
telephone poles, and rights of way to compete against existing utilities.
New energy firms should be able to use portions of the distribution systems
of oil and gas companies in order to compete in fuel and electricity markets. New health care companies should be able to obtain favorable regulation that helps them enter otherwise closed markets.[34] A new, frankly
pro-entrepreneur antitrust policy should aim to increase productivity gains
by encouraging both small and big firms to introduce new technologies.
These gains would translate into a higher standard of living and higher income for Americans.

The administration should pursue international treaties applying the
new American antitrust policy to foreign markets. An international antitrust policy would open new competitive opportunities in Asian markets.
Any such policy would preclude state-owned companies from remaining in
a market. State-owned firms inevitably obtain special legal and financial advantages to assist them in competition with private (and foreign) firms.

An international antitrust paradigm would bar governments from dis-
criminating against American firms competing in foreign markets. Trade
negotiators have debated this topic for years to no good outcome; it is time

for a major push toward a fair policy. In a world of rising international competition, American firms need a much more powerful effort by the American government to insist at the highest level on global competition according to the principles of a new entrepreneurial competition treaty.

Entrepreneurial firms can die from delay. They have limited money to spend on attacking markets. When it is gone, they may quit even if possibly on the verge of success. Therefore, government needs to decide antitrust issues promptly. To this end, Congress should eliminate the complicated processes that require multiple agencies to examine mergers and other antitrust questions in sequence. At the same time, Congress should order regulatory agencies to change their rules, if necessary, to accommodate the results of proposed mergers. The historic divorce between the Justice Department's antitrust enforcement and the competition regulations of various agencies has never made much sense. It primarily creates intergovernmental confusion. Government should craft a single antitrust policy. The Justice Department and administrative agencies should have an integrated, unified method of enforcing it, with no political intervention.

Growing the Market

Population growth will make the United States an increasingly attractive market in the twenty-first century. Americans will number nearly 400 million by 2050. With such a valuable and unified market at their disposal, firms that compete and win in America can expect to obtain ample investment resources and big profits. However, American firms will do even better if they bring more people into the consuming class to which they sell.

The United States can increase and unite the production and consumption power of North, Central, and South America. Instead of bringing Mexican workers into the United States by means of inadequate border policing, the United States can tie the Mexican and other Latin economies tightly into a common American market. The United States would benefit by creating social benefits for citizens of other countries in the Americas. Instead of dismantling its own social security system, it could create such plans in all the countries of the Americas at a level commensurate with the needs in those countries. For example, it could contribute matching funds for helping citizens of Latin American countries start savings accounts that will be invested in Pan-American stocks and bonds. Personal accounts for all the Americas would greatly expand the prospects of all U.S. firms.

An all-Americas market from Tierra del Fuego to Alaska could count about 800 million consumers. In such a market, firms from the United States could achieve brand recognition, efficient distribution, and great customer loyalty. Such hopes inspired the Chile–United States Free Trade Agreement in 2003, which in turn built on the Mexico–United States agreement called NAFTA (North American Free Trade Agreement) in 1993. By contrast, CAFTA—the Central American Free Trade Agreement of 2005—made a mockery of free trade when the Bush administration agreed, in the course of winning the vote from southern and Great Plains representatives, to perpetuate agricultural subsidies that impoverished many developing nations by denying their farmers the capability to earn even subsistence incomes.

The United States has historically made little concerted effort to create strong economic and social linkages between it and the rest of the American cultures. It was deterred by the centuries of connection between Latin countries and the European countries from which their immigrant populations came. The United States spent billions on attacking the drug trade in the southern continent but much less on economic development. As an example, until the 1990s American communications firms invested in oceanic optical cables west to Japan and east to Europe, but built little or no capacity heading south. The U.S. government paid much less attention to education, health care, and political reform in South America than to the tyranny in Cuba—a country with 4 percent of the population of South America.[35]

In 2000 the average per capita income in the six largest Latin American countries measured 35 percent of the American level.[36] If Latin America were to grow as fast as China, then by some time in the 2030s, the region could equal the U.S. economy's size in 2005. The combined Americas' economy would then be as or more powerful than China's. Any firm operating in the Americas would have the opportunity to obtain scale and scope invaluable in competing with Asian rivals. Particularly if the globe fractures into regional trading blocks, the United States will need a Pan-American market.[37]

American hardware and software firms do not require that all their customers have Western-style buying power. They can sell cell phones and secondhand computers to people who earn as little as $1,000 a year.[38] If American information firms penetrate foreign markets they can provide new, cheap solutions for education, health, and other social goals that the forces of large-scale global finance only indirectly address. For example, about 400 million children in the developing world currently have no likelihood of obtaining an education. In the face of population growth, coupled with the traditional model of brick-and-mortar schools, lecturers, and books on paper, the lack of funds will cause the uneducated population to grow to nearly a billion within fifteen years. If educators distributed Apple iPods or Hewlett-Packard computers as primary teaching tools, they could teach at a cost per student that decreased on the same declining curve as Moore's Law—doubling price performance every eighteen months. If an iPod can carry all the songs ever sung, or a laptop connect to all the thoughts ever expressed, then of course any teaching material or methodology can be contained in these inventions. Teachers will no longer repeat information. They will reveal it. They will show how to learn, not what to learn.

Hardware and software can deliver information in any language or any form—graphic, aural, numerical, pictorial, or alphabetic—at no meaningful extra cost. Economic development programs, then, can aim to deliver hardware and software goods dedicated to both commercial and social purposes. Families and communities can combine spending power to buy goods that offer economic, entertainment, and other intangible value. These new distribution channels would stimulate more rapid development of local small businesses. Information economies in the developing world could perpetuate indigenous culture while also connecting the locale to the efficiencies of the developed world's economies.[39]

American entrepreneurs will benefit by adding the developing world to their addressable markets. As long as entrepreneurs have a fair chance to enter the new markets, the increased size of these markets will increase the incentive to create new goods and services. If firms from the United States can establish distribution chains and brand recognition in the developing world, then they might win loyalty from the new consuming classes of Africa, Asia, and Latin America.[40]

The near future provides a glittering prospect of developing the world and integrating the next billion consumers into the American economy.[41] Not surprisingly, China understands this strategy. Its government engages aggressively with developing countries. China imports more from the developing world, even while it exports to the developed world economies. In effect, it sends money from rich America to poor countries and hopes for more than their gratitude in the course of time. China plans, ultimately, to export Chinese manufacturing to these growing economies in return for importing commodities.[42]

The United States has long hoped that as its firms succeed commercially in the developing world, they will transmit democracy, almost as if it were a benign virus carried by competition. In the Golden 90s, as American firms achieved much success worldwide, at last more than 50 percent of the world's population lived in democracies. Democratic capitalism seemed triumphant. Now the Chinese development model has as much or more appeal to many countries than America's. But along with the Chinese approach may come one-party rule and statism, instead of multiple parties and free elections. If that occurs, the 1990s would represent the high-water mark for democracy.[43]

The twenty-first century will be the age of growth, but few now see the United States as the inspirational or economic leader of that growth.[44] However, the United States could lead the world in bridging the age-old gulf between the haves and the have-nots, within its own national borders and around the world.[45] All humanity can achieve a high standard of living. A global elite of wealth, fame, and accomplishment can exist along with a high living standard for everyone else in the world. An egalitarian world need not require complete income equality; it merely has to reject appalling inequality. If America uses its astounding wealth to eliminate not only poverty but the absence of opportunity for everyone, its own entrepreneurs and citizens will be better off.[46]

Hand Up, Not Handout
Public Wealth and Private Gain

When reformers argue for more public goods—like roads and broadband networks—the goal is not necessarily free services for the masses, but less cost for industry. A sound economic policy for the United States should be based on providing more public goods. In transportation, communications, and energy markets, the wise goal should be to reduce the costs all firms pay for these input services. In each of these markets, the rule of law should aim to produce lower costs. In communications, those costs can approximate nearly zero per byte of information. Under such policies, existing firms will become more efficient. Importantly, start-ups will obtain the advantage of lowered costs for competing against existing firms.

All firms eventually must charge more than their costs. A start-up, however, typically loses money for up to four or five years before it begins to cover its costs. The investors know that they have to pay for product development, marketing, and sales efforts before they can expect much revenue. The start-up's executives usually decide that they cannot enter an existing market unless they charge at least 10 percent below what the existing firms charge, because otherwise customers will not take the risk of switching to the unknown new firm. The existing firms presumably recovered their cost in the past, however, and can compete with the start-up rival by lowering their price at least to the cost of maintaining their existing business—a much lower cost than originally incurred to found their businesses. Both the incumbent and the start-up have to pay for necessary inputs, such as energy and communications services. These costs are embedded in every product. The higher the costs, the less output of all goods and services. In addition, as costs go up, start-ups have to raise more money, and that reduces entrepreneurial activity. In the long run all firms in a market will pass their costs on to their customers, but in the short run the established firm can pay bills for necessary inputs while the start-up has to shift money from product creation to pay for heating, air conditioning, or broadband.

To promote efficiency and entrepreneurship, the rule of law should reduce the cost inputs necessary for all firms in a market. As an example, when the new competition in communications markets lowered the cost of services in the 1990s, start-ups and incumbent firms in all industries paid less for the necessary input of communications services. That gave a boost to new competition in all industries. Lower cost for a necessary input also makes all firms more productive. That creates greater wealth for the society and often increases employees' income.

The rule of law should not lower costs for some firms to the disadvantage of others. It should not aim to discriminate for or against start-ups. The law ought to aim for efficient firms to win, not caring whether an old firm defeats an upstart rival or a new firm topples a has-been incumbent. But law can create new public goods that lower costs for everyone, and by doing so help start-ups overcome the disadvantage of incurring costs before they can recover them and also make all firms more efficient.

When the government built the interstate highway system, fast-food franchises and motel chains built their new businesses at its interchanges. Similarly, dot-coms and established firms used the public good of the Internet to help new ventures succeed, and thereby expanded jobs and income in the United States. In the twenty-first century the government should create as another public good a high-speed broadband that reaches every American everywhere. From every place in America, and whether stationary or mobile, everyone ought to be able to go on the Internet at a price so low that everyone would always choose to log on. The stimulus to electronic commerce, small business growth, and job creation resulting from this public good—in effect a virtual interstate highway and local road system, combined with access to all existing media—would produce a significant gain in the size and productivity of the economy.[47] Beyond that, a universal access system would provide a medium for the development of new businesses, just as in the 1940s and 1950s broadcast television contributed quickly and surprisingly to mass marketing, suburban culture, new brands, and a substantial increase in annual economic growth. For about $10 billion to $20 billion, the government can make up the difference between what people are willing to pay for broadband and what the telephone and cable companies charge to cover their costs. That would represent about 3 percent of the five-year spending on roads, highways, and bridges authorized by Congress in 2005.[48]

Broadband will provide a platform for new commercial activities, such as concurrent game playing (as in Korea) or in-home medical examinations.[49] If everyone has access to the new medium, new content will create new cultural ties—just as broadcast television did in the last century. Unlike broadcast television, however, broadband permits individuals to associate with each other. They conduct their own transactions, as in the case of eBay; create their own content, as in the millions of blogs; or collaborate in compiling content, as in the open encyclopedia called Wikipedia. In a broadband society, a few content sources cannot so readily shape the culture as they did during the TV age. Broadband can stimulate cultural change, as television, radio, and telephone did in their enfant terrible days. Potentially, broadband will accelerate change, because of its capability to transfer information rapidly among its users. Broadband also can encourage associations across geographic, racial, and even linguistic lines that other media—newspapers, television, telephony, and movies—cannot so easily cross.[50] For these reasons, broadband shifts commercial and political power to end users. By doing so, it undercuts the advantages of incumbents and therefore increases the opportunity for entrepreneurs to compete.[51]

Worth What You Can Borrow

Every start-up executive knows the difficulty of persuading venture investors to spend the money necessary to build the chip, write the software, do the marketing necessary to attack the opportunity that may not even exist. These investors perform the useful function of allocating capital wisely, to the benefit of society. However, investors have difficulty assessing the prospects of start-ups. By definition, early-stage ventures usually require modest initial investments. They also often involve explorations of immature and unpredictable markets. Moreover, since start-up entrepreneurs usually have skimpy experience, they ask for a certain suspension of disbelief on the part of investors. For these reasons, entrepreneurs pursuing modest opportunities, such as local retail or service businesses, may have difficulty attracting investors. To remove this obstacle, government should create a large market of microlenders. It would consist of firms that focus on loaning small amounts to small businesses. The government should charter firms, as it did Fannie Mae and Freddie Mac in order to promote home ownership, in order to issue low-cost loans under $10,000 and even under $1,000.

Setting aside some portion of government spending for small businesses also could stimulate entrepreneurship. Particularly in technology markets, government can provide a start-up with an early opportunity to find an important customer. Start-ups, however, will not have the lobbying budgets of big firms. If they need to depend on political influence for government contracts, they will lose. To have a chance at some federal money, they need laws that require government agencies to give small businesses some contracts and a transparent bidding process for awarding the contracts.

Government should offer tax advantages for sellers who use the Internet. By relying more on the Internet, American commercial firms would become more efficient. To achieve a different type of efficiency, government should buy fuel-efficient transportation and lease energy-efficient office space. The government of course does not need to make a profit on its commercial transactions. Although government ought not waste the public's money, its spending can provide volume in demand, so that sellers of new products would have an easier opportunity to introduce their offerings.

Government makes between one-fifth and one-fourth of purchases in America. No other single buyer has as much power to influence demand for goods and services. That power could be exercised to encourage entrepreneurship.

All Together Now

An entrepreneur bets against the present, gambling on the overthrow of the status quo. The start-up takes a technology risk: can the product be made? It takes a market risk: will anyone buy it? The founders take a risk on people: have they recruited the right team? The team members take an economic risk: can I afford to work for less now in return for a payoff later? The investors take a financial risk: if the business incurs loss for some time, will it eventually turn a profit? The firm takes a competitive risk: will someone else make the product more quickly and at a lower cost? Risk and reward constitute two sides of the same coin—the start-up firm's bet of time and money now in return for reward in the future. To promote a culture of entrepreneurship, law should minimize some unnecessary risks and enhance rewards.

The New Deal liberal program in American politics smacks of income redistribution and is not well suited for promoting entrepreneurship. In a culture of entrepreneurship, success should earn large rewards. The right tax policy is neither to suppress consumption nor to take too much from those who have earned high incomes. A sound policy for entrepreneurship is to decrease the taxation of options and other forms of equity commonly owned by risk takers in small companies, and to decrease the taxation of incentive-based bonuses in big companies. Unearned income and assets, by contrast, are fit targets for increased progressive taxation.

Law should not reduce business risk, but it can reduce personal risk. Large businesses hedge against risk in many ways—for instance, they buy insurance, phase capital investment over time, avoid long-term contracts, buy and sell derivatives to guard against currency fluctuations. Because of these techniques, the big firm can take more risks. Individuals need government to give them similar techniques. Government should provide everyone insurance against natural calamities. It also should insure individuals against career risk. Yale economist Robert Shiller suggests livelihood insurance as part of the safety net: "Whichever [career] you choose, you're taking a risk." So, he concludes, individuals ought to be able to buy insurance against the downside so as to take a chance on the upside by investing time and money in obtaining specialized training in a new field.[52]

Individuals should know that they will have health care and retirement pensions no matter what happens.[53] In the last half of the twentieth century, the United States promised social security benefits, free education to war veterans, and Medicare for seniors. These benefits encouraged Americans to accept poor job security. The workforce became fluid and mobile. That led to increased efficiency and more risk taking by everyone. As an unfortunate by-product, nearly one-sixth of the population has no health insurance.

In previous decades, the U.S. government could count on companies to provide economic security under adverse circumstances—such as poor health or retirement—that in poorer countries the state had to guarantee in return for the support of its citizens. In the twenty-first century, American firms could or would no longer play the role of surrogate government.[54] Some faced so much global competition that they could not afford such costs. Others avoided such costs by relocating jobs in other countries. Either way, American government could no longer count on employers to provide employees the retirement, health, unemployment, and other income guarantees granted in the previous half century.

Gene Sperling, economic adviser to the president in the Clinton administration, argues for increased national savings by passing laws that encourage middle- to lower-class Americans to save for retirement. He says the outcome will be less wealth inequality. Although these goals are laudable, less income inequality is much more important than less wealth inequality. More public goods, which provide the equivalent of income gains, will benefit all Americans more than retirement savings. Improved standards of living, which result from increased public goods and higher income, are more important to people than increased savings. More public spending on education, greater encouragement of career risk taking, and other widely available benefits all are more important to the well-being of the whole society than tax incentives encouraging more retirement savings.

People do not like to gamble when it comes to health care or retirement pension. As long as these elements of security are lacking, people will be less willing to take risks in business. The absence of laws guaranteeing health care and minimum defined-benefit pensions discourages entrepreneurship in America. The law should tilt individual decision scales in favor of taking chances.

In the conservative way of thinking, if people bear sole individual responsibility for their well-being, then everyone will be more motivated to work hard. Americans do not need government help to overcome some aversion to work, except possibly for the inheritance class that argues for estate-tax repeal. For the most part, the country's citizenry works itself to death. Americans need to work less when they instead should be seeking more education. They need to be less trapped into seeking the security of dead-end jobs when they should be joining start-ups.

If everyone has assured education, health care, and pension insurance, all will be less dependent on the care of a particular large employer or a union. People will be able to move more readily from job to job, or region to region, or skill to skill. They can take chances, knowing that they and their families will not be helpless or destitute if the risks they take do not produce rewards every time or right away.[55] By adopting such confident attitudes, individuals will make the American economy more supple, re-silient, and productive.[56]

From 1975 to 2000, the probability that a firm in the top 20 percent of a market would fall out of that category in five years approximately doubled, from about 8 percent to 16 percent. The probability was even higher for information technology firms. In telecommunications, for example, bank-ruptcies went from nine between 1991 and 1997 to seventy-six from 1997 to 2002.[57] The stock market boom and bust undermined stability, but in-tense global competition, increasing returns to winning companies, and radical differences in efficiency among rivals are leading to a higher mor-tality rate for technology firms. In a more entrepreneurial economy, the death toll *should* rise. Laws should be changed so as to ease the impact on individuals of this enhanced uncertainty and thereby obtain societal sup-port for risk taking.

According to what economists call prospect theory, "the emotional drop from losing something is considerably greater than the emotional lift from gaining the exact same thing" by a proportion of roughly two to one. Therefore, if a million Americans lose a job and then get a new one at the same pay, that million will feel twice as bad about losing their jobs as they will about gaining new work.[58] This theory gives insight into the degree of pain and anxiety endemic to America because job loss and job creation is so much faster in the United States than in less turbulent, less creative, less dynamic societies. Research also shows, however, that op-portunities coupled with freedom enable individuals to achieve substan-tial happiness.[59] A stronger safety net—job loss insurance, health care in-surance, free education—will mitigate "emotional drop" and permit the elixir of opportunity and choice to increase the cultural commitment to entrepreneurship.

Principles of Technology Applied to Entrepreneurial Culture

The architectures of technology shape opportunities. The integrated circuit (or "chip") launched a half-century's worth of technological firms and created uncounted value—probably a meaningful fraction of the globe's $40 trillion of production.[60] The integrated circuit produced rapid and continuous change, substantial cost reduction of existing goods and services, and leadership by small new firms instead of large existing firms. At bottom, the value proposition of the integrated circuit was that it could become more complex without increasing the cost. Gordon Moore, co-founder of Intel, predicted in 1965 that the technologists could make the chip double in the number of circuits, or processing capability, every two years without becoming more expensive.[61] That meant firms could build computers that every two years saved more documents, displayed more colorful pictures, contained more applications, and cost no more than when they offered much less value. They could make cellular telephones that every two years advanced in some way—by allowing users to download ring tones, take photos, watch television—and cost no more than when they were just ways to talk. Without adding to the cost of the set-top box, cable companies could add more and more channels in their packages.

Moore's Law also meant that every firm was chained to a rapidly turning wheel of new product creation. After all, any firm that made the next version of any chip-containing product better, faster, and cheaper than an incumbent might then supplant the established firm. The technology of the integrated circuit in itself dictated rapid turnover of products, continual and fierce competition, productivity gains, and increasing wealth generation. The integrated circuit's technology defined the culture of entrepreneurship in its founders' home states of California (Robert Noyce) and Texas (Jack Kilby).

By contrast, the automobile processes of Ford and General Motors turned out cars that varied much more by style than by rapid increases in performance. Personal invention mattered less; employees became parts of a complex production machine. The automobile was to the first half of the twentieth century what the chip was to the second half. But it led to a culture of rank, scale, and consumer marketing. Its processes stifled entrepreneurship at the same time that the integrated circuit inspired it.

The chip sparked what Andy Grove famously called "paranoia," in large part because any entrepreneur in the world could acquire enough of the scientific knowledge behind the chip to compete with any incumbent in the market. The chip's technology made entrepreneurs learn the lessons of working hard, fast, and furiously. If a firm desired to maintain advantage, it had to make ever-better products. Moreover, the chip did nothing for a user until a firm built a system that used it in combination with software and various other parts, each of which worked only in conjunction with the others. The chip's technology taught its acolytes not only to expect vigorous competition but also to look for partners, complementors, and cooperative parties as allies in creating value.

Behind the chip's technology lay the science of quantum mechanics. In the first half of the twentieth century, Max Planck, Albert Einstein, and Niels Bohr uncovered new and nonintuitive relationships among time, mass, and speed. For the nonmathematicians who watched the geniuses work, at least three lessons emerged. First, the past did not predict the future; no rules foreordained that particles would end up in one place instead of another. The sun was only statistically probable to rise in the east; there was a chance that tomorrow dawn would break in the west. Second, no particles acted independently; other particles affected any particular particle even if the relationship was inexplicably "spooky," as Einstein put it. Third, particles were also waves; waves, particles. At most one could say that when measured in the past any object appeared as a particle; to describe its future behavior, best to call it a wave.

Translated from the language of mathematics, these three precepts became the key beliefs of the quantum culture of entrepreneurship. First, anyone can hope to become the next great creator of a product, a business, an idea, a style, or a new thing. No rule or ordered system dictates outcome. Out of ten start-ups, one or two will succeed, and no one can pick the winners in advance. Chance plays a very large role. Second, no invention wins on its own merits. A start-up depends on collaborators, complementors, influencers, partners to succeed. Third, entrepreneurial action does not move forward in a predefined path. Its actual progress can be measured only in the past, after the breakthrough event of a successful tapeout, a big contract, an initial public offering. In the moment, enterpreneurship is like riding a wave, heading for a wipeout or enjoying a long trip on the surf of success.

As Grove said, whatever technology can do, it will do.[62] To process speech will require six times the complexity of the computing behind e-mail. For a computer to say good morning to its owner will require two times more. All these miracles will come to pass, but how, when, and where they occur matters crucially to the entrepreneurs trying to create and capture new value. The challenge for Americans is making sure that, given the uncertainty of knowing what products will be of value, the collective efforts of entrepreneurs produce wealth for Americans.

To lead in entrepreneurship, a society must hold to the three quantum beliefs: it has to launch many new initiatives so as to have at least a few successes; it has to create an ecosystem of suppliers, complementors, and buyers; it has to move forward in many directions at once, because the best path is uncertain. Every two years, according to Moore's Law, the product market will be redefined.[63] Still, the leading firm has a good chance to remain the leader as long as it retains a creative culture. The leading nation can remain the leader if it sustains a culture of entrepreneurship.

Entrepreneurial Leadership
Risk-Taking and Risk-Reducing Leaders

Former treasury secretary Robert Rubin, unlike most accomplished business executives, superbly mastered the art of government. His experience at the risk-oriented Goldman Sachs trading desk taught him how to run the nation's fiscal policy. "At the core of [my] outlook," said Rubin, was "the conviction that nothing can be proven to be certain." Therefore, "you have to have the stomach for risk." Risk taking built a distinctive culture: Rubin worked in an "environment [that] was highly entrepreneurial and often seat-of-the-pants. . . . Management was accomplished by yelling—all day long."[64]

While others yelled, Rubin applied statistical reasoning to his judgments. He learned to give "appropriate weight to what might occur under remote, but potentially very damaging, circumstances."[65] Federal Reserve Chairman Alan Greenspan, Rubin's intellectual partner who shaped American monetary policy, followed the same method. A 90 percent probability of suffering a $10 million loss attracted less of their attention than a 10 percent probability of a $900 million loss: probability times loss equals the amount of attention the downside deserved. By this method, the two of them created the most salubrious combination of fiscal and monetary policy in the history of the United States.

Rubin and Greenspan gathered voluminous information, but only by guessing could they reach a final judgment. Events flowed in many directions, like a wave, and could be measured, like a particle, only when in the past. They tried to assess probabilities. They assumed the past was at least partly a prologue to the future. For example, they believed that certain trends put Americans at risk over time: too much energy consumption in a market of diminishing supply, too little education, too much government borrowing, increased spending on health care, climate change. Perhaps no calamity will ensue from any of these developments. The future, after all, is uncertain, and luck can favor anyone. Based on the lessons of the Rubin-Greenspan thought partnership, however, it should be axiomatic that leaders in government, as in business, should mitigate risk. Dangerous trends should be forestalled. If Chinese entrepreneurs might win major markets, Americans should compete more vigorously. If carbon consumption threatens the environment and the economy, then the United States should pass laws encouraging noncarbon energy now, before a crisis occurs.[66] Future benefits and future costs must be discounted to the present. The government should not spend more than it raises unless the benefits exceed the cost over time.[67]

At diverse times of crisis, leaders of the American government have made many remarkably wise decisions. As a result, the United States is the most successful large government since the Roman Empire. However, even as computers have enabled people to master ever greater complexity, American political leaders feel increasingly overwhelmed by the challenges of governing. They cannot rationally believe elections give them mandates, much less guidance. They are overwhelmed by the demands of fund raising. They are frustrated by the inefficiencies of tripartite federalism. They expect to be misunderstood, but even when their words rally support for some action, they doubt that they will be able to translate their intentions into results. In their frustration, they blame the voters, the media, and each other. They wash their hands of outcomes. Where no one takes responsibility, corruption flourishes. Bad apples spoil the bunch. The departure of the good leaves the less-good behind. Government becomes more populated by the incompetent, ignorant, and indifferent. Patronage overwhelms professionalism; loyalty trumps expertise.

To manage over time a sensible response to China, America needs to use the talent at its disposal. The Chinese Communist Party cannot be the only government that trains its leaders. The United States needs to root out graft. It needs to recruit talented people into government. It needs to empower capable people to use the law toward good goals. These steps would reduce the risk of bad decisions on crucial matters.

Government leaders should start by changing the process of organizing the allocation of authority. Good planning helps. Law should require a president, within sixty days after each congressional election, to submit a plan of organization for the administration for the next two years. Proposed changes in cabinet and agency structure will become law, barring a two-thirds vote to the contrary in each house of Congress. The president should make no more than 1,000 appointments. An independent, nonpolitical personnel agency should recruit qualified people for the several thousand positions now filled by patronage. The administration's shortened list of political nominees should be confirmed or rejected by the Senate within sixty days after appointment.

Every quarter each cabinet, subcabinet, and agency chief should produce for public examination a statement of goals, measurements of success, and a self-evaluation according to such goals. All such measures become, in time, paperwork processes. However, they also provide a healthy way to hold those in office accountable for success and failure. Most government action involves administration of funds or use of law to accomplish some specific goal, such as improving education or ending the drug trade. Stating goals and using efficient means to achieve them should be normal practice in government.

By organizing government better, leaders will create better opportunities for coordination among the many arms and agencies of the rule of law. Most goal-oriented programs succeed when they coordinate the activities of a broad group of interested parties, the way a software operating system organizes applications programmers. Perhaps nothing is more important to effective government than coordinating collective action by nongovernmental parties. For instance, in the 1996 Telecommunications Act, Congress ordered the Federal Communications Commission to issue regulations that ensured Internet access in every classroom in the United States. By the early oos the United States had exceeded every other country in introducing the Internet into classrooms. More than 80 percent had access. Unlike almost any other aspect of education, poor children had about as much access to this new resource as rich children.

The secret of the "e-rate" program's success was that it matched federal funds with money raised by local school districts. Poor districts had to contribute as little as 10 percent, rich districts as much as 60 percent, but every district had to pay something. For that reason, funds went only to those who had demonstrated serious interest in the program. The beneficiaries became owners. In making the commitment to pay something, the school districts had to think through the uses of the Internet. They became active participants in creating educational value from Internet access.

Congress could have simply ordered the army to run networks through the walls of classrooms. But changes in behavior, not changes in buildings, produce enduring success. Top-down mandates were not likely to encourage schools to learn how to use the Internet. By relying on local users to initiate the e-rate connections, the policy produced rapid cultural change. As of 2005, more than half of teachers said that computer technology had changed the way they taught "a great deal." More than three-fourths of teachers used new technology to communicate, do research, plan lessons, teach in class, keep records. Nearly two-thirds considered themselves to have become advanced users of computers.

Apart from organizing and coordinating better, government leaders should hold themselves accountable for taking a long view. Bob Rubin inspired others to look around the blind curve of immediate events. In that way he established the value of conduct in the present that will produce benefits in the future.

Technology leaders also can lead Americans to think forward, then reason backward. Their inventions always bring the future into being. What technologists discover, like the fruit of the forbidden tree, makes the difference between good and evil directions for humanity. Technology leaders bear more responsibility for society's direction than other people, because they know the power and likely consequences of their inventions. They, like Rubin and Greenspan with respect to economic activity, can see more clearly than others where their works will take society.

The big bang spawned myriad alternative universes that have unfolded in parallel through 10 billion years of cause and effect, pattern and accident. On some more Edenic Earth, cold fusion and cheap solar power preceded the invention of the Model T. On that version of our planet, no one now fears cataclysmic global warming. On that other pathway of probability, penicillin preceded bubonic plague, and the Black Death was never more than a bad cold. Nevertheless, we live on this humanity's one knowable world. In this reality we have godlike power to choose among infinite paths into the undiscovered future. Technologists therefore cannot escape the burden of leadership. By deciding what to work on and when to work on it, technologists select the future of the world.

J. Robert Oppenheimer never could decide whether he should have

helped invent the atomic bomb. He was, however, a hero, because he recognized the meaning of Hiroshima. He took responsibility for creating the
risk of the world's end, even though he had not acted alone and surely
someone eventually would have build the A-bomb if he had not led the
team.[68] Not every technology leader must elect between the incineration
of cities and the continuation of a world war. But all technology leaders
can be heroes if they see how their inventions choose certain paths for humanity among the infinite possible directions.

Virtuous Cycles

Reform in America depends on the replacement of failed leadership with a new breed of entrepreneurial leader. Marc Andreessen defined the necessary traits of an entrepreneurial leader this way: "Impatient.
Intolerant of the status quo. Open minded. Uncomfortable. Unhappy.
Unsatisfied with his lot in life. Unsatisfied with the way the world works.
Wanting to eat at a restaurant he can't afford."[69] Those characteristics a
culture could tolerate, or reject. As a culture ages, the hierarchy of power
and wealth may gradually lose these attributes. But when Andreessen arrived in Silicon Valley, America liked those traits.

When he reached age thirty-three in 2004, Andreessen was eight years
past his appearance on the cover of *Time* magazine. He doubted if he
could succeed in a big way again. "After a while when you get older you get
too far from the technology," said Andreessen. "The fundamental breakthroughs often come from people in their twenties. The problem isn't really physical age. It is that as you get older you get a more fixed view about
how things work. Your brain isn't as full in your twenties. To be an entrepreneur later on you have to try to get past that. You have to surround
yourself with younger people. I find people in their sixties, seventies, and
eighties who can still be teenagers. I think it is a choice."

Andreessen acknowledged the importance of the rule of law in promoting entrepreneurship: "You need a capital base and university research
and appropriate government tax policies." But culture mattered. "Most
importantly," he said, "America needs to think of entrepreneurship as a
natural birthright that has many potential enemies. With that thought, and
a pool of fundamentally dissatisfied people, America will see useful results,
and investment gains."

Steve Case summarized his version of American culture this way: "We
have had entrepreneurial culture in our country since America was founded.

Risks have been different in different times. For at least twenty-five years now technology has been the key area of entrepreneurship. But what continues to be remarkable is the ability of this country to have a culture of entrepreneurship. Most countries and companies get stifled, become static, as they grow larger."[70]

John Doerr, one of the greatest of Silicon Valley venture capitalists, proved the value of continuous disruption. Doerr was born in St. Louis, Missouri, in 1951. He always wanted to start a business, because his father had started a business—distributing the new invention of consumer air conditioners in humid, hot St. Louis early in the long boom of post–World War II America. Doerr received an engineering degree at Rice University and attended Harvard Business School. Fortunately for America, he did not take finance classes. Luckily, he did not get a job offer from either of the top two consulting firms to which he and most of the class applied. Best of all, he did follow his college girlfriend to California.

What made Doerr want to leave the path of wealth creation through finance and management that almost all his classmates took? "I wanted to start a company with some friends," said Doerr. "I wanted it to be a technology company. Subliminally, I felt individuals could gain unprecedented power and freedom from enabling technologies. And besides, what a thrill to have a machine follow your instruction. I had no notion of macroeconomics or globalization or wealth creation. It was much more geeky than that. It was more cool and neat if we could write the software and the machine follow the instructions. Gates still talks that way. Lots of Americans felt that doing this mattered. And also people were willing to pay me for this fun."[71]

Doerr got a job at Intel; the company had started only a few years earlier. Its four CEOs in the twentieth century—Bob Noyce, Gordon Moore, Andy Grove, and Craig Barrett—each had a doctorate in science and understood well the research establishment of America. Doerr lacked a doctorate, although he possessed master's degrees in engineering and business administration. More than that, he had a boundless belief in the power of science to change life.[72]

In Doerr's first summer at Intel he traveled to Europe with Andy Grove. Grove and his young acolyte signed on two big companies as customers for computer chips. They trained a European sales force—a handful of people. Doerr stayed at Intel until 1980 and left in the early days of the personal computer. He joined the venture capital firm where he still works. In the twenty-five years from 1980 to 2005 he founded or invested early in dozens and dozens of firms, including Andreessen's Netscape and the most famous start-up of the 00s, Google.

Can the entrepreneurship of Andreessen, Case, and Doerr be taught to others? "You can't teach entrepreneurship. Some would disagree with me. But that's what I've seen," said Doerr.

Andy Rachleff, another famously successful Silicon Valley venture capitalist, agreed: "Entrepreneurs cannot be trained. They are born. An entrepreneur has to be visionary. You can't hire vision. You can hire execution. Vision is the ability to conceptualize continually compelling products and services."[73]

If entrepreneurs are like gold—discovered, not manufactured—then still they must be found.[74] Doerr, Rachleff, and other Silicon Valley investors worked in a veritable Sutter's Mill of entrepreneurial prospecting. But the gold came to them: would-be entrepreneurs drove from Illinois, flew from India, knocked on door after door—like aspiring actors or writers—looking for a chance. A culture of entrepreneurship encouraged them to dream; a Silicon Valley culture of risk taking welcomed them. Rachleff counted since 1980 only about 300 to 350 American information technology start-ups that reached $100 million in revenue. Those in the charmed circle accounted for America's tremendous growth in productivity, income, and jobs. The process of winnowing thousands of firms down to a few hundred successes made the Valley and America rich; most small firms mainly wasted time and money. Paradoxically, because any entrepreneur faced long odds, the culture needed to encourage as much risk taking by as many entrepreneurs as could be found. Out of this process, new leaders emerged.

Behind all revolutions in conduct and performance lies change in perception. For the United States to compete successfully with China, all Americans have to see a new vision. They need to seek inspiring goals. They have to want to solve the impending catastrophe of global warming, end global poverty, and extend individual freedom through peace and economic development.[75] They need to take responsibility for their society's actions.[76] An aspiration to make a heaven of earth should animate the American historical narrative in the twenty-first century.[77] This story will attract the zeal and creativity of entrepreneurs. Perhaps the breed is born, not made, but entrepreneurs can more easily be uncovered and supported by a society that embraces vision and adventure.[78]

5

America the Hopeful

A political victory, a rise of rents, . . . or some other favorable event raises your spirits, and you think good days are preparing for you. Do not believe it. . . . Nothing can bring you peace but the triumph of principles.

—RALPH WALDO EMERSON, *SELF-RELIANCE*

The Power of Ideas

The greatest power to change culture stems from ideas. The greatest way to express ideas is through stories. In the Golden 90s technologists led the world in telling tall tales. They spun fantastical futures. At the zenith of the boom, narrators abounded and audiences swelled. Conferences multiplied like kudzu vines. *Forbes* and *Fortune* and Vortex and VON, on and on the hosts proliferated. They summoned the technorati, money guys, and media types to Aspen, Telluride, Sundance, Laguna Beach, and even the stodgy old Waldorf Astoria, where the hype had paraded many times before. The people with money and power they put on platforms to tell stories to an audience of people hungry for money and power. All democratically slung around the neck their first names on lanyards. They stashed stacks of business cards with the same leap of hope that inspired the rest of America to buy lottery tickets. At the zenith of the era the zeitgeist found its epitome when broadcast television and the Internet converged to buy the Declaration of Independence. Long before there was an Internet, when the transistor had just emerged from Bell Labs in the late 1940s, broadcast TV redefined the American experience and reinvented the art of telling stories. For more than fifty years, even during its recent innings of "reality TV," it has never ceased to narrate. Anyone who could tell a story had a fair chance to lead through that medium. That explained the otherwise inexplicable election of Ronald Reagan to the role of Great Communicator. That gave Norman Lear a chance to lead through ideas.

Norman Lear is among the greatest of the film and television producers of the 1970s. The greatest of his achievements was *All in the Family* (1971–79). In that series, he helped set up the Reagan Revolution by embodying the classic Democrat-cum-Republican, in the form of Archie Bunker. That homophobic, xenophobic, sexist, uneducable, overworked, unfit, irritable, domineering, cranky, entrepreneurial cab driver supposedly narrated a liberal tale of tolerance. Through him, Lear brought offensive attitudes into the open. Lear's didactic message was that the audience should learn to live and let live, laughing at Bunkerism while rejecting its values.

Time and television marched on, and the sitcom mutated into Seinfeldian nihilism and Friends-ish raunchiness. Still, Lear never lacked the capacity for new ideas. He was a born entrepreneur. In 2000, he decided he would save democracy by telling the story of democracy. By chance, Lear learned that Sotheby's intended to auction the Declaration of Independence. In some countries, the private sale of the birth certificate of the nation might seem, well, unseemly. Not in the United States. The auction house put up for sale one of only twenty-five copies of the Dunlap printings of Thomas Jefferson's original handwritten manuscript. (That, at least, can be viewed in the National Archives.) Only four private parties owned one of the Dunlap Broadsides; this acquisition opportunity was rare.

Sotheby's intended to sell the Declaration online, through its own start-up company, Sothebys.com. However, for the benefit of potential pre-Internet bidders, the denizens of the nation's premier islands of wealth could view it at one of the company's posh stores. So Lear found it right around the corner from his Beverly Hills office. As soon as Lear saw the broadside, according to his colleague Marty Kaplan, he began to cry at the prospect of using it to inspire patriotism in millions of Americans.[1] Like any great showman, he intended to put the Declaration in the center ring of a Barnum and Bailey circus of fervor for the idea of America. And he would put cameras on it; from Lear's point of view, nothing happened in America except insofar as it happened on television.

Because in June 2000 the boom was still in bloom, the Internet had to be considered. For that dimension, Lear called David Hayden. Lear had met Hayden at a conference on creative entrepreneurship.[2] Hayden had helped invent software for exploring the vastness of the Internet. The name he gave that software, Magellan, revealed his penchant for history and arguably foreshadowed his business fate. Then he founded a company, Critical Path, which built e-mail systems for corporations.

By spring 2000, Hayden had on paper nearly a billion dollars. He had stepped down from executive leadership, as founders in Silicon Valley do when invention and vision give way to management and execution as the firm's important attributes—and when the founders have so much money they conceive of initiatives beyond the range of ordinary people. Hayden's vision was a Net utopia. In April 2000 he went to Rome to speak at a World Bank forum on financing development in developing countries. He said, in a long and passionate speech, "The Internet will create . . . if it hasn't already . . . the environment connecting everyone on the planet in commerce and communication. The Internet can be the platform for sustainable distribution of capital and wealth. By sustainable, I mean quite simply, if we don't share all this, it's not sustainable on any scale. Remember commerce does not mean just money."[3] Hayden meant that the Internet would distribute not only money but also ideas and values.

Lear saw that Hayden knew how to pitch ideas. Hayden's wealth mattered too.[4] No one knew what the Declaration of Independence would sell for. The nouveau riche of the Net might pay anything for anything. After all, six years earlier, Bill Gates had paid $30.8 million for Leonardo da Vinci's Codex—his book of drawings and mirror-reversed secret scribbles. Gates also had assembled the world's largest collection of Napoleon's letters. These two testaments to creative genius—the one technological and artistic, the other political and military—he had on display for lucky guests to see in his capacious house dug Hobbit-style into a hillside on the shores of Seattle's Lake Washington. The library, a work of art in wood, bore the disarming quotation carved below the cupola: "He had come a long way to this blue lawn, and his dream must have seemed so close that he could hardly fail to grasp it."[5] If the richest man in the world wanted fabulous textual artifacts for home decor (including a tonic of literary irony), then so might any of the dozens of new Internet billionaires trump Lear's vision by selecting the Declaration for a wall hanging. For the Net rich, that acquisition would be a lagniappe in comparison to, say, a home on a Pebble Beach fairway, a collection of historic military airplanes, or the world's tallest-masted yacht.[6]

Only days remained until the June 30 auction. Lear called Hayden and pitched his concept. In the proverbial Internet nanosecond, Hayden plunged for half the purchase price.[7]

Because the new partners were comfortable with virtual meeting, the appointed day found Lear at his Vermont vacation house and Hayden on his plane heading to California. The auction, which Sotheby's held online, started at 9 a.m. Eastern time. The new partners constructed their bidding strategy on a telephone conference call, and had an assistant on the ground enter their bids over the Internet—a combination of old and new technologies that parroted the Lear-Hayden partnership itself. The bids ran all day. One rival—known by paddle number in a nod to the old way of bidding in person—emerged as the chief contender to the Lear-Hayden camp. Sotheby's keeps bidders' names confidential, so Lear found out only later that he had fought a liberal versus conservative contest, as was the dominant political theme of the year 2000. Rival Lew Lehrman, a well-known Republican from New York and former CEO of Rite-Aid Corporation, started like Hayden and Lear with little money and ended up with a great deal of it. Perhaps he also shared with Lear and Hayden the same vision of the use of the Declaration—any political perspective, of course, can generate patriotic feelings. But Lehrman did not have Internet wealth, and he failed to beat the winning bid of $8.14 million, including commission. Sotheby's announced the next day that no one had ever paid so much for a document from American history or for anything at all auctioned on the Internet.

Lear and Hayden appeared at a press conference in New York on July 1 and set forth their joint idea. Lear told CNN, "We intend to travel it across the country because it is the living document that set this nation up. . . . And it lives today, and those words are for everybody. We want to remind everybody of them." Hayden added the new dimension: "The Internet represents a global outreach of communication, and that this document represents the first incredible statement of democracy and liberty in the world is a great—it's ironic, but it's also a great, momentous convergence."[8]

By contrast, Sotheby's showed a little defensiveness. Selling to a private buyer, as opposed to enshrining the artifact for public purpose, did not pose any problem in their way of thinking—Harvard, Yale, and the Library of Congress, not to mention various state historical societies, had copies. One could not even say the Dunlap Broadside was priceless, because the market had settled the question of its value. However, selling it online did trouble the staid, hierarchical, privileged elites of the art auction world. For them, preserving cachet and limited access to auctioned items was how the system maintained both high prices and caste status. Even worse, the Internet had lured Sotheby's into a partnership with the distinctly egalitarian Amazon.com for the purpose of selling sports memorabilia and "general fine art" with an average price of $500. But what if fine art were sold, like every other object, in auctions on eBay? A mass market would set the price. Truly popular opinion, instead of the judgment of an elite, would determine value. And if the populace talked about art on the Net, they could conclude that a toilet bowl is just a toilet bowl. Not only ideas, but the way ideas are exchanged, makes culture change.

In buying the Declaration, Lear and Hayden proposed to revitalize the political democracy with the same urgency that the Net brought to democratizing business. But their political start-up met the same fate as most new ventures started at the peak of the boom: it collapsed for lack of money. Within six months of the acquisition of the Declaration, Critical Path missed its projected revenues. Not long after, the news carried reports of accounting irregularities, alleged phantom transactions, the resignation of the CEO, the return of Hayden to that job, his second departure a little later. As a minor consequence of the disappearance of most of Hayden's wealth, Lear had to buy Hayden's half of the Declaration—for an unannounced price.

In the wake of this restructuring of the venture, Lear continued his quest. On July 4, 2001, Mel Gibson, Michael Douglas, Kevin Spacey, Whoopi Goldberg, Benicio Del Toro, Renee Zellweger, and Winona Ryder taped a dramatic reading of the Declaration of Independence in Philadelphia. Lear put the show on television, posted it on the Web, and sent tapes of it on a trip around the country along with the Lear Declaration. The campaign he called "Declare Yourself." The artifact was intended to inspire nonvoters to register and vote.

Meanwhile, an extraordinary story of democracy's woes had already played out in the presidential election of 2000. In the next round, in 2004, registration and turnout, as Lear had foreseen, were critical. As Lear did not anticipate, the Internet, mobile communications, and brilliant attack tactics generated a record turnout of the Bush administration's base. Lear's registration drive seemed small and anachronistic in comparison to the power of the administration's high-tech and below-the-belt election machine.

Everything was wrong with Lear's notion. He was hopelessly behind modern get-out-the-vote techniques. He chose the wrong medium. He did not use the technology of the time. While he was carting the Declaration of Independence around the country, the youngest generation of voters was declaring independence from the substance and procedures of the old politics. As overblown as Hayden's rhetoric might have been, perhaps his absence deprived Lear's venture of the necessary insight into how America is changing in the twenty-first century. To keep up with the country, Lear needed to aim for cultural change with the medium of the moment, as he had done in putting Archie Bunker on broadcast TV. He needed to use the new tools of reform that technology offers. To change American culture, every reformer now needs to put a new message into the new medium, and yet reform needs to be as ambitious as Lear's grand, goofy plan: to renew participatory democracy in a disaffected society that has lost a sense of how to cure its own woes.

The Medium Is the Means

An America that graduated both Bill Clinton and George W. Bush from college in the famous year of student revolt, 1968, and then twice elected each of them president plainly has some explaining to do. Are Americans so dazed and confused that when the electoral coin comes up heads they go one way, and when it comes up tails they follow another leader in a completely different direction? Apparently, at least since the collapse of the Soviet Union, the United States has lacked a center to its politics. It was simpler to describe the national purpose when an enemy with enough bombs "to make the rubble bounce" threatened the country's survival. If the country cannot share common ideas about itself, it cannot reform its culture to meet the China challenge.

As president, George W. Bush has tried to renew cold war verities by uniting the country around a war on terror. Certainly, ever since twentieth-century technologies produced an armory of weapons of mass destruction, anyone's worst fears have had plenty of grounding in reality. As far as imagination can see into the future, people will have reason to dread the harm others may cause them. However, the terrorist cause presents no challenge to America's culture. The nihilism and horror of terrorism can never have an appeal beyond a desperate few in broken societies. Only if the reaction to terrorism distracts the country from addressing its problems will America find its values at risk.

Nor is China an enemy of the United States. China will send battalions of entrepreneurs to compete with American firms. All of Asia will launch armies of workers to compete with Americans. But China has no need to threaten America militarily. Nor does the prevailing Chinese culture, whether it is statism, fascism, or neocommunism, present an appealing alternative to the American system of wealth creation and individual freedom. At present, the Chinese challenge is economic, not cultural. In that sense, it is no different than the broad Japanese challenge of the 1980s or the many market rivalries between European and American firms for the last half-century.

To meet the challenge of China, and the other economic rivals that inevitably will rise up, the United States will have to address its own problems in more benign ways than through war. Increasing inequality of income and opportunity threaten the nation's ability to reform the architectures of culture. Leaders need to bring the country to a new agreement about its purposes.

For more than three decades, the generation of '68 has disagreed over American culture. The ground, however, has shifted under the feet of that generation's leaders. Both Bill Clinton and George Bush grew up in a middle-class country, although they were born on the opposite sides of that broad swath. That definition of the United States is evaporating. The two presidents were raised to choose between democratic capitalism and authoritarian communism. China does not fit in either category. Nor does the emerging American information society, with increasing returns and winner-take-all results, follow the rules of either industrial or state-directed economies. Who will redefine the essence of the American culture?

As America looks for leaders in the current century, the generation of '68 may not necessarily provide them. Younger Americans may step forward. However, from wherever the new leaders come, to succeed they will need to adopt the one truly sound idea that had its heyday in 1968 and has rooted itself deep in the Internet: the renewed belief in the transcendent value of finding one's individual identity.[9] That is the central animating principle of any reform agenda for America. That is the chief purpose of entrepreneurship in social, business, or personal life.

Encouraging a search for individual identity is a far more ambiguous pursuit for a national political leader than galvanizing a faction in opposition to a particular idea. For example, Bill Clinton found it difficult to describe his centrist policies in sharp contradistinction to existing ideologies. But his reform of legal architecture produced an extraordinary surge of entrepreneurship. Under his leadership, the structure and function of American technology led to unparalleled wealth creation.

By contrast, George Bush assembled his political support from shards of identity by means of group classification—the religious right, social conservatives, oil and gas businesses, the military, white southerners—that were effectively a mirror image of the Democratic Party's special-interest-group supporters. He motivates his followers by resurrecting cold war militarism. His agenda does not acknowledge the tears in the fabric of the American society. It classifies Americans by groups and intensifies distrust among groups. The Bush presidency's system of liberty is state-directed and militarily supported, much like the America of the 1950s instead of the 1960s. An individual under this approach is defined the way institutions of power prefer, and not by his or her own choices.

Identity, happily, is the major project of the Internet. Kim Cameron, architect of identity at Microsoft, has promulgated what he calls the seven essential laws of digital identity.[10] The laws emphasize the human or real-world person's power to choose different digital identities. The person determines how much information to communicate through each digital identity, providing as little as necessary to enable the identity to function. Other actors gather the least possible information about each identity that is necessary to enable the commerce, communication, or collaboration desired. Underlying all the laws is an emphasis on empowering the real-world individual, protecting that real-world individual's privacy, and limiting the power of sellers and institutions to turn the real individual into the subject of their discourses.

These laws of identity bring into cyberspace, the space defined by the Internet, a sensibility of individual freedom that is a worthy bequest of the 1960s. It is not a surprise that Cameron was at Woodstock in 1969. He is a member of the two presidents' generation. Like those two leaders, he saw that in the 1970s and 1980s American law was restructured so as to assert the rights of individuals in a highly paradoxical way. People obtained personal rights insofar as they belonged to impersonal groups. Individuals could not choose their groups; the law chose the groups and assigned individuals to them. The architecture defined people by race, ethnicity, language, geography, income, disability, religion, age, gender, sexual preference, and (it sometimes seemed) diction.

It was all well-intentioned. This architecture was designed to produce fairness and equality of opportunity. The modern project would be realized by taxonomy.

Business followed suit. With more thorough execution than the legal structure could manage, businesses became the mavens of classification, filling their ranks like Noah's Ark with at least one pair of every group. Television, always the mirror of conventional society (rarely a window on the future), reinforced the theme. From *The Cosby Show* to *Will and Grace,* television cast in its shows the rainbow ensemble of American society.

Group rights suffer from a lack of parallelism. Racial groups can intermarry, for example, but the right to marry does not extend to all groups defined by sexual preference. Group rights can produce, in application, rigid conventions of political correctness. Nevertheless, by extending rights to easily defined groups since the 1960s, America has led the world toward a broad expansion of individual rights.

Individuals, however, want something more. Media descriptions of groups diminish individual variation. Group definition limits a person's sense of individual choice and difference. It constrains the freedom to act as one wishes, to be let alone, to be known on one's own terms. Who wants all the time and in all situations to be known by skin color or sexual preference? After all, postmodernists are right to see group classifications as imposed by outside forces instead of reflecting free choice. How, then, can individuals obtain the power of group rights without accepting the constraints of group definition? Answering that question is the purpose of the emerging Internet community, and Kim Cameron's rules.

A digital identity, Cameron says, is "a set of claims made by one digital subject about itself or another digital subject."[11] One might claim to be a member of a group that has, in the physical world, rights conferred by law. But one might also present oneself as a number or a quirky username or a bidder for an item auctioned on eBay or a commentator on a blog. In the medium of the Internet, one's digital identity is not stereotyped by the architecture of the law. Institutions do not control the discourse that exercises power over the identity. Using digital hardware, software, and the networked medium of the Internet, the real-world individual creates digital identities that act as agents for specific purposes. J. P. Morgan defined culture as the way of life of someone who has more than two servants. In cyberspace, culture is the way of life of individuals who have many digital servants.

Cameron asks that we "project ourselves into a future where we have a number of contextual identity choices." He imagines identities for browsing, private interactions, community collaboration, employment, credit, and citizenship. These identities would be on one's desktop, used on multiple networks, stored in innumerable databanks. For the real-world individual, the experience of managing these identities will not be more difficult than handling multiple credit cards, a driver's license, mortgage payments, health care, and a job. All those are different forms of identity.

Digital identities, however, are much more centered on the individual than the identities conferred through the cards, accounts, visas, and passports of the paperbound world, as illustrated by the following points. (1) An individual typically does not have to seek permission for a digital identity, while the application process in the physical world gives the granting power to, for example, the health maintenance organization or home insurance provider.[12] (2) The digital identity does not bring one into the ambit of state control, as a driver's license does. (3) A digital identity can protect one from invasions of privacy, whereas a credit card exposes the real-world individual to telemarketing, credit checking, and other annoyances of financial marketing. (4) A digital identity need not necessarily be commercial in the sense of an employment contract, even when one is using it to collaborate on creating an online encyclopedia, book, or software application. (5) An individual typically can create a digital identity as quickly as a password can be typed; by contrast, a paper-shuffling bureaucracy makes an expensive and lengthy process out of granting its permission slip. (6) Whereas a real-world identity pins an individual to a place, such as a voter's registration card will do, a digital identity enables the individual to roam the virtual world. (7) In the physical world one's identity defines an individual as distinct from a community. Through a digital identity, however, an individual finds and joins one or more communities. One can become an eBay bidder, a Yahoo! user, a Skype telephone networker, or a participant in any number of other groups. Typically, these groups offer ways for the individual to connect with others for collective action, as opposed to the real world's ways of using identity to distinguish people from others. Because the digital identity negotiates common ground with other identities, it naturally seeks scale. By altering the preferences of a digital identity, an individual can select a buying club with the greatest number of members, which in turn will obtain the lowest possible prices. Similarly, the individual can call for a boycott, fund a candidate, build an online protest movement. Anyone in the real, physical world might try to do the same thing but faces high transaction costs. The barriers of having to cold-call people on the telephone, or arrange a meeting, or organize a march are often insurmountable. A digital identity faces no obstacles. (8) Most important, a digital identity can be smart, while the physical identity is a dumb target of the advertisements and rules imposed by others. The smart identity can get the best price for any purchase; the answer to any question; the directions to any restaurant; the evaluations of any movie, given by people whose identities resemble one's own identity. Such is the eight-fold path of digital usefulness.

Digital identities will change the politics of both rich and poor countries. In the words of a character in the Turkish novel *Snow:* "Mankind's . . . biggest deception of the past thousand years is this: to confuse poverty with stupidity."[13] The dispossessed have always obtained access to technology later than the citizens of the developed countries, but they use it just as well. That is one of the lessons the Chinese people are teaching to their own state, as blogging represents to Beijing the biggest threat to state censorship since Tiananmen Square.

Some will contend that digital identity has meaning only to hypereducated technophiles. In fact, the most proficient users of such identities today are the youngest people in any country. More than 80 percent of American children have used the Internet by the time they are sixteen, and in not many years this number will approach 100 percent in most countries, just as television over about two decades became part of every child's experience in the United States, Europe, and ultimately Asia.[14] In text messages, social networks, e-mail, and Internet chat rooms, young people go by numerous alternative identities as readily as their parents might have responded to nicknames in their own youth.

The younger citizens of the United States will agree with a report from the Berkman Center for Internet and Society of Harvard University. It describes the Internet as becoming a "social network . . . architected so that every individual could have complete control over her own relationships and activities. . . . The open platform would be a 'free nation' [used] for a wide variety of personal, professional, commercial and civic interactions and transactions."[15] Responding to this vision, politicians are beginning to understand that the Internet is permanently altering the electoral and governing process. Every new medium eventually does that. Broadcast television entered American society in the late 1940s and early 1950s. By 1960, it was the medium through which the presidential election was decided. From that date to the present, political leaders have used it to obtain popular consent on everything. In its time in office the Bush administration made television an ally in a permanent campaign for public support. It brought the mainstream media into concert with its political goals. It managed its image frame by frame, sound bite by sound bite. It perfected the use of television as a platform for running the nation. Some medium always has that role for a governing power. The question for the Internet is what power will best master its capabilities.

The Internet already reaches the majority of voters. Soon it will connect to everyone, all the time, through wireless and wire-based devices. It will absorb broadcast television and then extinguish it. Inevitably, the Internet will become the medium through which politics is conducted, just as television was in its time. The question for the country is what kind of politics will result.

For the purpose of individual fulfillment, Internet politics could be very different than the other-directed, money-saturated, and deceptive governing that takes place on television today. The Internet already is a disruptive force. After all, somehow the American public fell out of its trancelike support for the misguided Iraq invasion. The administration did not change its version of the news. Congress did not discover much of anything. Yet somehow an alternative version of events in Iraq, perhaps one much closer to the truth, reached the American people and caused them to turn against the president.[16] Apparently, the technology of the microprocessor and the medium of the Internet produced such a proliferation of access to alternative reporting, analysis, and opinion that government, even in league with media conglomerates, could not frame or contain all the truths about the reality of Iraq. In the information society of America as it exists today, everyone is showered with disinformation, but still most people can obtain an accurate gestalt. The age of cover-up may have given way to the epoch of uncovering.

Whether digital identities over the Internet have the capability to produce organized demands for changes in legal architecture remains to be determined. According to Everett Ehrlich, a Clinton appointee in the Commerce Department, "anyone with a Web site and a server, a satellite transponder and about $100 million can have—in a matter of months— much of what the political parties have taken generations to build."[17] The price tag of $100 million can be mustered by many groups (as shown by the couple billion dollars spent on elections every two years already), and technology will only bring that number down. The Internet may be the medium that breaks the two-party system. In apprehension of that risk, the two existing parties are rapidly trying to respond to it, as they had to do with respect to television, and radio before that. No matter what they do, however, the Internet may shift political power from a few small groups of politicians and money people to many large groups assembled through individual choice. That is the logic of its decentralized technology.

Decentralization in politics, as in business, means that start-ups have a better chance to succeed. The grass roots will be fertile ground for leaders. Under this version of future politics, people can efficiently form groups of like-minded identities, commit to fund candidates, conduct interviews, choose a leader, argue the case, and battle for votes. People, organizing and acting with the efficiency of digital identities, might move assuredly to make parties and candidates align with their wishes.

In the politics of today, the parties define people by race, income, neighborhood, and voting patterns. They knock on doors and drag subjects to the polls. Political power comes from the managing of information by the leaders of campaigns, who are effectively the leaders of the parties and increasingly the leaders of government. This system has made a mockery of informed choice. It has demonstrated, as law professor Peter Shane has said, "the fragility of the idea that the dispersion of power is central to freedom."[18]

In the politics of the Internet, by contrast, the people would choose their identities, band together, and where necessary select representatives. Moreover, direct democracy looms as a potent alternative to the palsied version of republican government that exists today. A new version of the classic liberal, nonparty vision is emerging. It happens to be precisely what the writers of the Constitution envisioned. For the framers, the "Internet" was the transcontinental world of arts and sciences reflected in print and conversation, but as archaic as their media seem, their ideal of a disinterested leader still appeals to modern Americans. If the Internet provided the medium for a heated but nonparty politics, Americans probably would choose that over broadcast TV as the way to pick a government.

Similarly, through collaborative work on the Internet, individuals can create and alter the architectures of technology. The Internet's architecture spreads power to the edge of the network. Individuals can compute, store, manage, and distribute information with growing efficiency. That premise lay in the business plans of Google, Skype, and numerous other start-ups that have created huge participating audiences without selling through complex and expensive distribution channels. Moreover, because of the decentralization of power, individuals, as Yale law professor Yochai Benkler has explained, are more inclined and able to engage in value creation without operating through commercial markets. In other words, they can give away more goods and services for free, and by collaboration can make free services more valuable.[19]

Mancur Olson argued that "the larger the group, the farther it will fall short of providing an optimal amount of a collective good." A collective good is one that cannot feasibly be withheld from anyone in the group. Only in small groups, Olson contended, can individuals achieve common interests, including the provision of public goods.[20] But if Benkler is right, the flexibility and simplicity of collaboration on the Internet means that people can obtain on a large scale, outside of the formality of laws, the same or similar results that Olson claimed large groups could not accomplish.

Suppose that, as Benkler says, "individuals . . . work in collaboration . . . not organized in firms and . . . [not choosing] their projects in response to price signals."[21] In such groups, organized through digital identities and not by the management of centralized firms, they might agree to provide each other any number of public goods. Individuals in a neighborhood might band together to bury power lines, install fiber-optic cable, and give themselves cheaper electricity and cheaper Internet access. Today they have to wait for a mayor to provide leadership, and too often big firms and red tape hornswoggle the mayors and other local governing authorities of America. On the Internet people's digital identities can offer assurance contracts—a promise to act only if enough others make the same promise—and see if an adequately large network of buyers exists to pay the up-front costs.

Groups can assemble to create and share goods and services of many kinds. Already, groups organize their own cooperative education, vacation plans, job placement, and book clubs on the Internet. In only a little while, groups of scale could assemble to acquire health care, vaccines, and insurance, to name only a few public goods. They could effectively take into their own virtual hands the job of reforming the distribution of services that government and industry have delivered in such unsatisfying fashion.

It will be thought that all this is fanciful. Yet it is precisely the scale of change that broadcast television caused. Brands, marketing, product creation, geographic location, store design, home ownership, city planning, and language were all radically changed by television. The surprise would be if the Internet did not have such sweeping effects when it achieves, as it surely will in time, complete saturation of the population. In any case, the growth in electronic commerce, the shift in advertising from print to Web, and the creation of new Internet brands already prove the case.

Political leaders from the traditional American left may find that in networked societies there is a less compelling need for the state to provide many public goods. Similarly, leaders from the conservative right, enamored of oligopoly, may see that big firms cannot do as good a job as Internet-based solutions in providing goods that voters demand. Health care is a shattered system in the United States today. Liberals may not be able to install a government monopoly, but conservatives will draw increasing ire until the system is fixed. The Internet may be the only workable way to provide better and cheaper health care, through electronic records, preventive medicine via broadband, and so forth. Even if politicians do not advocate it, individuals acting collectively may create that sort of system on Net. Several such efforts were launched in the 1990s, and although they failed, others will try in the future as technology costs go down and the online population rises to 100 percent.

Internet politics will not necessarily turn out to be different than broadcast TV politics. America's new leaders themselves will decide the outcome. As the late Senator Daniel Patrick Moynihan wrote, "The central conservative truth is that it is culture, not politics, that determines the success of a society. The central liberal truth is that politics can change a culture and save it from itself."[22] The American political system plainly needs saving from itself. A large majority of Americans see that. As Moynihan noted, the goal of a new progressive politics should be cultural change that the large majority welcomes. To respond to Chinese and global competition, that change should be the expansion and encouragement of entrepreneurship.

An expansive entrepreneurial culture will be manifested in an increasing number of new business firms, and a larger number of new great firms. It will have as its vital idea a conviction in the value of individual fulfillment. Technology's architecture, revealed most particularly in the Internet, will be able to inspire that conviction in everyone.

In the new culture, Americans can return to the world of individual adventure that industrialization and complexity have blurred over the past 500 years. That world was the Renaissance. When it was in full flush, the great Italian goldsmith and sculptor Benvenuto Cellini (1500–1571) described it in one of the first modern autobiographies. No better tale of personal entrepreneurship, with wild swings of success and failure, glory and disaster, war and love, has ever been told. As a lesson of his experience, he observed, "When fortune misses the target it's as if nothing had happened. Certainly, people say: 'You'll learn your lesson for next time.' But in fact next time is always different and never the same as expected."[23]

Although most Americans think of themselves as conventionally middle class, in their unique personal lives they live as large as Cellini did in long-ago Italy. The exasperating charm of the American culture is that no American ever does learn his or her lesson. No matter, because the next time is always different and unexpected. Still, Cellini's reliance on skill and pluck is not easily replicated by everyone. Hardly anyone, after all, can carve a Christ for a king or wield a lethal sword in a duel. Most people are going to have to work in groups in order to succeed in the brand new day of Chinese competition. A few can design video games that sweep the world or make movies that everyone watches. But most people will need to focus on more down-to-earth tasks. To make goods and services that win in global competition, they will work in teams. To nurture creativity on a local level, they will build self-contained communities linked by preference, friendship, geography, or other negotiated bonds.

This is in form the same sort of paradox as group rights—to give an individual freedom, define the person as part of a group. The difference is that in a culture of entrepreneurship, individuals can choose their groups, instead of submitting to the selections made by the system. They can choose with whom they work, share ideas, vote, do business. In doing so, they inevitably will choose leaders. These leaders may come from positions of institutional power, such as elected office or corporate board rooms. Such influencers of opinion as Oprah Winfrey, Matt Drudge (!), Markos Moulitsas Zúniga (Daily Kos), and Bono have shown that leadership can come from unexpected places. America's new leaders, in any case, will flourish in the exchange of ideas in the new medium.

The new leaders of the Internet-based American culture may not think of their decision making as similar to principles of quantum mechanics. But they will naturally understand uncertainty, collaboration, and probabilistic thinking. They will see the future as a wave spreading out into many alternative pathways. They will see that change is inevitable and that Americans have to react smartly to change.[24] They will know that collaboration among individuals is the method by which consensus will be built and a pathway selected. They will intuitively or scientifically grasp that reducing severe risk is the way to maximize productive risk taking.

These precepts are not enough to inspire Americans. America's leaders have to provide more. They have to appeal to the dream that everyone in the world knows to be the genius of the American culture. It is not only a dream of continuous wealth creation for everyone. It includes, but goes beyond, that promise. Anyone who would lead America must aim to realize heaven on earth. That was the bedrock of the country's founding beliefs and it is the beacon that calls people to America today. No one will arrive there in this life, but Americans are still young enough and confident enough to believe that they can lead the world further in that direction than any other human community has ever done. America's new leaders will be those who renew the culture's selfless, immodest, and utterly hopeful commitment to saving the world.

Introduction

1. Aiming at a rival's best sector is not necessarily a wise national strategy. "The model suggests, for a developed country, a focus on rapidly evolving industries and, for a less developed country, a focus on industries where productivity advances are *not* occurring rapidly." Ralph E. Gomory and William J. Baumol, *Global Trade and Conflicting National Interests* (Cambridge, Mass.: MIT Press, 2000), 56. The United States should take this advice, but it does not; China falls in the latter category but acts in part as if it were in both categories.

2. "Based on revised IMF data, . . . the remainder of the world economy—some 70% of global output—collectively accounted for only 2% of the cumulative increase in world GDP over the 1995 to 2002 time frame. . . . America's 98% contribution to the cumulative increase in world GDP growth over the 1995 to 2002 period can be broken down as follows: About two-thirds of it appears to reflect growth disparities, and about one third is traceable to currency shifts." Steven Roach, "The Long Road," Morgan Stanley Web site, May 14, 2004, at http://www.morganstanley .com/GEFdata/digests/20040514-fri.html.

3. Paul D. Reynolds, "Entrepreneurship in the U.S.: 2004 Assessment," June 1, 2005, at www.entrepreneurship.fiu.edu/pdf/part_01.pdf.

4. In the series of years from 1990–91 to 2001–02, new business births outnumbered business deaths every year, except the first and the last. In 1990–91, deaths exceeded births by 5,000; in 2001–02, the negative outcome was 17,000. See Small Business Administration, "Employer Firm Births and Deaths by Employment Size of Firm, 1989–2002," at www.sba .gov/advo/research/dyn_b_d8902.pdf.

5. This book does not claim that the two Bush administrations had sole responsibility for negative entrepreneurship in the negative years that occurred in their tenures. However, the governmental response to the 1990–91 net downturn in new business creation did contribute positively to the succeeding Golden Age of entrepreneurship. The very different response to the 2001–02 negative business creation was not as wise.

The speculation here is that the business birth rate correlates to job creation; that new business birth correlates in the short and long term to economic expansion; that the higher the new business birth rate, the greater the American income per capita; that increase in the new business birth rate in the future is essential for Americans to maintain income growth in the face of new competition from China. Furthermore, although venture capitalists usually provide less than 10 percent of the money for new business births, and perhaps only 1 percent of the number of new businesses created, the theory here is that the firms they fund contribute disproportionately to all these asserted positive outcomes.

6. Figures come from http://yhoo.client.shareholder.com/faq.cfm#5-12; http://investor.ebay.com/faq.cfm; and http://investor.google.com/faq .html#gci3.

7. See conference proceedings for Entrepreneurship in the Twenty-first Century (hosted by the U.S. Small Business Administration Office of Advocacy and the Ewing Marion Kauffman Foundation, Mar. 26, 2004), 7 (and sources cited therein), available online at http://www.sba.gov/advo/stats/ proceedings_a.pdf. But see Steven J. Davis, John C. Haltiwanger, and Scott Schuh, *Job Creation and Destruction* (Cambridge, Mass.: MIT Press, 1996), 57, 81 (arguing that small business contributes less to net job creation than commonly thought).

8. See U.S. Census Bureau, "Statistics of U.S. Businesses: 2001," at http:// www.census.gov/epcd/susb/2001/us/US—.HTM.

9. See Charles Dickens, *Nicholas Nickleby*, where Micawber says, "Annual income one pound, annual expenditure nineteen shillings and sixpence; result happiness. Annual income one pound, annual expenditure one pound and sixpence; result misery."

10. Gomory and Baumol, *Global Trade*, 4. ("A developed country such as the United States can benefit in its global trade by assisting the substantially less developed to improve their productive capability. However, the developed country's interest also requires it to compete as vigorously as it can against other nations that are in anything like a comparable stage of development to avoid being hurt by their progress.")

11. This book articulates a theory of entrepreneurship in the sense that literary and cultural studies assert theories: "A theory . . . is speculation . . . an explanation whose truth or falsity might be hard to demonstrate." Jonathan D. Culler, *Literary Theory: A Very Short Introduction* (Oxford: Oxford University Press, 2000), 2. The purpose is to inspire individuals to pursue cultural reform in a systematic, urgent, and analytical manner.

12. Larry Lessig's brilliant *Code* expressed the great insight that software created an architecture as powerful as law. Lawrence Lessig, *Code and Other Laws of Cyberspace* (New York: Basic, 2000), 4–6. My contention here is that law, technology, and leaders make up three distinct architectures. Another of Lessig's works, *Free Culture*, sparked interest in the cultural effects of law and technology. See generally Lessig, *Free Culture: How Big Media Uses Technology and the Law to Lock Down Culture and Control Creativity* (New York: Penguin, 2004).

13. Entrepreneurship is "an effect, rather than a cause, the product of discourses [architectures] which attempt to analyse, describe, and regulate the activities of human beings." Culler, *Literary Theory,* 7. Entrepreneurship creates possibilities for individuals in society, including the possibility of changing law, technology, and leaders as well as their leadership in order to enhance or minimize future entrepreneurship.

14. In the words of Jim Clark: "At that moment [when Netscape went public], I had the pleasure of knowing that whatever else others had done, none of this could have happened without me. This feeling, of having been absolutely essential to something extraordinary, is the kind of pleasure that doesn't come often in life." Jim Clark with Owen Edwards, *Netscape Time: The Making of the Billion-Dollar Start-Up That Took on Microsoft* (New York: St. Martin's, 1999), 251.

15. In October 2005, the U.S. Census Bureau estimated the world population at 6.47 billion. See U.S. Census Bureau, "World Population Information," at www.census.gov/ipc/www/world.html. It estimated that the global population would exceed 9 billion in 2050, of which more than 5 billion would be in Asia.

CHAPTER 1: Looking East Toward the Dawn
Epigraph. Marco Polo, *The Travels of Marco Polo, the Venetian.* Edited and translated by William Marsden, re-edited by Thomas Wright (Garden City, N.Y.: Doubleday, 1948), 114.

1. Polo's *Travels* was a "merchant's handbook." Jonathan D. Spence, *The Chan's Great Continent: China in Western Minds* (New York: W. W. Norton, 1998), 11. Mixing practical details about commercial opportunity with descriptions of fantastic marvels, it apparently aimed to encourage Chinese trading ventures, such as Polo's father and uncle had undertaken. In the 00s, American business visitors to China churned out Polo-grams by the truckload, typing insight and ignorance on the ephemeral mediums of e-mail and PowerPoint.

2. See Frances Wood, *Did Marco Polo Go to China?* (Boulder, Colo.: Westview, 1996), 149. ("That Marco Polo himself might not have gone to Karakorum, let alone Peking, seems more likely . . . than that he wrote everything he knew from a view of Peking.")

3. See "Marco Polo," Wikipedia, at http://en.wikipedia.org/wiki/Marco_Polo.

4. Wood, *Marco Polo,* 10, 149 (Christopher Columbus obtained a copy of Marco Polo's *Description of the World* [usually known as *The Travels of Marco Polo*] from London in 1498; that book with his annotations is in Seville, Spain).

5. "As we look back across the cycle from 1620 to 1960 [of Western advisers to China], we can observe the standpoint of superiority from which the Western advisers approached China. This superiority sprang from two elements: the possession of advanced technical skills and a sense of moral

rightness." Jonathan D. Spence, *To Change China: Western Advisers in China* (New York: Penguin, 1980), 290.

6. This anecdote came from a personal conversation with Kissinger in 2004. Nixon and Kissinger admired China's centralized power, asserting that Mao Zedong and his retinue possessed "enormous calculation and cunning." Spence, *The Chan's Great Continent*, 218. Like many other Westerners, those two cold warriors projected on the screen of China their own self-images.

7. Hegel thought that China was "outside" the "march toward freedom in the world," and that only "the dynamic forces emanating from the West" could bring it into world history. Spence, *The Chan's Great Continent*, 210. Marx and Weber developed distinctive arguments to explain China's backwardness. Ibid., 210–12. Wittfogel elaborated with his theory of rice-growing China's "hydraulic despotism." Ibid., 218.

8. Jonathan D. Spence, *The Search for Modern China* (New York: W. W. Norton, 1991), 7.

9. Jonathan D. Spence, *God's Chinese Son: The Taiping Heavenly Kingdom of Hong Xiuquan* (New York: W. W. Norton, 1996), xxi.

10. The overthrow of the last Qing emperor in 1912 led to nearly two decades of fighting among regional warlords. Millions of Chinese died of disease, famine, and violence. The Japanese invasion of 1931 started a fourteen-year Asian war that eventually involved every major power in the world and ended only with the American atomic bombing of Hiroshima and Nagasaki. About 3 million Chinese soldiers died, according to Chiang Kai-Shek, the Nationalist leader. Peter Calvocoressi and Guy Wint, *Total War: The Causes and Courses of the Second World War*, part 2 (New York: Pantheon, 1972), 1223. Counting civilians, the number exceeded 10 million. From 1945 the Communists battled the Nationalists until Mao drove Chiang to Taiwan in 1949. Another 2 to 3 million Chinese died. The Chinese lost another million in the Korean War from 1950 to 1953. From 1959 to 1962 Mao's Great Leap Forward produced famine and violence that took the lives of 20 to 40 million people. Spence, *The Search for Modern China*, 583. From 1966 to 1971, the Great Proletarian Cultural Revolution killed another half million, although some give much higher numbers. The labor-camp death toll during Mao's long rule could have been up to 20 million. Mao is usually considered the most murderous ruler in world history.

11. Eric Hellweg, "Microsoft's China Gamble," *CNN/Money.com*, Mar. 5, 2003, at http://money.cnn.com/2003/03/05/technology/techinvestor/hellweg/.

12. Bruce J. Dickson, *Red Capitalists in China: The Party, Private Entrepreneurs, and Prospects for Political Change* (Cambridge: Cambridge University Press, 2003), 34.

13. "It is not inevitable that China will continue to grow rapidly enough to

equal or surpass eventually the growing per capita incomes of the US and Western Europe," according to the Becker-Posner Blog. Problems include "a disastrous capital market . . . highly inefficient public enterprises . . . a prematurely aging population." Another risk is that while "authoritarian regimes do not grow slower on average than democratic governments, they do have more unstable growth rates than democracies." Finally, "as countries get richer, they often introduce policies that retard further progress." By contrast, "the US can continue to do well . . . if it provides a good environment for new companies, flexible labor and product markets, sizeable investments in human capital and technology, and an open attitude to new ideas, immigrants, and different ways." Becker-Posner Blog, "Will China Become the Leading Nation of the 21st Century? Perhaps Not!," Apr. 3, 2005, at http://www.becker-posner-blog.com/archives/2005/04/will_china_beco.html.

14. The state in China even built churches, trying to manage the rise of conversion to Christianity from six million in 1980 to about 45 million by 2005. Charles Hutzler, "Mixing Religion and Noodles Lands Ms. Su in Hot Water," *Wall Street Journal,* June 2, 2005.

15. Spence, *In Search of Modern China,* 747. Bill Clinton on a trip to China in 2005 said, "The more China grows and diversifies economically and opens up to the rest of the world, the more there will have to be some room for dissent." Associated Press, "Clinton: China Must Tolerate Dissent to Continue Growth," *Wall Street Journal,* Sept. 11, 2005.

16. See Edward W. Said, *Orientalism* (New York: Vintage, 1979), 204 ("the more advanced cultures . . . have rarely offered the individual anything but imperialism, racism, and ethnocentrism for dealing with 'other' cultures"); see also 331–32 (the "development and maintenance of every culture require the existence of another, different and competing *alter ego. . . .* Each age and society re-creates its 'Others'").

17. Spence, *In Search of Modern China,* 733. (The "Three Highs" were what a man needed to persuade a woman to marry: "high salary, an advanced education, and a height over five feet six inches.")

18. Adding populations of China, India, and the former Soviet Union. Clyde Prestowitz, *Three Billion New Capitalists: The Great Shift of Wealth and Power to the East* (New York: Basic, 2005), 3.

19. Some have looked at the works of China and despaired. Ted Fishman wrote that Chinese wishes will be America's commands. William Grimes, "Car Clones and Other Tales of the Mighty Economic Engine Known as China," review of *China, Inc.: How the Rise of the Next Superpower Challenges America and the World,* by Ted Fishman, *New York Times,* Feb. 15, 2005. Fishman also claimed that "China has little problem setting the rules of the game and no problem breaking them." Ted Fishman, *China, Inc.: How the Rise of the Next Superpower Challenges America and the World* (New York: Scribner, 2005), 294. In truth, Beijing struggled to impose

orders on provincial governments. Chinese businesses faced World Trade Organization rules, challenging foreign markets, and the inexorable discipline of global financial markets.

20. See generally Dickson, *Red Capitalists*.

21. David Sheff, *China Dawn: Culture and Conflict in China's Business Revolution* (New York: Harper Business, 2002), 43, 47.

22. In urban China, as of 2003, people spent on average only about $800 a year. But that number was rapidly increasing. Matsushita, a Japanese manufacturer, put its first plant in China in 1983. One employee said that in China any successful product would be imitated by local rivals at lower cost in less than a year. "We always have to be one step ahead," said the Matsushita representative. "If we can survive here, we'll be able to survive globally." Ginny Parker, "A Tricky Transition in China," *Wall Street Journal*, Nov. 23, 2004.

23. In 2005, handset sales for consumption in China reached about 100 million units, of which most were priced between $100 and $200. The source here is Telegent Systems, where the author is a member of the board of directors. This is not publicly accessible information.

24. The source here is internal analysis by McKinsey & Company, the strategic management company, where the author is a senior adviser. This is not publicly accessible information. Hereinafter, all such analysis will be referred to as McKinsey analysis. In 2003, Chinese telephone penetration was about 40 percent. China Telecom, *Statistical Annual Report of China's Communications in 2003*, cited in a Nov. 12, 2004, report by the China Telecom Development Strategy Advisory Committee, of which the author is a member. Even though China's leading mobile and fixed-line companies were the world's largest in number of subscribers, they could expect 70 percent (mobile) and 50 percent (fixed line) increases in customer base within three or four years.

25. The prodigious difference in quality of life for workers was revealed in an index developed by the Asian Labour News. As of 2005, a McDonald's employee in China had to work three hours and fifty-eight minutes to earn enough to buy a Big Mac from his or her employer. In the United States the average was thirty minutes. See Rising Hegemon Blog, "How Long Does It Take to Buy a Big Mac?" June 6, 2005, at http://rising-hegemon .blogspot.com/2005/06/how-long-does-it-take-to-buy-big-mac.html. Thomas Friedman wrote that Chinese workers are hungry for American jobs; he ignored the fact that by the mid-00s the bulk of Chinese workers were working to avoid hunger. See Friedman, *The World Is Flat: A Brief History of the Twenty-first Century* (New York: Farrar, Straus, Giroux, 2005).

26. David Ricardo, "The Iron Law of Wages" (1817), available online at http://www.fordham.edu/halsall/mod/ricardo-wages.html.

27. In the United States in 2004, the average per capita income was $33,000,

ranging from $45,000 in Connecticut down to $25,000 in Mississippi. However, the U.S. median income that same year was only $24,000. (In 2004, real median *household* income was $44,000, unchanged in real terms from 2003.) The median income represents the point at which half of incomes are higher and half are lower. The average is much higher than the median because the average is dragged up by the very rich, whose income vastly exceeds that of the half of income earners below the median. In terms of how most Americans experience income, the median matters more than the average. In terms of the whole economy's buying power— that is, in terms relevant to most businesses—the average is probably more important than the median.

28. McKinsey analysis.
29. McKinsey analysis (from 26.4 percent to 41.8 percent). In developed countries, however, about 70 percent live in cities.
30. Indeed, China expects to increase the number of students in postsecondary education from 11 million in 2000 to 16 million in 2005. Chinese students seeking education outside their own country have increased applications to several European countries, but applications to American graduate schools dropped 45 percent in 2004. Sam Dillon, "U.S. Slips in Attracting the World's Best Students," *New York Times,* Dec. 21, 2004.
31. New goods and services in the 00s were defined by users and collaborators, as much or more than by unitary producers. Eric Von Hippel, "Innovation by User Communities: Learning from Open Source Software," *MIT Sloan Management Review* (Summer 2001).
32. "China, as it seizes control over certain [technology] standards, can put its mark on what kind of products reach its markets." Jack Goldsmith and Timothy Wu, *Who Controls the Internet?* (Oxford: Oxford University Press, 2006), chap. 6.
33. When American consumers discover that their material world is shaped and directed by Asian teenagers, they may not care any more than they minded where chow mein or the Lexus came from. But when American firms see that the defining edge of technological change in their market lies in Asia, they know they need to be in that country.
34. In 1990, Harvard's Michael Porter advocated vigorous domestic competition and local centers of excellence as keys to building successful entrepreneurial firms. See Porter, *The Competitive Advantage of Nations* (New York: Free Press, 1990). China put his advice into practice. Regional specialties were emerging—consumer electronics in Guangdong, telecom equipment in Hangzhou, semiconductors in Tianjin. Evan Ramstad, "The Technological Rise of China Was Speedy—and Just the Beginning," *Wall Street Journal,* Dec. 20, 2004. A Chinese commentator on information technology argued in 2004 that a "healthy development" of the Chinese computer industry depended on better enforcement of pro-competitive antitrust laws, the development within the country of a complete value

chain, and the creation of a "consumer-dominated" base of public opinion. Fang Xiangqian and Fang Xingdong, *A Challenge to Intel: Blog China* (Beijing: China Customs Press, 2004), 264–65. Chinese entrepreneurs were prepared to advocate intensely competitive domestic markets as the training grounds for their global challenge. Nothing should have worried American entrepreneurs more, especially as the American government in the oos relaxed antitrust enforcement, favored consolidation, and rebuffed consumer advocacy.

35. In Datang, China, factories make nine billion pairs of socks a year. More than 100,000 buyers come from around the world to Datang's annual sock festival. Cities of sweaters, children's clothing, underwear, and neckties are nearby. Low wages, high efficiency in machinery and techniques, and economies of scale produce big winners in global markets. David Barboza, "Made Elsewhere/Textile Enclaves: In Roaring China, Sweaters Are West of Socks City," *New York Times,* Dec. 24, 2004.

36. In his famous Southern Tour of 1992, Deng said that "foreign-funded enterprises . . . are good for socialism." Joe Studwell, *The China Dream: The Quest for the Last Great Untapped Market on Earth* (New York: Grove, 2003), 56. His message was an open-armed welcome to investment from overseas Chinese, numbering 30 million in Hong Kong, Macau, and Taiwan, and another 30 million in areas beyond those territories, which the PRC expects eventually to control. Ibid., 63. It was also intended to reach multinational corporations committed to "globalization," and it did greatly increase foreign direct investment in China.

37. "Chinese President Hu Jintao is emerging as an unyielding leader determined to preserve the Communist Party's monopoly on power and willing to impose new limits on speech . . . to do it." Philip P. Pan, "Hu Tightens Party's Grip on Power," *Washington Post,* Apr. 24, 2005. Indeed, the seventy-two-year-old doctor who exposed the Chinese government's initial cover-up of the SARS epidemic was, for his pains, put under house arrest until he "changed his thinking" about Tiananmen Square. See Philip P. Pan, "China Spares Dissident Prison Term," *Washington Post,* June 12, 2004.

Eric Schmidt, CEO of Google, said that the "entire power elite . . . is under attack by the emergent online culture." Asked how the online culture would change China and India, he answered, "These answers are culturally dependent." Personal interview, 2004. In other words, China would have free speech when its culture so demanded, not when the United States might wish.

38. Jack Goldsmith and Tim Wu wrote in 2006, "China is trying to combine the world's fastest growing economy and internet population with among the world's most extensive state propaganda systems. . . . Only time will tell whether the sheer volume of information now available in China will erode the Communist Party's position. But it hasn't happened yet. . . . [China] is proving that a country can reap the benefits [of] the internet . . . without

also changing its political system. . . . China has turned American companies like Cisco and Yahoo into its primary agents of state control." Goldsmith and Wu, *Who Controls the Internet?*, 2–3. They made at least two key points: First, modern technology does not intrinsically assure the triumph of freedom; only a rule of law can do that. Second, at least as of the 00s, the Chinese rule of law aimed at using technology to maintain centralized power.

39. Any American discussion of Chinese culture is prone to what William James called the "psychologist's fallacy"—the "confusion of [one's] own standpoint with" the mental state being reported. William James, *The Principles of Psychology*, vol. 1 (1890; repr., New York: Dover, 1950), 196.

40. Joseph A. Schumpeter, "Development" (1932), available online at http://www.schumpeter.info/Edition-Evolution.htm.

41. Jeffrey Madrick saw the primary causes of economic development as "the size and expansion of markets" and the "availability of information." Madrick, *Why Economies Grow: The Forces That Shape Prosperity and How We Can Get Them Working Again* (New York: Century Foundation, 2002), 3, 4. He agreed with Schumpeter that "entrepreneurialism is the great source of economic growth," but argued that it "requires a context" and was not by itself "a human trait that stands alone." Ibid., 7. Madrick considered the rule of law to be an effect, not a cause, of expanding markets and widespread information.

42. Some "Confucian" values promote entrepreneurship, according to Geert Hofstede: perseverance, ordering relationships by status, thrift, and a sense of shame. Hofstede, *Cultures and Organizations: Software of the Mind* (New York: McGraw-Hill, 1997), 168–69.

43. Personal interview, 2004. In American culture, three beliefs gird popular support for entrepreneurship. Americans believe people have a right to be cranky, opinionated, selective in choice of companions, prone to dissent and disruption. They also believe even loners should show enthusiastic team spirit when there is work to be done. Finally, Americans believe in private property and personal gain: what's mine is mine, what's yours I might take in a fair fight or good deal, virtue may be its own reward but hard work should pay off in money, and people should enjoy the material world because you only go around once. Adhering to these values, American entrepreneurs, according to myth and many real examples, display individual thinking, team play, and healthy acquisitiveness. A culture of entrepreneurship celebrates these virtues.

44. Sheff's portrait of entrepreneurs in China emphasized their ambition, hard work, and patriotism. They were, in his account, not much concerned about political reform. Tiananmen Square shocked them but also warned them away from interfering with the party's efforts to maintain control. Nor were they engaged in work that is truly accessible to Westerners. They may be trained in the West, supported by Western expertise and funds, and

even married to Westerners. But for Western entrepreneurs China was too huge, too impenetrably complex, and too daunting; China in short belonged to the Chinese, according to Sheff's account. By contrast, the national origin of entrepreneurial CEOs was scarcely noticed by Americans. See generally Sheff, *China Dawn*.

45. Dickson, *Red Capitalists,* 23, 67, 84, 122.

46. "China's Polluted Environment," *Economist,* Aug. 19, 2004.

47. According to a McKinsey analysis, China accounts for 46 percent of global growth in aluminum demand, 55 percent of global growth in iron ore, 98 percent in refined copper, and 69 percent in coal.

48. China's imports of oil in the twenty-first century will shape the global energy market, influencing what companies rule and what prices prevail. The United States played that role in oil markets in the twentieth century and chose to create Arabian Gulf client states with its buying power. China's full strategy has not yet been revealed. See Andrew Browne et al., "Asian Rivals Put Pressure on Western Energy Giants," *Wall Street Journal,* Jan. 10, 2005.

49. In 2005 one consulting group argued, "Many outsourcing deals are tantamount to strategic divestitures and joint ventures." In other words, they were ways to deploy assets, not just means to pay lower labor costs. David Craig and Paul Willmott, "Outsourcing Grows Up," *McKinsey on Finance* 14 (Winter 2005), 1.

50. Manufacturing is important in maintaining any country as a world power. Louis Uchitelle, "Factories Move Abroad, As Does U.S. Power," *New York Times,* Aug. 17, 2003. Indeed, in 2003 Senator Joe Lieberman said the move of semiconductor manufacturing overseas was "an imminent threat to national security." See Office of Senator Joe Lieberman, "Lieberman Calls for Pentagon Action to Halt Offshore Migration of High-Technology Manufacturing," press release, June 2, 2003, available online at http://lieberman.senate.gov/newsroom/release.cfm?id=207744. Information technology can hardly be less important, since the winning firms in information technology affect the way people buy, sell, express themselves, learn, work, and even love. Moreover, winning information technology firms typically hold their leads for many years and bring along with them a suite of developers and other camp followers that elaborate on the designs of chips, software, genetic maps, and every other technology.

51. Senator Lieberman asserted that the "migration of high-end chip manufacturing to East Asian countries, particularly China" was "a result of concerted foreign government action . . . [including] direct and indirect subsidies to their domestic semiconductor industries, exacerbated by changing market conditions." See letter to Hon. Donald H. Rumsfeld from Joseph I. Lieberman, June 2, 2003, available online at http://lieberman.senate.gov/newsroom/release.cfm?id=207744.

52. Since 1985, more than 120 million new businesses have started in China.

See Fishman, *China, Inc.* The information technology sector was predicted to grow at more than 18 percent a year based on demand from business alone. China accounted for more than half the growth in the global telecom equipment market, and Chinese vendors took increasing share in that market. Cisco, however, had more than 50 percent market share in 2003 and was increasing its share. The battle royal between Cisco and its Chinese competitor Huawhei, with its market share below 10 percent, will continue throughout the 00s (see Chapter 2). Any American should want Cisco to prevail, even if to do so Cisco must send investment and jobs to China.

53. See National Center for Education Statistics, "Fast Facts: Most Popular Majors," at http://nces.ed.gov/fastfacts/display.asp?id=37.

54. See Asia/Pacific Cultural Centre for UNESCO, "National Literacy Policies: China," at www.accu.or.jp/litdbase/policy/chn/.

55. According to Robert Solow, Nobel Prize–winning economist, the key to productivity gains was firms not just using technology but also learning how to organize themselves to do so. Jon E. Hilsenrath, "Behind Surging Productivity: The Service Sector Delivers," *Wall Street Journal,* Nov. 7, 2003. The necessary organizational techniques were transmitted by consultants and migrating businesspersons from the West to Asia.

56. In 2003 more foreign investment went to China than to any other country; the United States had previously led in this vital category. See Diana Farrell, Paul Gao, and Gordon R. Orr, "Making Foreign Investment Work for China," in "Special Edition: China Today," *McKinsey Quarterly* (2004).

57. On September 30, 2005, the Bureau of Economic Analysis (BEA) released statistics demonstrating that in August 2005, Americans' personal income decreased $5.3 billion (or 0.1 percent) and disposable personal income decreased $7.4 billion (or 0.1 percent). Personal consumption expenditures decreased $47.2 billion (or 0.5 percent). This tiny decrease in consumption, combined with weak income growth, still meant that Americans' personal savings—as a percentage of disposable personal income—was down to −0.7 percent (from 1.4 percent in June 2004). See BEA, "News Release: Personal Income and Outlays," Sept. 30, 2005, at http://www.bea.gov/bea/newsrelarchive/2005/pio805.htm.

58. For example, TechFaith (symbol CNTF), a firm that designed cell phones (it did not make a product or sell to an end user), went public in 2005 and as of November had a market capitalization of $6 billion. The thirty-four-year-old founder, D. F. Dong, had been a Motorola sales executive in Beijing until he persuaded thirteen Motorola colleagues to start the firm.

59. In late 2004, a writer in *PC Magazine* commented, "You really begin to miss the aggressive technology rollout of the nineties. There is nothing going on anymore." John C. Dvorak, "False Promises, Failed Initiatives," *PC Magazine,* Oct. 19, 2004, 67. He meant in the United States: in China everything was happening faster, bigger, and cheaper.

60. "Many imaginable options for dealing with our economic problems are also

precluded by rhetorical norms reflective of values, enshrined in impressions of history." Richard E. Neustadt and Ernest R. May, *Thinking in Time: The Uses of History for Decision Makers* (New York: Free Press, 1988), 205. In other words, culture—including the way a society talks about its values and beliefs—sets the range of choices for economic behavior.

61. Clay Christensen and Michael Raynor state that "processes and values" are an organization's culture. Christensen and Raynor, *The Innovator's Solution: Creating and Sustaining Successful Growth* (Cambridge, Mass.: Harvard Business School Press, 2003), 188. Those interested in reforming culture should consider legal and technological processes as the structural underpinning of culture (architectures), and values and beliefs as the warp and woof of culture's web. Reformers then can change architecture in ways that alter culture; their changes succeed only to the degree that they have cultural effects.

62. Kaushik Basu quotes Abhijit Sen's advice to the Indian government on a currency issue, noting that Sen concludes with the observation that for his advice to be followed "the existing culture in government must be turned upside down." Basu, *Prelude to Political Economy: A Study of the Social and Political Foundations of Economics* (Oxford: Oxford University Press, 2003), 168. Basu says, "This is virtually tantamount to saying that the advice cannot be followed." Ibid., 168–69. But really it is the same as calling for cultural reform so that the advice can be followed and the discussion of architectural change can begin.

63. Clifford Geertz, *The Interpretation of Cultures* (New York: Basic, 1973), 44 ("culture is . . . a set of control mechanisms . . . for the governing of behavior").

64. Rick Perlstein called for "a long-term time horizon" for a political movement. Perlstein, *The Stock Ticker and the Superjumbo: How the Democrats Can Once Again Become America's Dominant Political Party* (Chicago: Prickly Paradigm Press, 2005), 8. He aimed at increasing the number and opportunities for "professionals." Professionals are entrepreneurs. See ibid., 16–17. "It is crucial to build a political movement that will endure beyond particular electoral contests." Ibid., 73. Any such movement will seek reform, and that reform should self-consciously and self-descriptively concern cultural change for and by entrepreneurs.

65. The Chinese government ordered China-based Web sites and blogs to register, with the punishment for noncompliance ranging up to more than $100,000. The government developed a system for tracking down violators over the Internet (which had nearly 90 million Chinese users as of mid-2005). See Associated Press, "China Orders All Blogs to Register," *MSNBC.com*, June 7, 2005, at http://www.msnbc.msn.com/id/6448213/did/8131497. The government installed surveillance cameras in Internet cafes, and between February and April 2004, it inspected 1.8 mil-

lion such cafes and closed thousands. "China Continues Internet Crack-down," *CBC News*, Oct. 31, 2004, at http://www.cbc.ca/story/world/national/2004/10/31/china_internet041031.html. The Chinese government forced Yahoo! to turn over information about the e-mail of a journalist who later was convicted under state secrecy laws and sentenced to ten years in jail. Elaine Kurtenbach, "Yahoo Founder Explains China E-Mail Move," *USA Today*, Sept. 10, 2005, at http://www.usatoday.com/tech/news/2005-09-11-yahoo-explains-china_x.htm. The extent of state supervision of speech and conduct was much less than in previous decades but far beyond the intrusions of government in the West. If Chinese firms accepted such constraints and also were responsible for the future design and operation of the global Internet—as leading firms have been in the past—then the Chinese government could also track Americans' use of the Net. The Chinese might even constrain Americans from using the Internet, at least outside American borders, in ways that the Chinese did not like, such as sending e-mails to China. Economic power can encourage any sort of political behavior. "China Orders Web Sites, Blogs to Register with Government," *Wall Street Journal*, June 7, 2005.

66. Alexis de Tocqueville, the famously perceptive observer of the United States in its formative decades, noted these attributes: everyone worked, many worked more than one job, women ran small businesses out of their homes, people moved to find new jobs, people moved up in rank as they made money and so there was no real ranking outside of monetary success. See generally Tocqueville, *Democracy in America: The Complete and Unabridged Volumes I and II* (New York: Bantam Classics, 2000). Even if Max Weber was not completely right, in America at least the Protestant ethic and capitalism converged into one pervasive attitude of everyone being on the make.

67. Paris lionized Benjamin Franklin for being a pragmatic creative genius who fused scientific discovery with the manufacture of new products that changed the way people lived. Franklin—always in start-up mode—founded a chain of print shops, a lightning rod company, the post office system, a lending library. On his death in 1790, he left a 200-year trust for "married tradesmen [in Philadelphia and Boston] under the age of 26" to help them start in business. Philadelphia loaned some of the interest to individuals, and in 1990 on the 200th anniversary of Franklin's death dedicated the $2.25 million to scholarships for high-school students going into college in the sciences. See Clark DeLeon, "Divvying Up Ben: Let's Try for 200 More," *Philadelphia Inquirer*, Feb. 7, 1993.

68. See Patrick Kreiser, Louis Marino, and K. Mark Weaver, "Correlates of Entrepreneurship: The Impact of National Culture on Risk-Taking and Proactiveness in SMEs" (paper presented at the U.S. Association for Small Business and Entrepreneurship Conference, Reno, Nev., Jan. 17–20, 2002), 13

("national leaders should enact policies aimed at changing predominant cultural values in order to encourage national levels of entrepreneurship"). Risk taking is an important component of entrepreneurship.

69. Benjamin Franklin thought scientific inquiry less important than public service; Thomas Jefferson thought the opposite. Edmund S. Morgan, *Benjamin Franklin* (New Haven: Yale University Press, 2003), 26. In effect, they debated the relative importance of law (Franklin's preference) and technology (Jefferson's), two of the architectures that shape culture. The third, leadership, Franklin and Jefferson demonstrated amply.

70. Geertz wrote that "a country's politics reflect the design of its culture." Geertz, *The Interpretation of Cultures,* 311. The culture supports political forces—groups of actors—that try to create a rule of law. Some actors seek a legal architecture that sustains and perpetuates the culture. Others, called reformers, revamp legal architectures in order to change the culture.

71. By 2003, the South Korean government's policies of low cost and high bandwidth had drawn about three-quarters of the population to broadband Internet, about three times the American penetration. "Korea Leads Broadband Horserace," McKinsey analysis. In the United States, meanwhile, the chairman of the Federal Communications Commission ridiculed the need for a "universal service" policy for broadband, comparing it to giving a Mercedes-Benz to everyone. The difference between a publicly shared road (broadband) and a private car (the movie or e-mail sent over the broadband connection) apparently was lost on him. He drove a BMW, by the way.

72. See Jonathan Weisman and Jim VandeHei, "Road Bill Reflects the Power of Pork," *Washington Post,* Aug. 11, 2005. As Thomas Bleha argued, the "United States is the only industrialized state without an explicit national policy for promoting broadband." Bleha, "Down to the Wire," *Foreign Affairs,* May–June 2005.

73. Basu argues, as a core theorem of law and economics, that "whatever behavior and outcomes in society are legally enforceable are also enforceable through social norms." He breaks it into two corollaries: (1) "what can be achieved through the law can, in principle, also be achieved without the law," and (2) "if a certain outcome is not an equilibrium of the economy, then no law can implement it." Basu, *Prelude to Political Economy,* 117 (italics omitted). To escape circularity and provide a blueprint for cultural reform, it is better to note that nothing is legally enforceable unless it is culturally acceptable. Legal architecture encourages certain cultural belief, but if prevailing culture does not accept a law, the society will change that law, either by formal action (repeal, reversal) or informal disregard (as of speed limits, for example). If the culture accepts a law, the economy will mirror that acceptance.

74. "Von Neumann Architecture," Wikipedia, at http://en.wikipedia.org/wiki/Von_Neumann_architecture.

75. Whether one acts out of reasoning, "gut feel," economic calculus, religious mandate, or an irresistible urge just to talk, by any such action every person contributes in some measure to the shaping of culture.

76. Roberto Guizeta, then CEO of Coca-Cola, said that technology permits people to manage complexity but leadership is required to manage change. Personal conversation, 1996. Harvard Business School professor Richard Tedlow makes a finer distinction: managers manage complexity and leaders make changes. Changes have effects; they are part of a sequence of cause and effect that alters possibilities. Personal conversation, 2005.

77. Otto von Bismarck, quoted in William Manchester, *The Last Lion: Winston Spencer Churchill, Visions of Glory* (New York: Little, Brown, 1983).

78. Some academics have argued that individual leadership was not an important cause of behavior. First, the concept of leadership was thought to be too vague. Second, organizations appeared to produce the same results without reference to any specific leaders. Joel M. Podolny, Rakesh Khurana, and Marya Lisl Hill-Popper, "Revisiting the Meaning of Leadership," in *Research in Organizational Behavior,* vol. 26, ed. Barry Staw and Roderick M. Kramer (Greenwich, Conn.: Elsevier/JAI Press, 2005). The derogation of individual ability to change the world suited the academy's abandonment of 1960s idealism. In the Golden 90s, however, the charismatic and successful leader made a return to consciousness, whether in the image of a very popular president or the numerous self-defined new entrepreneurs who changed culture. Not many people doubt the ability of leaders to persuade others and thereby create action and meaning; the academy is catching up to common sense.

79. "If we learn anything from the history of economic development, it is that culture makes all the difference." David S. Landes, *The Wealth and Poverty of Nations: Why Some Nations Are So Rich and Some So Poor* (New York: W. W. Norton, 1999), 516. This is culture "in the sense of the inner values and attitudes that guide a population." Ibid. More than 100 NASDAQ-listed technology companies started in Israel, none in Finland, even though both societies number about five million people, many of whom have very advanced training. McKinsey analysis. Luck cannot be the only explanation.

80. Do architectures create culture, only to have culture then produce architecture, so that a circular, unchanging system results? Legal architecture often seems to create a circular motion machine. But technology and leaders produce changes that alter culture's web of meaning, and sometimes changes in law also occur.

81. Reformers always seek a reliable equation of cause and effect. No matter how specific or punitive, laws do not produce predictable outcomes; results can be perversely contrary to intentions. Similarly, technologies have unforeseeable effects. Leaders may take decisive action but in retrospect have taken their people in the wrong direction. However, reformers will achieve

results over the long term if they change culture. Law, technology, and leadership will in the aggregate probably produce predictable changes in action and belief.

82. The fabricators of these architectures all can be described as entrepreneurs; see generally Paul Du Gay, ed., *Production of Culture/Cultures of Production* (London: Sage/Open University, 1997). But perhaps it would be more precise to think of them as individuals making decisions about law, technology, and historical actions that are intended to foster a culture of entrepreneurship. That culture will be manifested in high productivity gains and rapid turnover of goods and services.

83. Grove said, "What I had in mind is this. Technological advance is often controversial because it tends to upset the status quo, the balance of power. . . . Luddites . . . can impede the progress of technology . . . , but technology works around them and always prevails. Whatever is technologically possible, will happen." Vikas Kumar, "The Original Mr. Chip: The Andy Grove Interview," *Times News Network,* June 2, 2005, at http://economictimes.indiatimes.com/articleshow/1130750.cms.

84. Researchers in the United Kingdom have received a grant to develop human teeth from stem cells in 2005. The end of dentures would be welcomed by the old and produce unimaginable benefits for the young. See "Stem Cells Transplanted to Where Your Tooth Fell Out Will Soon Make a New Tooth for You," *Medical News Today,* May 4, 2004, available online at http://www.medicalnewstoday.com/printerfriendlynews.php?newsid=7922.

85. According to Nikolas Rose and Peter Miller, the "modes of government should . . . be analyzed in terms of their governmental technologies . . . through which authorities . . . give effect to governmental ambition." Rose and Miller, "Political Power Beyond the State: Problematics of Government," *British Journal of Sociology* 43, no. 2 (1992), 175. But technology is not easily captured by governmental authorities; it empowers the non-authorized as well.

86. Some argue that culture precedes law: Lawrence Friedman wrote that in the 1800s, "the law in action reflected the general culture; and that culture was a culture of enterprise, of growth, of progress." Lawrence M. Friedman, *Law in America: A Short History* (New York: Modern Library, 2002), 53. But then where does culture come from and who can change it? Some people want to change culture, others to preserve it, and both use law for their purposes.

87. Thomas Kuhn stressed the role of social convention—culture, if he would permit—in encouraging or limiting science. See Kuhn, *The Structure of Scientific Revolutions,* 2nd ed. (Chicago: University of Chicago Press, 1970). The combination of personal initiative and science is entrepreneurship, which culture might stimulate, honor, and welcome, or might disrespect and discourage.

"A . . . political culture might look at a PC and see it as the pinnacle of communitarian striving, the proud handiwork of noteworthy gross tons of government and private-sector collaboration. And when startups are viewed without rose- (or mica-) libertarian-tinted glasses, it's easy to see how most of them are *collectivist* enterprises." Paulina Borsook, *Cyberselfish: A Critical Romp Through the Terribly Libertarian Culture of High Tech* (New York: Public Affairs, 2000), 234. In other words, American culture decides how Americans interpret the power of technology; a different culture could apply the same technologies in totally different ways.

88. "Believing, with Max Weber, that man is an animal suspended in webs of significance he himself has spun, I take culture to be those webs, and the analysis of it to be . . . an interpretive one in search of meaning." Geertz, *The Interpretation of Cultures*, 5. "Culture is the fabric of meaning in terms of which human beings interpret their experience and guide their action; social structure is the form that action takes." Ibid., 145. "Culture provides the link between what men are intrinsically capable of becoming and what they actually, one by one, in fact become." Ibid., 52. Entrepreneurs are made in the context of culture. Individuals can be entrepreneurs only if their culture permits.

89. "Even if . . . there are fewer and fewer in the way of distinct and recognizable 'cultures' in the contemporary world . . . , the fundamental assumption that people are always trying to make sense of their lives, always weaving fabrics of meaning, however fragile and fragmentary, still holds." Sherry B. Ortner, ed., introduction to *The Fate of "Culture": Geertz and Beyond* (Berkeley: University of California Press, 1999), 9. "'Culture' . . . must be located and examined . . . [inter alia] as the grounds of agency and intentionality in ongoing social practice." Ibid., 11. In other words, culture provides purpose to people in their daily acts. It informs and includes their attempts to reform or resist reform of the architectures of culture.

90. Business school and other academic researchers have concluded over the last twenty years that "culture [is] the result of entrepreneurial activities by company founders, leaders of movements, institution builders, and social architects." Edgar H. Schein, *Organizational Culture and Leadership* (New York: Basic, 1973), xi. Leadership is separate from management and concerns "creating and changing culture." Ibid. Entrepreneurship emanates from culture. Culture is "the deeper level of *basic assumptions* and *beliefs* that are shared by members of an organization." Culture indeed is "*learned*" as a response to "a group's problems of *survival* in its external environment and its problems of *internal integration*." Ibid., 6. "Culture . . . is a *learned product of group experience* and is . . . to be found only where there is a definable group with a significant history." Ibid., 7. What is true for firms is also true for societies as large even as America.

91. Samuel Huntington calls America's "core culture" a cluster of "religious beliefs, social and political values, assumptions . . . , and . . . institutions." Samuel P. Huntington, *Who Are We? The Challenges to America's National Identity* (New York: Simon and Schuster, 2004), 18, 30. Institutions belong in the shaping category of architecture, but otherwise this definition of the shifty word "culture" will do. Huntington emphasizes in this cluster the "American Creed" with key elements that include, among others, "the rule of law, . . . the rights of individuals, . . . individualism, the work ethic, and the belief that humans have the ability and the duty to try to create a heaven on earth." Ibid., xvi. This creed is reified in entrepreneurship, and to the degree Huntington is right, entrepreneurship contributes to national security and power over international affairs.

92. In the early 1800s "Americans believed in their own inevitability. They separated religion from the state, but their confidence was based on a mystical faith in their chosenness." Madrick, *Why Economies Grow,* 186.

93. "Economic culture is defined as the beliefs, attitudes and values that bear on the economic activities of individuals, organizations, and other institutions." Michael E. Porter, "Attitudes, Values, Beliefs, and the Microeconomics of Prosperity," in *Culture Matters: How Values Shape Human Progress,* ed. Lawrence E. Harrison and Samuel P. Huntington (New York: Basic, 2000), 14. Porter summarizes "a whole series of supportive attitudes and values: [creation of new goods and services] is good, competition is good, accountability is good, high regulatory standards are good, investment in capabilities and technology is a necessity, employees are assets, membership in a cluster is a competitive advantage, collaboration with suppliers and customers is beneficial, connectivity and networks are essential, education and skills are essential to support more productive work, and wages should not rise unless productivity rises, among others." Ibid., 22. Most belong in the architecture of law; some of these "supportive" elements concern leadership acts (investment); and a few (connectivity and networks) are technological. The values of a "productive" culture are the values of entrepreneurship: a belief in progress, wealth creation, disruption, change, individual freedom, initiative, hard work, skepticism.

94. In *Collapse: How Societies Choose to Fail or Succeed* (New York: Viking Adult, 2004), Jared Diamond argued that when societies collapse they often do so quickly, for some or all of five reasons—environmental damage, climate change, changes in trade, new enemies, and the society's response. He seemed to mean that societies succeed or fail depending on how they react to change. See also Diamond, "The Ends of the World as We Know Them," *New York Times,* Jan. 1, 2005.

95. In the 1920s, Russian economist Nikolai Kondratiev observed in the world capitalist economy cycles or waves, fifty to sixty years in length, "consist[ing] of an alternation of periods of high sectoral growth with periods of slower growth." See "Kondratiev Wave," Wikipedia, at http://

en.wikipedia.org/wiki/Kondratiev_wave. The Industrial Revolution's material gain followed, roughly, Kondratiev waves of twenty-five years up, twenty-five years down, during which, according to Schumpeter, one set of economic "innovations" exhausts its profit potential, and a new set takes its place. Eric J. Hobsbawm, *The Age of Empire, 1875–1914* (New York: Vintage, 1989), 46–48. A similar pattern apparently fits the Third Industrial Revolution, as the information age perhaps will produce growth from about 1995 to 2020, after a period of downturn from 1970 to 1995. These patterns are not well proved, but the fundamental social change of growth puts every culture at risk. With economic growth, cultures do not clash; architectural change disrupts them from within.

96. "The key to prosperity in the 1990s was the interaction between entrepreneurs and political leaders in both parties who prevented the established interests from blocking new competitors." Paul A. London, *The Competition Solution: The Bipartisan Secret Behind American Prosperity* (Washington, D.C.: American Enterprise Institute Press, 2005), 173.

97. E-mail to Reed Hundt from Richard S. Tedlow, Harvard Business School Professor of Business History, Dec. 11, 2005. ("The history of American business during the past century and a quarter has been the history of the development of new products and services. American consumers have far more choices about how to spend their disposable dollars today than they did in the past. And that is good, because America is about choice.")

98. American economic history is "the most successful economic story ever." Brad DeLong's Semi-Daily Journal, "Econ 113 Opening Lecture Notes," Jan. 18, 2005, at http://www.j-bradford-delong.net/movable_type/2005-3_archives/000187.html. America was in 2004, at current exchange rates, six times as well off as the world average, three times as well off measured by purchasing power parity. Ibid. The United States was second in terms of competitiveness as of 2005, according to a World Economic Forum survey. See World Economic Forum, *Global Competitiveness Report, 2005–2006* (Geneva: World Economic Forum). But "the country's technological prowess is offset by [inter alia] concern regarding . . . public finances." Ibid., xv.

99. Porter, *Competitive Advantage of Nations*, xiii.

100. Ibid., 87.

101. From 1995 to 2000, the prices of domestic and international long distance and wireless dropped continuously, and the forward price of a 2002 contract for high-speed optical transport from New York to Los Angeles dropped more than 90 percent in less than four months in 2000. In the same time period telecommunications spending increased its share of gross domestic product (GDP) at a rate of about 4.3 percent per year, going from about 4 percent to about 6 percent, even while the overall size of the economy increased at nearly the same rate. McKinsey analysis. As prices dropped, consumers purchased so much more communications services

that the total volume and total revenue went up. The proliferation of start-ups and the advances in technology (architectural choices) contributed to this result. Government and business leaders embraced all this change.

102. The 1960s were "perhaps the first time . . . history and society were apt to be understood through the movements of its youth." Andrew O'Hagan, "Back in the US of A," review of *Magic Circles: The Beatles in Dream and History,* by Devin McKinney, *New York Review of Books* 51, no. 9 (May 17, 2004), 4, available online at http://www.nybooks.com/articles/17112. Just as the Beatles personified, and helped make, those movements in the 1960s, so Marc Andreessen, Steve Case, and thousands of other self-created technology businesspersons did in the 1990s.

103. They did not all come for pecuniary reasons. Jerry Yang of Yahoo! explained that "we created Yahoo as a hobby while students at Stanford—we never thought it would become a business. We did it for every reason other than making money. We did it because we loved it." Steven Ferry, "An Interview with the Chief Yahoo," *Visions,* Feb. 1999.

104. Elizabeth G. Chambers et al., "The War for Talent," *McKinsey Quarterly* 3 (1998), 44–57. See S. L. Bachman, "Silicon Valley Dons a Brave Face, Despite Worries," *Yale Global,* Apr. 28, 2004 (stating that in 1998, Chinese and Indians operated 25 percent of high-tech firms in the Bay Area); Juan Enriquez, *As the Future Catches You: How Genomics and Other Forces Are Changing Your Life, Work, Health and Wealth* (New York: Crown Business, 2001), 192 (noting the large number of immigrants in Silicon Valley, where, it is stated, one-third of all CEOs were Indian or Chinese). Others have noted the remarkable success of Indian immigrants in Silicon Valley. For example, Michael Lewis has discussed the creation of the Indian Institutes of Technology in the 1960s, which created a cadre of great technical talents who could also speak English; many of them went to Silicon Valley and benefited from the boom. Michael Lewis, *The New New Thing: A Silicon Valley Story* (New York: Penguin, 2000), 105–11.

105. Brad DeLong's Semi-Daily Journal, "Compensation Share," Jan. 22, 2004, at http://www.j-bradford-delong.net/movable_type/2004_archives/000099.html.

106. Entrepreneurship is not important because it equates to small firms and America should become a nation of shopkeepers. It is not a good goal for everyone to run a family business, especially if that business consists of selling goods and services made in some other country. Entrepreneurship is important because small firms pressure large firms to invest in new goods and services and because some few small firms can become very large, important firms.

107. "Opsware Inc.: On the Record: Marc Andreessen," *San Francisco Chronicle,* Dec. 7, 2003. See also John Micklethwait and Adrian Wooldridge, *A Future Perfect: The Challenge and Hidden Promise of Globalization* (New York: Crown Business, 2000), 210–12. According to Micklethwait

and Wooldridge, the entrepreneurial culture of Silicon Valley is characterized, in part, by a belief in meritocracy, a bias toward youth, an openness
to immigrants, a high tolerance for failure and "treachery," collaboration,
risk taking, reinvestment in companies, enthusiasm for change, and wealth-
sharing within companies. "The business of creating and foisting new technology that goes on in Silicon Valley is near the core of the American experience. . . . [The United States] is the capital of . . . material prosperity, of a
certain kind of energy, of certain kinds of freedom, and of transience," and
Silicon Valley "is distinctively us." Lewis, *The New New Thing,* xvi.

108. Clayton M. Christensen rightly argued that an "organization's structure
and the way its groups learn to work together can then affect the way it can
and cannot design new products." Christensen, *The Innovator's Dilemma*
(New York: HarperCollins, 2003), 34. He might have said that culture
affects entrepreneurship.

109. The IPO earned the company $140 million in cash, despite the fact that
the seventeen-month-old business had yet to earn a profit. See Anthony B.
Perkins, "Netscape? Wake Up and Smell the Java," *Wired Magazine* 3,
no. 11 (Nov. 1995).

110. PricewaterhouseCoopers et al., *Money Tree Survey: Q3 2005 Results,* available online at http://www.pwcmoneytree.com/exhibits/
05Q3MoneyTreeReport.pdf.

111. As Andreessen said, "In the startup world, you're either a genius or an
idiot. You're never just an ordinary guy trying to get through the day."
Personal interview, 2004.

112. The employment-to-population ratio was about 61 percent at the depths of
the 1991 recession and about 62 percent in 2004. It peaked at about 65
percent in the Golden 90s. Similarly the share of economy allocated to paying labor was at a low in 2004 that had been matched only in the 1966 recession. Corporate after-tax profits were 9.6 percent of GDP in 2004, the
highest level achieved since such records were first kept in 1947. Firms,
plainly, were succeeding from 2001 to 2004, while individuals by and large
were not. Brad DeLong's Semi-Daily Journal, "Levels and Rates of
Change, Jake, Levels and Rates of Change . . . ," June 23, 2004, at http://
www.j-bradford-delong.net/movable_type/2004_archives/001072.html.
    Between 1997 and 2001, worker share of American total income went
from about 64 percent to nearly 67 percent. Since total income itself grew
in this time period, the larger pie and larger share of the pie for workers
translated to long-denied income gains for nearly everyone. But in the early
2000s the workers' share declined to a degree that offset total income
growth. The pie got a little bigger but the workers' slice shrunk. As a result, except for the top 20 percent in income, the rest of the country's citizens made less money. Brad DeLong's Semi-Daily Journal, "Compensation
Share," Jan. 22, 2004, at http://www.j-bradford-delong.net/movable_type/
2004_archives/000099.html. That would continue to be true, in all likeli-

hood, unless one or both of two changes occurred: first, an increase in entrepreneurial activity drawing on high-wage skills and, second, a reallocation of income from corporations to employees.

113. The outcome would be worse if workers gave up on finding new work and withdrew from the fray. That was happening by the mid-00s. See Angry Bear Blogspot, "Is the Labor Market Strong or Weak?" June 3, 2005, at http://angrybear.blogspot.com/archives/2005_06_01_angrybear_archive .html, citing the Bureau of Labor Statistics.

114. See David Leonhardt, "U.S. Poverty Rate Was Up Last Year," *New York Times,* Aug. 31, 2005.

115. See generally Timothy J. Hatton and Jeffrey G. Williamson, *The Age of Mass Migration: Causes and Economic Impact* (New York: Oxford University Press, 1998), chap. 8.

116. In May 2005 Andy Grove, then Intel's chair, said that outsourcing was "going to bring competition on a scale and in areas that never existed before. . . . It's just a lot bigger than any of us can understand today." Vikas Kumar, "Outsourcing to Change Lives in India," *Times News Network,* June 2, 2005, at http://economictimes.indiatimes.com/articleshow/ 1129649.cms. He continued, "Outsourcing is the . . . relatively minor indication of a much longer, much more significant secular trend that's best described as a very large portion of the world joining the electronic community that has only existed in the US for all practical purposes. . . . The phenomenon . . . is the joining of a whole country and the educated workforce of that country into a global network of intellectual property generators." Vikas Kumar, "The Original Mr. Chip: The Andy Grove Interview," *Times News Network,* June 2, 2005, at http://economictimes.indiatimes .com/articleshow/1130750.cms. See also Carl Bialik, "Outsourcing Fears Help Inflate Some Numbers," *Wall Street Journal Online,* Aug. 26, 2005, at http://online.wsj.com/public/article_print/0,,SB112488992778121 8 01,00.html (statistics on outsourcing).

117. "If you can describe a job precisely . . . it's unlikely to survive. Either we'll program a computer to do it, or we'll teach a foreigner to do it," were the words of Frank Levy, MIT economist, quoted in the *Wall Street Journal.* David Wessel, "The Future of Jobs: New Ones Arise, Wage Gap Widens," *Wall Street Journal,* Apr. 2, 2004. Any job exists in the space around something that is incompletely known, like how to create electronic health records or cure cancer. In that area, people need to invent goods, services, and processes. All employees use some inventions, whether a shovel or a data center. As the inventions become more competent, the employee's role becomes mechanical, routinized, unvarying, low-paid, outsourced, and offshored. Ultimately, if the machine becomes perfectly skilled, no human needs hiring. All valuable jobs in the future of American work, then, must be entrepreneurial. They must involve unsolved problems and difficult tasks, where the human being does what the machine cannot.

118. For most Chinese, Indians, and other Asians to develop the skills to com-

pete against Western workers will take several decades, because the populations are so big and poor education is endemic. See Jagdish Bhagwati, Arvind Panagariya, and T. N. Srinivasan, "The Muddles Over Outsourcing," *Journal of Economic Perspective* 18, no. 4 (Fall 2004), 108. But for a significant number of Chinese and other Asians to compete for at least 30 percent of jobs in America will take only a few years. See Vivek Agrawal and Diana Farrell, "Who Wins in Offshoring," in "Special Edition: Global Directions," *McKinsey Quarterly* (2003), 37–41. Bhagwati, Panagariya, and Srinivasan argued, "The dynamic U.S. economy grows by a continuous infusion of new products and processes, which in turn offers a stream of new jobs." Bhagwati, Panagariya, and Srinivasan, "The Muddles Over Outsourcing," 31. But more jobs at higher wages in the future depend on whether the United States adds to its average levels of "technology, human capital, and physical capital, and [works] not too far from full employment." Ibid., 32. Their argument implied that American culture must be "dynamic"— meaning entrepreneurship based on scientific advance, new investment, and experimentation in new ways to make new goods and services.

119. McKinsey Global Institute, *The Emerging Global Labor Market: Part I— The Demand for Offshore Labor Talent in Services* (June 2005), 6–7, available online at http://www.mckinsey.com/mgi/reports/pdfs/ emergingglobalabormarket/Part1/MGI_demand_executivesummary.pdf.

120. See generally Martin Wolf, *Why Globalization Works* (New Haven: Yale University Press, 2004).

121. See generally Ralph E. Gomory and William J. Baumol, *Global Trade and Conflicting National Interests* (Cambridge, Mass.: MIT Press, 2000). From May 2004 to May 2005, spending on manufacturing in the United States rose by nearly 25 percent, although it remained far below the amounts spent in the best years of the Golden 90s. "Manufacturers Spend More on Plants," *Wall Street Journal,* July 5, 2005. The lesson was that manufacturing did not have to leave the United States completely, and in particular a more aggressive rule of law designed at encouraging domestic manufacture might produce some positive results.

122. Paul Samuelson, "Why Ricardo and Mill Rebut and Confirm Arguments of Mainstream Economists Supporting Globalization," *Journal of Economic Perspectives* (Summer 2004).

123. Indeed, in the first half of 2004, one-quarter of new hiring growth occurred in restaurants, temp agencies, and building services. Stephen Roach, "America's Job-Quality Trap," Morgan Stanley Web site, July 9, 2004, at http://www.morganstanley.com/GEFdata/digests/20040709-fri.html. These jobs would not increase wages in America.

CHAPTER 2: The Uprooting of American Business

1. In the 00s Western corporations began to adopt enterprise risk processes in order to cope with potential events—to bring surmise, speculation, and surprise into the realm of planning. See Committee of Sponsoring Organi-

zations of the Treadway Commission (COSO), *Enterprise Risk Management-Integrated Framework,* Executive Summary, Sept. 2004. Indeed, by early 2005 more than 90 percent of firms adopted some form of enterprise risk management as a way of doing business. Stephen Gates and Ellen Hexter, "Beyond Compliance: The Future of Risk Management," *Executive Action,* no. 132 (Jan. 2005), 1. A significant long term risk was whether a firm participating in global trade could survive without a major presence in Asian markets.

2. These three strategies can be called: "fight 'em, join 'em, and roll over."

3. The Japanese car companies became somewhat American to enter the United States in the 1980s. They succeeded in convincing many Americans that they were more desirable employers than their rivals, General Motors and Ford.

4. Industries in trade in 2002 paid wages nearly 60 percent higher than industries not in trade. They had much higher productivity, many more patents per employee, and they participated in many more markets. The obvious conclusion was that Americans would be better off if more worked in trade industries and if the country's firms competed in the maximum number of markets. See Michael E. Porter, "The Economic Performance of Regions," *Regional Studies* 37 (Aug./Oct. 2003), 560; see also Marc J. Melitz, "The Impact of Trade on Intra-Industry Reallocations and Aggregate Industry Productivity," CEPR Discussion Paper No. 3381, Centre for Policy Research, 2002–05, available online at http://econpapers.repec.org/paper/cprceprdp/3381.htm.

5. Kevin M. Murphy, Andrei Shleifer, and Robert W. Vishny, "Industrialization and the Big Push," *Journal of Political Economy* 97, no. 5 (Oct. 1989), 1003–36.

6. For a communications firm, the total number of customers on the network creates value for each customer. According to Metcalfe's law, the value equals the square of the number of customers. A large company can assure each new customer that he or she can contact all the existing customers. A small company's similar promise carries less value. All other things being equal, no customer will subscribe to a small company, unless for some reason (such as government intervention) the small company can connect a communication to the big company's customers. Unless the small company somehow shares the network effects enjoyed by the big company, the winner will take most of the customers.

7. Microelectronics contributed, for example, as much as 10 percent of the value of an automobile by 2003. The chip was everywhere.

8. Big winners tend to be very big winners; small firms tend to be forced into tiny niche and local markets. Indeed, the winners in the Chinese textiles and clothing markets were expected to win more than 50 percent of the global market by 2007. Mei Wong and Greg Hitt, "China Sets Export Duties on Textiles, Easing Tensions," *Wall Street Journal,* Dec. 14, 2004.

9. Where firms can obtain increasing returns as they increase market share, then one can predict that one firm will probably dominate the market, but no one can predict which one. The most efficient does not necessarily win. "History becomes all-important." W. Brian Arthur, *Increasing Returns and Path Dependency in the Economy* (Ann Arbor: University of Michigan, 1994), 27 (footnote omitted). History, as Arthur called it, includes decisions to invest before others do, decisions to cluster certain technological entrepreneurship in a particular geographic area, or even random chance. This pattern of history creates an architecture, in this book's terminology, because it opens some possibilities and forecloses others, creates some results and denies others.

10. In information industries, winners tend to amass the capital that gives them continued advantages against rivals in the future. For example, in 2004 Intel and Samsung each invested two to three times more capital than each of the firms in the second tier beneath these two global leaders.

11. Stanford engineers (Cisco is a shortened form of "San Francisco") founded the company in 1984. Cisco routers directed data packets from one computer to another and composed the essence of the Internet. See Steven Segaller, *Nerds 2.0.1: A Brief History of the Internet* (New York: TV Books, 1998), 244.

12. McKinsey analysis.

13. Thomas B. Edsall, "Labor's Divisions Widen as Membership Declines," *Washington Post*, Mar. 7, 2005. Unions claimed the communications industry as their most successful organization of labor. Until the breakup of AT&T in 1984, most jobs were unionized and pay was high. Since that date, the number of union workers in telephone and data services has fallen to half, in part because of technological advances and mergers within the telephone industry but also because the emerging Internet, cable, computing, and wireless industries were never organized. Particularly in technology industries, most workers will in the rest of the 00s feel on their own. Matt Richtel, "Unions Struggle as Communications Industry Shifts," *New York Times*, June 1, 2005. They might choose to fight for unionization but most will instead be more attracted by the ability to associate, share information, and come to agreement through Internet communication.

14. If all nations agreed to common global taxation with an international tax collector, they could tax corporations. No emerging nation would do that; it amounts to the relinquishment of national sovereignty from their perspective. Therefore nations can principally tax only that which it can keep within its borders: real property, income earned by its citizens domestically, and domestic consumption.

15. Executives want acceptance by every culture. They cannot act as ambassadors for the country of their origin. They must become citizens of the world, more than any nation, like tennis and soccer professionals, or entertainers. Michael Porter observed that a "firm must become part of the

culture, feel the local competitive pressure, and break completely into the network represented by the national cluster." Porter, *The Competitive Advantage of Nations* (New York: Free Press, 1990), 606 (footnote omitted). But a multinational firm has to become part of many national cultures. It must create a polyglot culture of its own and seek acceptance by every national or local culture where it lives, buys, or sells.

16. Andy Grove said in 2004 (in an interview with me), "The American treatment of the Asian challenge ranges from dismal to jingoistic with nothing in between. Will Americans face the fact that in some occupations winning consists of losing 10 percent of wages instead of 30 percent, 8 percent unemployment instead of 15 percent?"

17. In the 00s the United States argued that the World Bank should reduce loans in favor of direct grants. In practice, such a step would diminish the amount of money transferred through the World Bank to other nations and in turn spent on purchasing goods from American exporters.

18. If Latin Americans, Africans, and Asians could escape the poverty trap, they would consume products. American firms might sell those products, especially if their rich government ($2 trillion in annual federal spending) helped these new markets grow, but government leaders objected so vigorously to the methods of addressing poverty that they appeared not to care about alleviating the condition.

19. "The smaller a country is as compared to the rest of the world, the more it stands to gain from trade due to international economies of scale and the more it stands to lose via international diseconomies of scale." Elhanan Helpman and Paul R. Krugman, *Market Structure and Foreign Trade: Increasing Returns, Imperfect Competition, and the International Economy* (Cambridge, Mass.: MIT Press, 1987), 53. Given the shrinking size of its domestic market relative to the rest of the world, an American firm probably will lose in competition unless it wins in export or replants itself overseas. By comparison, in the Golden 90s the American market accounted for almost all global growth, so American firms rightly put their attention on their domestic market.

20. Horatio Alger's books sold over 20 million copies. See "Alger, Horatio," *Britannica Concise Encyclopedia* (2005), available online at http://concise .britannica.com/ebc/article-9005694.

21. As of 2004, more than 80 percent of American executives told a pollster that they would send more jobs overseas in the next year—more than double the percentage in 2002. Ken Brown, "Offshore Outsourcing Will Increase, Poll Finds," *Wall Street Journal,* Mar. 26, 2004. Similarly, IBM executives stated in mid-2003 that they needed to increase the firm's offshoring. No one expected offshored jobs to return. Steven Greenhouse, "I.B.M. Explores Shift of White-Collar Jobs Overseas," *New York Times,* July 22, 2003. Even if firms did not move job slots overseas, they sometimes moved job assignments, thereby avoiding hiring new employees in

the United States. See Louis Uchitelle, "New Reality Is Leaving Growth in the Mire," *New York Times,* July 20, 2003.

On the other hand, Jagdish Bhagwati, an effective pooh-pooher of offshoring worry, said that Craig Barrett, Intel's CEO, "exaggerated" when he said that Americans in technology faced global labor competition of unparalleled scale. Bhagwati said, "There is little evidence of a major push by American companies to set up research operations in the developing world." Jagdish Bhagwati, "Why Your Job Isn't Moving to Bangalore" (Op-Ed), *New York Times,* Feb. 14, 2004. In fact, that push was exactly what American companies needed to do over the next decade in order to compete in new markets.

22. In 1999, Chinese Premier Zhu Rongji, speaking at MIT, encouraged Chinese students to bring management and technological expertise back to their home country. David Sheff, *China Dawn: Culture and Conflict in China's Business Revolution* (New York: Harper Business, 2002), 91. Multinational companies obliged, using return-to-home programs to lower wages and provide skilled staff to their new facilities in China.

23. About 90 percent of foreign companies operating in China observe "virtually no enforcement" of intellectual property rights. American leaders assert that foreign companies lose about $50 billion a year in revenue they would be owed in China if intellectual property rights were enforced. "U.S. Business Groups Complain About Product Piracy in China," *Wall Street Journal,* Sept. 16, 2004. Indeed, in 2003, pirated software amounted to about 92 percent of all computer software installed in China. Jennifer Tan, "World Software Piracy Losses Double in 2003—Study," *Yahoo! India News: Technology,* July 7, 2004, at http://in.tech.yahoo.com/040707/137/2etsw.html.

24. See Patent and Trademark Office, "Frequently Asked Questions," at http://www.uspto.gov/main/faq/index.html.

25. The example of the U.S. government's anachronistic restrictions on the transfer of chip technology to China illustrates this point. The United States used legal architecture (an export ban) to keep American processing technology a head start over rivals in other countries. By contrast, Korea, Japan, and some cities in China try to confer competitive advantages on their citizens by providing them low-priced, high-speed access to the Internet. And almost all countries except the United States use public funds so as to lower the price and expand the penetration of brand new personal computers with the best of new chips. So instead of helping its citizens get smarter faster with new broadband services, the United States uses law to hamper the ability of its chip-making firms to invest in foreign markets. The United States has got its policy backwards: the law constrains the global activities of American firms while failing to support the competitiveness of American citizens.

26. In May 2003, *Harvard Business Review* editor-at-large Nicholas Carr, in a

widely read article, asserted that for American businesses "the IT buildout is much closer to its end than its beginning." Firms should spend less on information technology, follow others and avoid leadership, and worry about "vulnerabilities, not opportunities." Nicholas G. Carr, "IT Doesn't Matter," *Harvard Business Review* (May 2003), 10, 11. This discouraging commentary reflected and perhaps contributed to reduced investment in information technology by American firms. At the exact same time, on the other side of the world, many Asian companies and governments pursued the opposite strategy.

27. By itself, international trade, Paul Krugman taught in the early 1990s, does not produce productivity gains for Americans, and only productivity gains can in the long run increase the standard of living for Americans working within the borders of their own economy. Krugman, *Peddling Prosperity: Economic Sense and Nonsense in an Age of Diminished Expectations* (New York: W. W. Norton, 1994), 268.

    In the United States, net investment in the business sector in 2003 was 60 percent below the level of the boom's zenith in 2000. Stephen Roach, "The Day After Tomorrow," Morgan Stanley Web site, Nov. 1, 2004, at http://www.morganstanley.com/GEFdata/digests/20041101-mon .html#anchor0.

28. Ruy Teixeira, "The Myth of the Investor Class," *American Prospect* 14, no. 5 (May 1, 2003), available online at http://www.prospect.org/print/ V14/5/teixeira-r.html.

29. Firms with market capitalization greater than $500 million have lower cost of capital than those below that level. Robert S. McNish and Michael W. Palys, "Does Scale Matter to Capital Markets?" *McKinsey on Finance* 16 (Summer 2005), 23. For this reason also American firms will seek growth in rising markets, because faster-growing firms have greater market capitalization per dollar earned.

30. By the mid-00s directors of American firms began to study the health of their corporations in terms of market position, organization, and position in culture. Robert F. Felton and Pamela K. Fritz, "The View from the Boardroom," in "Special Edition: Value and Performance," *McKinsey Quarterly* (2005). Such inquiries focus on opportunities in China and rising Asia.

31. Garry Wills, *Exploring America: The Federalist* (New York: Penguin, 2001), 270 ("America has to be explained, historically, in terms of the Enlightenment, of the code of public virtue").

32. When a Chinese state-controlled oil company bid for ownership of an American oil company, many in the United States became alarmed that America might lose control of essential energy assets. Keith Bradsher, "China's Oil Setback: The Fallout," *New York Times,* Aug. 3, 2005. They should have worried instead that under the rules of shareholder democracy no American corporation should reject the transfer of any assets to Asian

buyers if the price is high enough. The voters in shareholder democracy after all are committed not to preserving American freedom or security but to maximizing wealth—and that is what the law says they should have as their purpose.

33. See "Excerpts from an Interview with John Kerry," *Wall Street Journal Online,* May 3, 2004, at http://online.wsj.com/article/SB108353849188699 786.html.

34. U.S. Census Bureau, "Miami-Dade Leads Nation in Percentage of Foreign-Born," *U.S. Department of Commerce News,* at http://www.census .gov/Press-Release/www/2003/cb03cn66.html; U.S. Office of Immigration Statistics, *Yearbook of Immigration Statistics, 2004,* at http://uscis .gov/graphics/shared/statistics/yearbook/YrBk04Im.htm.

35. McKinsey Global Institute estimated that the United States economy captured 78 percent of the value created by offshoring jobs. McKinsey Global Institute, *Offshoring: Is It a Win-Win Game?* (Aug. 2003), 13. That value included reduced costs for consumers, higher profits for companies, new revenues obtained by offshoring companies in the country they sent jobs to, and new work found by displaced American workers. Forrester Research predicted that about 3 percent of American jobs would be offshore by 2015, and according to McKinsey, American businesses would gain a 50 percent increase in profits from those job shifts. McKinsey Global Institute, *Offshoring,* 10. No wonder that American businesses wanted to shift jobs overseas. However, the additional value to the American economy might not go much or at all to employees' wages. Only 36 percent of displaced workers in one survey found jobs that matched or increased their wages. Ibid., 15. According to Paul Samuelson, it was "dead wrong" to say that "the gains of the American winners are big enough to more than compensate for the losers." Quoted in Steve Lohr, "An Elder Challenges Outsourcing's Orthodoxy," *New York Times,* Sept. 9, 2004 (internal quotation marks omitted). (Samuelson prescribed increased investment in science, research, and education. He presupposed that entrepreneurs would translate that investment into products sold in global markets.)

36. Only if full employment existed could free trade benefit American consumers as a whole. See Jeff Madrick, "Toward a Progressive View on Outsourcing," *The Nation,* Mar. 22, 2004, available online at http://www .thenation.com/doc/20040322/cavanagh/3 (citing economist Alan Blinder). Free education, greater incentives, surer safety net—learning, rewarding, and assuring—were necessary means to this end.

37. For example, by 2003, more than 70 percent of workers told a pollster that the government should prevent jobs from being offshored. K. A. Dixon, William M. Rodgers, and Carl E. Van Horn, "Laid Off: American Workers and Employers Assess a Volatile Labor Market," *Work Trends* 7, no. 1 (Apr. 2004). Many wondered, as Americans lost highly skilled jobs, "Can you keep going up the job chain?" William Daley, quoted in Bob Davis,

"Migration of Skilled Jobs Abroad Unsettles Global-Economy Fans," *Wall Street Journal,* Jan. 26, 2004. The Information Technology Association of America argued in 2004 that since outsourcing had transferred about 3 percent of technology jobs from the United States to other countries, it was only about half as big an issue as job loss attributed to the collapse of the stock market bubble. That was to be filed under "cold comfort." Rachel Konrad, "Study: Outsourcing Tech Jobs Helps the Economy," *Washington Post,* Mar. 29, 2004. Indeed, from 1999 to 2004, support for free trade from Americans making more than $100,000 a year dropped from 57 percent to 28 percent. Brad DeLong's Semi-Daily Journal, "American Mercantilism," June 25, 2004, at http://www.j-bradford-delong.net/movable_type/2004_archives/001084.html.

38. The theme of distrust of politicians was classically captured by Mark Twain in *The Gilded Age:* "'I think you are the best soul and the noblest I ever knew, Colonel Sellers! and if the people only knew you as I do . . . you would be in Congress.' [The Colonel] said gravely . . . 'Now I don't think there has ever been anything in my conduct that should make you feel justified in saying a thing like that.'" Mark Twain and Charles Dudley Warner, *The Gilded Age: A Tale of Today* (New York: Penguin, 2001), 370.

39. Measured by household income, from 1968 to 2001, the top 20 percent of Americans (in terms adjusted to reflect the value of the dollar in 2001) went from earning a mean of $81,000 a year to $146,000, a raise of 44 percent. By contrast, the income hike for the middle 20 percent was from $33,000 to $43,000, a 33 percent raise. In summary, 80 percent of Americans obtained a smaller slice of the growing national income pie. The top 20 percent obtained a larger slice from 1968 to 2001—specifically from a 43 percent share to a 50 percent share. U.S. Census Bureau, "Historical Income Tables: Income Inequality," at http://www.census.gov.

   Indeed, by the twenty-first century, a very wealthy class had grown into a global phenomenon. Wealth possessed by millionaires in the world amounted to nearly $30 trillion by 2004. Robert Frank, "Making Waves: New Luxury Goods Set Super-Wealthy Apart from Pack," *Wall Street Journal,* Dec. 20, 2004. In North America individuals with more than $30 million each purely in financial assets (that is, not counting real estate) controlled more than $3 trillion. Visible manifestations of such wealth included the rise in vacation-home prices in the locations favored by the very rich, such as Aspen and Palm Beach, and the tripling of the size of the luxury yacht market from 1997 to 2000. One of the leading yacht builders said that his customers liked the privacy and freedom that large boats granted their owners. In previous years, the American Dream had included the promise of privacy and freedom to everyone, not just yacht owners.

40. One of the fastest growing groups in America was college dropouts. As of 2000, men in their early forties without a four-year degree earned about $40,000 a year and those with such a degree made $65,000. About 75

percent of students enrolling in community college said they hoped to transfer to a four-year university; only about 17 percent did so within five years. David Leonhardt, "The College Dropout Boom," *New York Times,* May 24, 2005.

41. The Internet mitigated wage losses for many consumers by providing new benefits, not reflected in wages. See Tyler Cowen, *Marginal Revolution,* Apr. 14, 2005, at http://www.marginalrevolution.com. However, in part because the United States did not adopt any policies to subsidize Internet broadband access to people without a high ability to pay, these new technological benefits went disproportionately to more skilled workers. See Daron Acemoglu, "Technology and Inequality," *NBER Reporter* (Winter 2003), available online at http://www.nber.org/reporter/winter03/technology andinequality.html.

42. Only about a third of the millionaires' wealth came from compensation; at that level almost everyone was a capitalist investing in foreign markets, hedge funds, real estate that might never be visited, much less used. Only 30 percent made most financial decisions without an adviser. (Information technology enabled everyone in the United States to aggregate even very small amounts of money into large funds that advisers could guide into the astute diversification strategies that the millionaires use.)

43. These millionaires composed a country within a country, with a population almost as large as that of Italy. See Robert Frank, "Millionaire Ranks Hit New High," *Wall Street Journal,* May 25, 2005. They had their own cars, clothes, tutors, colleges, vacation destinations, doctors, lawyers, investment advisers, skin care products, food, and clubs. They exercised great political influence. By the oos, millionaires as a group accounted for perhaps 90 percent of political campaign funds and probably 10 percent of routine voters. As long as the rest of the population split on social issues like women's choice or affirmative action, millionaires might be the decisive swing block. No one could say if they would advocate policies that would be good for all citizens but expensive for them.

44. In the United States in the oos the middle class, as usually defined, shrank. The percentage of householders making between $25,000 and $75,000 (adjusted for inflation)—a range around the median of about $45,000 to $50,000—dropped between 1980 and 2003 from nearly 52 percent to just below 45 percent. Timothy Egan, "Economic Squeeze Plaguing Middle Class Families," *New York Times,* Aug. 28, 2004. The rungs in the country's income ladder were compressing at the bottom and stretching farther apart through the middle and at the top, so that climbing became harder for those who had the ambition to head upward. (Andy Grove deserves credit for the metaphor.) Indeed, Europeans at the bottom rung of the income ladder have a better chance of rising during their lifetime than those similarly situated in the United States. David Wessel, "As Rich-Poor Gap Widens in the U.S., Class Mobility Stalls," *Wall Street Journal,* May 13, 2005.

45. John Sargent, "An Overview of Past and Projected Employment Changes in the Professional IT Occuptions," *Computing Research News* 16, no. 3 (May 2004), available online at http://www.cra.org/CRN/articles/may04/sargent.html.

46. As a group of economists and other academics wrote in an open letter to the president, "The most commonly accepted measure of inequality [the Gini coefficient] . . . is far higher in the United States than in any other developed country and is continuing to move upward." Francis Aguilar et al., "Open Letter to President George W. Bush," Oct. 4, 2004, 2, available online at http://www.openlettertothepresident.org.

47. In the early 00s, nearly one in five American workers lost or changed their jobs. That meant nearly everyone in America had someone in their family or a next-door neighbor lose a job. Dixon, Rodgers, and Van Horn, "Laid Off." Silicon Valley, epicenter of boom and bust, lost 9 percent of its jobs from 2001 to 2002, amounting to more than half the job gains from 1998 to 2000. The high-siders of the Valley, however, hoped to find work in biomedicine; the Valley had the most biomedical companies of any city in the United States. Lawrence M. Fisher, "Job-Rich Silicon Valley Has Turned Fallow, Survey Finds," *New York Times,* Jan. 20, 2003.

48. Decreases in marginal income tax rates do not offer much benefit to those in the bottom half.

49. Robert Guy Matthews, "Recovery Bypasses Many Americans," *Wall Street Journal,* Aug. 31, 2005 (income fell for most in 2004); Carmen DeNavas-Walt, Bernadette D. Proctor, and Cheryl Hill Lee, *Income, Poverty, and Health Insurance Coverage in the United States: 2004* (Aug. 2005), 1, available online at http://www.census.gov/prod/2005pubs/p60-229.pdf (real median household income was unchanged between 2003 and 2004, but more were in poverty by 2004).

50. Among adults aged twenty-five to fifty-four, participation in the workforce in 2004 dropped to its lowest level since 1987. Approximately 66 million American adults were "not in the labor force" according to the Labor Department. Edmund L. Andrews, "A Growing Force of Nonworkers," *New York Times,* July 18, 2004.

51. The official poverty rate in 2004 in the United States was 12.7 percent, up from 12.5 percent in 2003. The number of Americans in poverty and the American poverty-rate percentage both increased every year from 2001. Both measurements declined every year from 1993 to 2000. See U.S. Census Bureau, "Poverty: 2004 Highlights," at http://www.census.gov/hhes/www/poverty/poverty04/pov04hi.html.

52. Gregg Easterbrook had made a career out of optimism—in *A Moment on the Earth* he claimed that environmentalists have changed the culture and the world is getting cleaner, and in *The Progress Paradox* he assembled a monumental grab bag of anecdotes showing that Americans (among some others) have a much better standard of living than in the past. See generally

Easterbrook, *A Moment on the Earth: The Coming Age of Environmental Optimism* (New York: Viking Adult, 1995); Easterbrook, *The Progress Paradox: How Life Gets Better While People Get Worse* (New York: Random House, 2003). Yet he concluded that the rich are not as happy as they ought to be. Worrying for the condition of the rich was in the 00s a deeply unnecessary task that engaged legions of politicians, lawyers, doctors, bankers, and writers. Yet none of the class jesters counseled entrepreneurship as a source of satisfaction.

53. In the 00s, America's political leaders and media commentators derided France for a host of alleged failings, including lack of entrepreneurship, no American Dream (!), laziness, arrogance, and an antidemocratic culture. These critics mocked the mirror. On the facts, the emerging class structure in the United States—power vested in the very rich, heavy taxation of the middle, scant ability to move up the ladder—resembled the stratified hierarchy of modern France. From 1970 to 2000, top incomes in France comprised primarily dividend incomes—the rich were "rentiers." In those decades, top American incomes were earned by working. But as Americans reduced the progressivity of income taxation and expanded the ability of the rich to preserve capital, the United States in the 00s created its own class of rentiers—more like a Kennebunkport than Texas style of governance. See Thomas Piketty and Emmanuel Saez, "Income Inequality in the United States, 1913–1998," *Quarterly Journal of Economics* (Feb. 2003), 37.

CHAPTER 3 : The Up and Down of Entrepreneurial Culture
in America

1. Thomas L. Friedman, "Learning from Lance" (Op-Ed), *New York Times,* July 27, 2005.

2. See Clyde Prestowitz, *Three Billion New Capitalists: The Great Shift of Wealth and Power to the East* (New York: Basic, 2005) (calling for a "broad competitiveness policy," 256, including legal measures directed at energy independence, increasing savings, taxing consumption, portable health care, wage insurance, higher pay for teachers, more subsidies for education, greater commitment to free trade, and improved physical infrastructure, 254–58).

3. Michael Lewis, *The New New Thing: A Silicon Valley Story* (New York: Penguin, 2000).

4. The argument is not that the nation needs an economic policy that selects particular sectors or particular jobs for favored treatment under the rule of law. Net job creation depends on specific circumstances of particular firms in individual markets: the phenomenon is idiosyncratic. See Steven J. Davis, John C. Haltiwanger, and Scott Schuh, *Job Creation and Destruction* (Cambridge, Mass.: MIT Press, 1996), 153–54. Policies aimed at saving certain kinds of jobs in certain firms, including the promotion of small

business generally, are not likely to produce good outcomes for the country. See ibid., 169 and generally 153–59 (chap. 7).

Indeed, skepticism should be directed even at favoritism for particular courses of study. As of the mid-oos individual choice of education and career paths appeared superior to other-directed centralized selection mechanisms. Individual firms appeared better able to choose what products to make and what markets in which to sell than any centralized system that might be imagined. Chaos and randomness played huge roles in personal and firm outcomes; stochastic and idiosyncratic explanations dominated. The argument here instead is in favor of embracing open markets for new entrants, open access to opportunity for both individuals and firms, and open use of public goods so as to minimize the advantages of incumbent firms and incumbent individuals in positions of power and wealth.

5. In U.S. manufacturing in the 1970s and 1980s, "shutdowns do not account for an unusually large fraction of job destruction during recessions, nor do startups account for an unusually large fraction of job creation during booms." Davis, Haltiwanger, and Schuh, *Job Creation and Destruction*, 34. Adding job creation and job destruction together with positive or negative job growth, the result is job reallocation: the number of job changes in a firm. Job reallocation studied by the authors exceeded 10 percent every year in virtually every manufacturing sector. Ibid., 37. This figure apparently may correlate to the number of firms started and ended annually. Both firm birth/death rate and job reallocation may be measurements of the entrepreneurship of an economy: the former tells us something about the rate of entrepreneurship among firms and the latter about the rate of career entrepreneurship among individuals.

6. "Large . . . firms account for most newly created (and newly destroyed) manufacturing jobs." Smaller firms create many jobs but also lose many. In addition, jobs at small employers and also low-paid jobs are not as durable as big employer jobs and well-paying jobs. Small business contributes much less to net job creation than commonly thought. See Davis, Haltiwanger, and Schuh, *Job Creation and Destruction*, 57, 81.

7. Brink Lindsey, "Job Losses and Trade: A Reality Check," Trade Briefing Paper No. 19, Cato Institute, Mar. 17, 2004, available online at http://www.freetrade.org/pubs/briefs/tbp-019es.html.

8. See generally U.S. Department of Labor, Bureau of Labor Statistics classifications, at http://stats.bls.gov/soc/socguide.htm.

9. According to surveys in early 2005 only half of U.S. workers were happy with their jobs, down from 59 percent in 1995. Adam Geller, "U.S. Workers More Dissatisfied with Jobs," *ABC News.com*, Feb. 28, 2005, at http://abcnews.go.com/Business/wireStory?id=538310. Larry Page, one of Google's co-founders, said in 2004 that "for 20 percent of your time, if you're working at Google, you can do what you think is the best thing to do." "Google Founders Keep 'Top 100' List of New Ideas," *Boston.com,*

Feb. 29, 2004, at http://www.boston.com/business/technology/articles/ 2004/02/29/google_founders_keep_top_100_list_of_new_ideas?mode =PF. Perhaps a good way to define the difference between working at Google and working at a nonentrepreneurial company is that at the latter, closer to 0 percent of one's time is self-directed. America in the future should aim to expand for everyone the ability to do "what you think is the best thing to do." Some individuals, including even Harvard MBAs, prefer to start their own businesses in order to exercise more control over their lives. Glenn Rifkin, "Reaching for Success but Not Too Much of It," *New York Times,* Sept. 1, 2005.

10. The argument here is not that start-up firms will be the source of new jobs and higher wages that offset job loss and income cuts at larger firms. That topic should be studied, but the probable conclusion is that most new net jobs and most wage increases in the future, as in the past, will be evidenced in big firms.

11. See NASDAQ, "Historical Data—NASDAQ-100 Index," at http://www .nasdaq.com/indexshares/historical_data.stm.

12. Homer, *The Odyssey,* trans. Robert Fagles (New York: Penguin, 1996), lines 1–2.

13. As one American technology businessperson working in Asia said in 2004: "An American firm has to be as Chinese as it possibly can be in order to survive. That is something that no one had to do in Japan. The United States in the 1980s was scared down to its toes about Japan, but Japan has one-half the population of the United States and one-half the GDP at the most. China has five times the population and it follows that it will have five times the GDP. It has a proactive government and a proud history. It was one-half the world economy in the 1600s and will be the same again eventually. My recommendation? My kids must learn Mandarin" (personal conversation). See also Tyler Cowen, *Creative Destruction: How Globalization Is Changing the World's Cultures* (Princeton, N.J.: Princeton University Press, 2002), 65 ("the cultural entities that survive tend to be large but to have complex and diverse inner workings").

14. See Modern Language Association, "MLA Language Map," at http:// www.mla.org/census_map.

15. Michael E. Porter, *The Competitive Advantage of Nations* (New York: Free Press, 1990), 6. A rising standard of living depends on labor and capital productivity. "The particular industry . . . is where competitive advantage is either won or lost." Ibid., xiii. A nation's firms may lose competitive advantage, and then the citizens of that nation might not experience a rising standard of living.

16. "Nations that are most successful in fostering entrepreneurship have consistently sustained growth and maintained low unemployment." Gene Sperling, *The Pro-Growth Progressive: An Economic Strategy for Shared Prosperity* (New York: Simon and Schuster, 2005), 86 (citation omitted).

17. See U.S. Census Bureau, "Statistics About Business Size (Including Small Businesses)," at http://www.census.gov/epcd/www/smallbus.html.

18. All quotations from and biographical data about Steve Case in this section come from a personal interview with the author in 2004.

19. Randy Komisar and Kent L. Lineback, *The Monk and the Riddle: The Education of a Silicon Valley Entrepreneur* (Boston: Harvard Business School Press, 2000).

20. According to Case, to be an entrepreneur, "you have to feel you have nothing to lose. Later in life you feel you have a lot to lose. You start getting the mentality of protecting what you have. You want to protect it so you aren't willing to roll the dice. If you have no money and no kids there's not much downside. It's hard for entrepreneurs to have second or third acts. You are less passionate. You are less likely to do it seven days a week, 24 hours a day. Not as likely to swing for the fences."

21. Personal conversation.

22. See Marshall McLuhan, *Understanding Media: The Extensions of Man* (Cambridge, Mass.: MIT Press, 2001), 7.

23. See David Held and Anthony G. McGrew, eds., *The Global Transformations Reader: An Introduction to the Globalization Debate* (Cambridge, Eng.: Polity Press, 2000), 3 (discussing how English became the Internet's lingua franca). See also Joseph S. Nye, Jr., *The Paradox of American Power: Why the World's Only Superpower Can't Go It Alone* (Oxford: Oxford University Press, 2000), 38 (because more Chinese are projected to be Internet users in the future, "many believe that in a decade or two, Chinese will be the dominant language of the Internet").

24. In *The Lexus and the Olive Tree,* journalist Tom Friedman criticized Silicon Valley entrepreneurs for failing to recognize the important role the U.S. government played in encouraging globalization, by which he meant, primarily, capitalism. Thomas L. Friedman, *The Lexus and the Olive Tree: Understanding Globalization* (New York: Farrar, Straus, Giroux, 1999), 134, 374. In his later *The World Is Flat,* he became more of a technological determinist, leaving national governments the role of providing Band-Aids for those hurt when the march of history destroyed their quality of life. Friedman, *The World Is Flat: A Brief History of the Twenty-first Century* (New York: Farrar, Straus, Giroux, 2005). Friedman's technological rapture ignored the essence of entrepreneurship—it comes from the people, not machines. It also ignored the real probability that technological programs will make some societies richer, stronger, and more dangerous to others. The culture he espoused in both books was a deracinated Monticello or year-round Davos. In it, winners in the genetic lottery excused themselves from responsibility for the global failure to redistribute wealth, stop war, or save the environment because their technologies, they presumed, in the long run would make everyone wealthy and democratic (with a very little "d").

25. John Perry Barlow, "A Declaration of the Independence of Cyberspace" (1996), at http://homes.eff.org/~barlow/Declaration-Final.html.

26. "Ira Magaziner Addresses Policy Conference," *Tech Law Journal*, May 12, 1998, at http://www.techlawjournal.com/internet/80512.htm.

27. Kaushik Basu described three types of norms: rationality-limiting (don't steal a wallet in a crowded bus because it is "simply not done"); preference-changing (a religion insists on not eating meat and eventually the adherent does not like meat); and equilibrium-selection (people drive on the right side of the road, even with no police around). Basu, *Prelude to Political Economy: A Study of the Social and Political Foundations of Economics* (Oxford: Oxford University Press, 2003), 72–73. Laws can merge into or come from norms. Ibid., 123. They have little force until identical to norms.

28. In order to serve a home with two high-definition television signals and another feed into a digital video recorder, an access network would have to provide almost twenty megabits per second. By 2008, entrepreneurs estimated, each household will require thirty to fifty megabits to meet reasonable expectations for demand from the Internet. However, no American government or business leader has a plan for connecting all households to such a high-speed network by that date.

29. According to AOL's policy director, George Vradenburg, other motivations for the merger included "taking the Internet to a new, higher level through digital media/entertainment, diversification of revenue streams to avoid impact of possible Microsoft pricing of MSN at zero, [and] timing advantages of robust valuation on AOL by Wall Street." E-mail from George Vradenburg to Reed Hundt, Nov. 8, 2005.

30. Andreessen said, "I grew up in Wisconsin and went to school in Illinois, and they just don't start companies out there. You just don't do it. . . . The culture is all wrong." David K. Allison, "Excerpts from an Oral History Interview with Marc Andreessen," Smithsonian Institution, June 1995, available online at http://americanhistory.si.edu/collections/comphist/ma1.html. Of course, thousands of companies started in the Midwest, but Silicon Valley funded and assembled technology start-ups at a unparalleled pace.

31. Andreessen gives much credit to Eric Bina, among others.

32. Personal conversation, 1994.

33. All quotations from and biographical data about Marc Andreessen in this section come from a personal interview with the author in 2004, unless otherwise noted.

34. For an interesting look at Jim Clark and his exploits, see Lewis, *The New New Thing*. For the text of the e-mail Clark sent to Andreessen, see Jim Clark with Owen Edwards, *Netscape Time: The Making of the Billion-Dollar Start-Up That Took on Microsoft* (New York: St. Martin's Press, 1999).

35. See "Remarks by the President and the Vice President to the People of

Knoxville," Knoxville, Tenn., Oct. 10, 1996, at http://www.ntia.doc.gov/
ntiahome/101096clinton.htm.

36. See generally Randall E. Stross, *eBoys: The True Story of the Six Tall Men
Who Backed eBay, Webvan, and Other Billion-Dollar Start-Ups* (New York:
Crown Business, 2000).

37. See generally James Marcus, *Amazonia: Five Years at the Epicenter of the
Dot.com Juggernaut* (New York: New Press, 2004); Robert Spector,
Amazon.com: Get Big Fast (New York: Collins, 2002).

38. National Venture Capital Association statistics, available online at http://
www.nvca.org/ffax.html.

39. See Technology Administration, "The National Medal of Technology
Recipients, 1985–2003," at http://www.technology.gov/medal/
Recipients.htm (Vinton G. Cerf and Robert E. Kahn, 1997).

40. On network effects, see Metcalfe's law (v equals n-squared where n is the
number of network users and v is the value of the network); "Metcalfe's
Law," Wikipedia, at http://en.wikipedia.org/wiki/Metcalfe's_law.

41. David S. Isenberg, "The Rise of the Stupid Network," *Computer Telephony*,
Aug. 1997, 16–26, available online at http://www.hyperorg.com/misc/
stupidnet.html.

42. "The signature trait of the boom was its from-the-ground-up quality. . . .
There had been a near-total collapse of the old financial order, in which a
person, if he wished to borrow money, must already have money." Michael
Lewis, *Next: The Future Just Happened* (New York: W. W. Norton, 2001),
55–56.

43. See Francisco de Goya's famous etching with the inscription "the sleep of
reason produces monsters," available online at http://www.metmuseum
.org/toah/ho/09/eusi/hod_18.64.43.htm.

44. In the mid-00s the United States continued to argue that ICANN, the Internet corporation for assigning names and numbers, set up by the United
States in 1998, would continue to run the addressing system of the Internet. It also insisted that the U.S. government control the servers that made
the system work. However, in time China and other Asian countries surely
would insist on some influence over these authorities. The sooner the
United States adopted a far-reaching policy of integrating the world's Internet communities, the better, but America's leadership had no such vision. See generally "Controlling the Internet," *Economist*, Nov. 18, 2004.

45. "Practical men, who believe themselves to be quite exempt from any intellectual influences, are usually the slaves of some defunct economist." John
Maynard Keynes, *General Theory*, quoted in Todd G. Buchholz, *New Ideas
from Dead Economists* (New York: Penguin, 1989), 219.

CHAPTER 4: Home Improvement

1. For this purpose, law includes constitutional provisions, treaties, statutes,
regulations, and procedures, whether these mandates create or deny rights;
tax or spend; affect local, national, or international issues.

2. See Steven Segaller, *Nerds 2.0.1: A Brief History of the Internet* (New York: TV Books, 1998); "Cisco Systems Fact Sheet," at http://newsroom.cisco .com/dlls/corpfact.html.

3. See Introduction, note 6.

4. In the early 00s Harvard, Yale, and most other top-ranked academic institutions announced plans to increase the size of their faculty and student bodies by significant amounts.

5. John Carey, "Flying High? Long the Innovation Leader, the US Now Has Serious Competition from Abroad," *Business Week,* Oct. 11, 2004.

6. It exceeded spending in South Korea by ten times.

7. Chinese and other Asian countries had advanced significantly in nanotechnology, energy efficiency, aerospace, and biotechnology, among other areas. Task Force on the Future of American Innovation, "The Knowledge Economy: Is the United States Losing Its Competitive Edge?" Feb. 16, 2005, 13–35, available online at http://www.futureofinnovation.org/PDF/ Benchmarks.pdf.

8. The federal government's investment in physical sciences, math, and engineering dropped from 0.25 percent of the GDP in 1970 to 0.16 percent of the GDP in 2003. Bill Roberts, "The End of Innovation?" *Electronic Business Online,* Oct. 1, 2004, at http://www.dlc.org/ndol_ci.cfm?kaid=140 &subid=293&contentid=252920. In November 2004, Congress repudiated a plan announced in 2002 to double the funding for the National Science Foundation and instead cut its budget. A physics professor who became a Republican congressman said, "I am astonished that we would make this decision at a time when other nations continue to surpass our students in math and science and consistently increase their funding of basic research." Robert Pear, "Congress Trims Money for Science Agency," *New York Times,* Nov. 30, 2004. From 1998 to 2003, Congress doubled the funding of the National Institutes of Health. Scientists opposing the NSF cuts explained that developing cures at NIH required in the long run more funding of basic research. Ibid.

   Private sector funding for life sciences went down between 1996 and 2004, suggesting that government spending might have displaced private spending. Federal support for research and development concentrated on military matters—44 percent went to missiles and aircraft. A sensible federal spending policy would lay the groundwork for industry's development spending by funding basic research in every field of actual and potential commerce. Linda R. Cohen and Roger G. Noll, "Is U.S. Science Policy at Risk?" *Brookings Review* 19, no. 1 (Winter 2001), 10–15. By the 00s, American firms had almost eliminated their previous support of basic research in order to emphasize work on projects that might produce commercial goods and services in less than two years. To maintain some cultural commitment to long-term invention, firms tried to maintain a commitment to creativity by sponsoring pep talks, tai chi classes, and meetings with people in unrelated disciplines. See Brian Bergstein, "IBM

Examines How Inventors Invent," *Red Orbit*, Sept. 27, 2003, at http://www.redorbit.com/modules/news/tools.php?tool=print&id=11110. Research, however, depended on funding professors and their projects.

9. Task Force on the Future of American Innovation, "The Knowledge Economy," 7. "Traditionally balkanized high-tech lobbying groups [were] remarkably unified . . . on the need to boost basic research funding at the federal level." Randy Barrett, "Banging the Drum for Basic Research," *National Journal Tech Daily*, Mar. 14, 2005.

10. Task Force on the Future of American Innovation, "The Knowledge Economy," 1. Asian universities in 2000 accounted for about 1.2 million science and engineering degrees, whereas North American universities awarded about 500,000. Ibid., 3. About 80 percent of global science and engineering students earned their doctorates outside the United States. Fewer Asian students chose to study in the United States, and even at the doctorate level, sought education in their home countries. Ibid., 5. (Some thought governments and businesses in other countries preferred stay-at-home students to those who had gone abroad.)

11. By the mid-00s, American citizens obtained a smaller percentage of U.S. patents than in previous years. Those granted had less importance economically or scientifically. See Erich E. Kunhardt, "Necessity as the Mother of Tenure" (Op-Ed), *New York Times*, Dec. 14, 2004. According to experts, as reported in the *New York Times* in 2004, "foreign advances in basic science now often rival or even exceed America's." William J. Broad, "U.S. Is Losing Its Dominance in the Sciences," *New York Times*, May 3, 2004.

12. Ed Frauenheim, "Brain Drain in Tech's Future?" *CNET News.com*, Aug. 6, 2004, at http://news.com.com/Brain+drain+in+techs+future%3F/2100-1008_3-5299249.html.

13. See Edward O. Wilson, *The Future of Life* (New York: Knopf, 2002).

14. Robert J. Gordon, "Technology and Economic Performance in the American Economy," CEPR Discussion Paper No. 3213, Centre for Policy Research, Feb. 2002, available online at http://papers.ssrn.com/sol3/papers.cfm?abstract_id=303760. In Gordon's words, "The fruits of innovation in telecom and biotech are both wondrous and partly unmeasured, and exactly the same could be said with even greater emphasis of all the great inventions dating back to the dawn of the first industrial revolution in the late 18th century." Ibid., 46.

15. Net job creation depends on specific circumstances of particular firms in individual markets: the phenomenon is idiosyncratic. See Steven J. Davis, John C. Haltiwanger, and Scott Schuh, *Job Creation and Destruction* (Cambridge, Mass.: MIT Press, 1996), 153–54. Policies aimed to saving certain kinds of jobs in certain firms, including the promotion of small business generally, are not likely to produce good outcomes for the country. See ibid., 169 and generally 153–59 (chap. 7).

16. In 2003, the Bush administration announced plans for manned space flight

to the moon. Irene Klotz, "NASA's Big Space Dreams Stumble on Cash Deficit," *Red Orbit,* Nov. 5, 2005, at http://www.redorbit.com/news/ space/295787/nasas_big_space_dreams_stumble_on_cash_deficit/index .html. On the importance of "better spending" on R&D, not just "more spending," see Gary McWilliams, "In R&D, Brains Beat Spending in Boosting Profit," *Wall Street Journal,* Oct. 11, 2005. McWilliams also notes that the benefits of R&D spending depend on firm culture.

17. Gene Sperling, *The Pro-Growth Progressive: An Economic Strategy for Shared Prosperity* (New York: Simon and Schuster, 2005), 74 ("workers [should] receive a 50 percent credit on all qualified education or training up to $15,000 per decade").

18. "U.S. Tops the World in School Spending but Not Test Scores," *USA Today,* Sept. 16, 2003 ("the United States spends more public and private money on education than other major countries").

19. The government eliminated all aid for many tens of thousands of students. Greg Winter, "Tens of Thousands Will Lose College Aid, Report Says," *New York Times,* July 18, 2003.

20. Although college enrollment is up, graduation is not up. Sperling, *The Pro-Growth Progressive,* 146.

21. Increasing college tuition contributed to a decreasing number of black students in colleges. Michael Dobbs, "Universities Record Drop in Black Admissions," *Washington Post,* Nov. 21, 2004.

22. Steve Lohr, "Microsoft, Amid Dwindling Interest, Talks Up Computing as a Career," *New York Times,* Mar. 1, 2004.

23. Laura Ascione, "Teachers' Tech Use on the Rise," *eSchool News,* Aug. 29, 2005, at http://www.eschoolnews.com/news/showStoryts.cfm?ArticleID =5835 (noting positive impact of technology on teaching).

24. The National Academy of Engineering in 2005 recommended more American investment in engineering research, better education from kindergarten on, and the creation of domestic "discover-innovation" institutes. National Academy of Engineering, *Assessing the Capacity of the U.S. Engineering Research Enterprise,* draft (Washington, D.C.: National Academies Press), 18–19.

25. In January 2005 Commerce Technology Undersecretary Phil Bond said, "We need to get better and faster in the way we create lifelong learners" because of "intense global competition." The Bush administration announced a plan to use technology more in education. However, the head of a consortium for school networking said, "Frankly, there is no money at the national level of leadership." Danielle Belopotosky, "Seven-Point Plan to Improve Educational Technology Released," *National Journal,* Jan. 17, 2005.

26. By 2005, Bill Gates's foundation had committed more than $2 billion to reforms in American education. Peggy Anderson, "Gates Foundation Puts $2.3B into Education," *ABC News.com,* May 15, 2005, at http://abcnews

.go.com/Business/wireStory?id=759251. In the 00s, wealthy Americans collectively had enough resources to pay for a national broadband network, a string of new schools for the whole country, or both. However, no leaders persuaded them to act together.

27. David M. Kennedy, *Freedom from Fear: The American People in Depression and War, 1929–1945* (New York: Oxford University Press, 1999), 184. Kennedy describes the efforts of the National Recovery Administration as "codes that amounted to nothing less than the cartelization of huge sectors of American industry under the government's auspices."

28. See Timothy F. Bresnahan, "The Economics of the Microsoft Case," Olin Working Paper No. 232, Stanford Law School, 2002, 2, available online at http://papers.ssrn.com/sol3/papers.cfm?abstract_id=304701. ("Schumpeterian competition typically combines elements of . . . three forces: divided technical leadership, epochal change and indirect entry.")

29. The alternative—a negotiated compromise involving an independent supervisor of a promise to disclose applications interfaces—would have enhanced competition in the mid-00s.

30. See *United States v. Microsoft Corp.*, 87 F. Supp. 2d 30 (D.D.C. 2000); *United States v. Microsoft Corp.*, 253 F.3d 34 (D.C. Cir. 2001) (en banc).

31. See *New York v. Microsoft Corp.*, 224 F. Supp. 2d 76 (D.D.C. 2002); see also *New York v. Microsoft Corp.*, 231 F. Supp. 2d 203 (D.D.C. 2002).

32. The Antitrust Modernization Commission, created by Congress in 2002, was chartered to overhaul competition policy in the United States. The commission was tilted, however, to lawyers and experts aligned with big companies. See Jonathan Krim, "A Less Public Path to Changes in Antitrust," *Washington Post*, May 12, 2005.

33. Andrew S. Grove, *Only the Paranoid Survive: How to Survive the Crisis Points That Challenge Every Company* (New York: Doubleday, 1999), 30 ("supercompetitive forces . . . ten times what it was just recently").

34. These assertions reflect the "essential facilities" doctrine. See *Aspen Skiing Co. v. Aspen Highlands Skiing Corp.*, 472 U.S. 585 (1985).

35. The illegal status of many Mexican workers blocks their progress up the American economic ladder. Anthony De Palma, "15 Years on the Bottom Rung," *New York Times*, May 26, 2005. These millions represented vast potential for entrepreneurship, as well as large contributions to tax receipts, if only politicians implemented a program for adding them to the legal workforce.

36. Jeffrey D. Sachs and Joaquin Vial, "Can Latin America Compete?" *Latin American Competitiveness Report, 2001–2002* (Geneva: World Economic Forum), 10, available online at http://www.cid.harvard.edu/cr/lacr _200102.html.

37. In spring 2005 the premier of China traveled to Bangalore to advocate that China and India "join hands together . . . to set a new trail in the IT business world." John Larkin, "Chinese Premier Seeks Closer Ties with India

to Lead in Technology," *Wall Street Journal*, Apr. 11, 2005. That should have alarmed American technological entrepreneurs. The huge population and rapid growth rate of India, as well as its commitment to liberty and the chaos of democracy in a multiparty, multiethnic state, beg the United States to create a permanent bond at least as tight as that between the United States and Great Britain in the twentieth century—for reasons that include the usefulness of such a relationship in negotiations with China over the future of humanity.

38. According to one research study, in developing countries, an increase of ten mobile phones for every hundred people increased national GDP growth by 0.6 percentage points. "Economics Focus: Calling Across the Divide," *Economist*, Mar. 12, 2005, 74.

39. Tyler Cowen, *Creative Destruction: How Globalization Is Changing the World's Cultures* (Princeton, N.J.: Princeton University Press, 2002) ("cross-cultural trade . . . liberates difference from the constraints of place").

40. As C. K. Prahalad and Allen Hammond wrote in September 2002, "Big, multinational companies [could] enter and invest in the world's poorest markets [and by] stimulating commerce and development at the bottom of the economic pyramid . . . could radically improve the lives of billions of people and help bring into being a more stable, less dangerous world." Prahalad and Hammond, "Serving the World's Poor, Profitably," *Harvard Business Review*, Sept. 2002, 4. The authors pointed out that the poor of the world, perhaps four billion people earning less than $2,000 a year, had large aggregate buying power, were willing to spend on consumer electronics (particularly cell phones and computers), and could even pay higher prices than middle-class consumers in developed countries. Ibid., 5. (In purchasing power parity, four billion people spend less than $2,000 a year, two billion between $2,000 and $20,000, and 100 million more than $100,000 a year. Ibid., 7.)

41. In 2004 worldwide PC shipments grew at nearly 12 percent. "Gartner Says Strong Mobile Sales Lift Worldwide PC Shipments to 12 Percent Growth in 2004," Gartner press release, Jan. 18, 2005, available online at http://www.gartner.com/press_releases/asset_117925_11.html. Because this rate exceeded global population growth by four times, in the fullness of time everyone in the world could expect to have a personal computer. The sooner the better for the United States, because as the site of the leading information sector of the economy in the 00s it would benefit from rapid increase in computerization.

42. China has adopted a similarly mercantilist strategy in Southeast Asia. China decided by the mid-00s to create a regional trading block at least as big as the American free-trade zone and the European Union market. The Chinese strategy created the risk that American firms would not be permitted to compete on the same terms in the Asian region. If large enough, that region could have great impact on the World Trade Organization, including

even the possibility of confining its reach to the West. In the late 1990s the United States traded admission to the WTO for a key to opening Chinese markets, but by the mid-oos the American inability to formulate an effective next step to free trade negotiations had permitted China to seize the initiative. Personal conversation with Charlene Barshefsky, Nov. 29, 2004.

43. Amy Chua argued that "the global spread of markets and democracy is a principal, aggravating cause of group hatred and ethnic violence throughout the non-Western world." Chua, *World on Fire: How Exporting Free Market Democracy Breeds Ethnic Hatred and Global Instability* (New York: Doubleday, 2003), 9. The rule of law includes markets and democracy, but, Chua argues, more important dimensions of law include wealth redistribution (267) and individual liberties (273). Chua identified the American Dream ("that anyone high or low can move up the economic ladder as long as they are talented, hardworking, entrepreneurial and not too unlucky," 196) as a cruel lesson to the "worse-off that their plight is the result . . . of their own deficiencies" (197). But Chua, like the Bush administration, omitted the Dream's complementary dimension that each generation should have, with exceptions only for those who did not seek work, a higher standard of living than its parents. That collectivist definition—we are all in it together—would appeal to the rest of the world.

44. Critics of global business argue that the growing power of corporations weakens nation-states and democracy. See, e.g., Noreena Hertz, *The Silent Takeover: Global Capitalism and the Death of Democracy* (New York: Free Press, 2001), 8. But governments should help their citizens start, and work for, firms that have that success. To that end, citizens should insist that their governments provide them with public goods and proper preparation.
    According to Tom Friedman, "The idea of America as the embodiment of the promise of freedom and democracy . . . is integral to how we think of ourselves, but it is no longer how a lot of others think of us." Friedman, "Love Our Technology, Love Us" (Op-Ed), *New York Times,* June 20, 2004. But perhaps the "others" value most in American culture the belief that Americans at any time could start a new business, get a new job, move somewhere new, take a chance, and bet confidently on future success. If that remained true, America could be "the embodiment of the promise of freedom and democracy."

45. Inequality of income has a negative impact on growth at all stages of development. Philippe Aghion and Jeffrey G. Williamson, *Growth, Inequality and Globalization: Theory, History, and Policy* (Cambridge: Cambridge University Press, 1998), 7. More "egalitarian distribution of wealth . . . will favor [disadvantaged people's] cooperation and thereby increase the level of output and the growth rate. . . . Excessive inequality . . . generates macroeconomic volatility." Ibid., 23.

46. Friedrich A. Hayek, a favorite thinker for conservatives, taught that wealth cannot be allocated in an egalitarian manner without destroying liberty and

ultimately breaking the wealth-creating machine of capitalism. See generally Hayek, *The Constitution of Liberty* (Chicago: University of Chicago
Press, 1978); and Hayek, *Law, Legislation, and Liberty, Volume 2: The
Mirage of Social Justice* (Chicago: University of Chicago Press, 1978). But
it did not follow that anyone had to be relegated to poverty in order to
assure liberty and wealth for the rest.

47. Ronald Coase said that the firm's size was a function of gathering information. If a big firm was ideal for assembling vast amounts of information
about price, consumer behavior, manufacturing processes and so forth,
then firms would be big. Quoted in Everett Ehrlich, "Q: What Will
Happen When a National Political Machine Can Fit on a Laptop? A: See
Below," *Washington Post*, Dec. 14, 2003. It followed, then, that as a result
of the advances of technology made vivid in the Golden 90s, small groups
could emulate big firms by using the power of networked computers to
gather information. In short, the Golden 90s should inaugurate the golden
age of entrepreneurship. The lesson is that if everyone in the United States
had cheap access to broadband, more entrepreneurial initiatives would
result.

48. In the twentieth century, law opened all communications networks to all
users. The telephone network, and the Internet itself, demonstrated four
kinds of openness: open to content, open to all other networks connecting
to it, open to all people, and open to all uses by other business. In the 00s,
however, the government, with the nod of the Supreme Court, repudiated
this approach for all networks. Under the new model—unlike that of any
country in the world—the U.S. government encouraged a few firms to
own communications networks and choose the degree of openness in ac-
cord with their best interests. Citizens and entrepreneurs will not be able to
look to government for solutions in the event the network owners discrimi-
nated against their content or use.

49. Chen Tianqiao, founder and chairman of Shanda, built a world-leading
company in the MMORG market (massive multiplayer online role-playing
games). Shanda in 2004 typically conducted online games with several hundred thousand concurrent users. The company anticipated doubling the
size of its user base about every six months. After all, said Chen Tianqiao's
colleague Gary Chang, "everyone lives a double life: one in the real world
and the other in a digital world." McKinsey analysis. It sometimes seems
that in the United States no one in the government lives in either world.

    The United States public and private sector could save more than $100
billion a year on health care costs if the government built a national
Internet-based clinical information network. Jon R. Duane and James
Kalamas, "The Case for Medical Data Online," *McKinsey Quarterly*, no. 1
(2005), 13. Such savings would more than pay for the cost of the network
within a matter of months.

50. To build global support for American values, the United States would ben-

efit more from global access to the Internet than from elections in emerging markets.

51. Information and communications firms generally contribute to the possibility of a "big push" in economic growth, principally because they help other
firms become more efficient in the making and distribution of their products. Kevin M. Murphy, Andrei Shleifer, and Robert W. Vishny, "Industrialization and the Big Push," *Journal of Political Economy* 97, no. 5 (Oct.
1989), 1023.

52. "Shiller Suggests Broad Plan to Reshape Social Security," *Wall Street Journal,* Aug. 1, 2003.

53. See "More Insurance," Eschaton Web site, Nov. 18, 2004, at http://atrios
.blogspot.com/2004_11_14_atrios_archive.html; see also Sperling, *The
Pro-Growth Progressive,* 193 ("what is needed is a Universal 401(k) system
for all Americans" [citation omitted]). "If the government is seen to sanc-
tion an uncertain environment where workers have no economic reliance,
an increasing number of people could decide that taking risks and investing
in training and education will still leave them vulnerable—stifling innovation and productivity in our economy." Ibid., 26.

54. By 2000, less than 10 percent of corporations believed that they owed a
commitment of job security to loyal and useful employees. As of 2003, employers still provided health care insurance to more than 60 percent of employees, but since only 2000, employers raised the price of that insurance
by 50 percent on average. And by 2003 only 20 percent of employees had
defined benefit plans for retirement. Peter G. Gosselin, "If America Is
Richer, Why Are Its Families So Much Less Secure?" *Los Angeles Times,*
Oct. 10, 2004. In order to avoid paying for the health care and other benefits owed new employees in America, firms asked existing employees to
work harder. Nearly two-thirds of American employees in 2004 said their
workload was increasing. Collectively their health suffered, according to
doctors. John Schwartz, "Always on Call and Anxious, Employees Pay with
Health," *New York Times,* Sept. 5, 2004. In a culture of entrepreneurship,
the right response to harsh work conditions would be to start or join a new
business; the wrong response would be to regulate employers more severely.

55. The argument for assuring economic security, then, is not based on fairness
or equity. It is not Rawlsian. It instead is about how to best achieve higher
economic growth.

56. As another step, government might extend the earned income tax credit by
creating a credit that employees would assign to any hiring employer. That
way the employers would have a greater incentive to hire, and to pay more
to new hires.

57. McKinsey analysis.

58. See Tyler Cowen, "How Does Sadness Affect Market Behavior?" *Marginal
Revolution,* Mar. 23, 2004, at http://www.marginalrevolution.com/
marginalrevolution/2004/03/index.html; see also Tyler Cowen, "Does

Money Make You Happier?" *Marginal Revolution,* Feb. 25, 2005, at
http://www.marginalrevolution.com/marginalrevolution/2005/02/
does_money_make.html (noting that happiness research showed by the 00s
that large negative changes produced substantial misery); "Mind Games:
Can Studying the Human Brain Revolutionise Economics?" *Economist,*
Jan. 13, 2005 (observing that people feel worse about disappointed expectations and happier about short-term benefits than they rationally should).

59. Cowen, "How Does Sadness Affect Market Behavior?"

60. Jack Kilby of Texas Instruments and Bob Noyce, then of Fairchild Semi-
conductor and later the co-founder of Intel, generally receive joint credit.
Their two companies litigated the intellectual property rights for many
years and resolved the matter by licensing the rights to each other. Leslie
Berlin, *The Man Behind the Microchip: Robert Noyce and the Invention of
Silicon Valley* (New York: Oxford University Press, 2005), 139–40.

61. Moore's Law is that the "complexity [of transistors on a silicon chip] for
minimum component cost . . . increase[s] at a rate of roughly a factor of
two per year." Gordon Moore, "Cramming More Components onto Integrated Circuits," *Electronics Magazine,* Apr. 19, 1965. Over the decades
since its 1956 promulgation, the "law"—which is a comment about technology, and not law—became an observation that a chip's performance
would double every eighteen months. Memory, hard drives, software, and
whole systems, however, do not adhere to Moore's Law. Moreover, the cost
of manufacturing chips at scale increases at a rate that may resemble the reciprocal of Moore's Law: that is, cost increasing every eighteen months to
two years. For this reason, some say only government-sponsored firms can
compete with industry leaders.

62. "Grove's Law"; see Chapter 1, note 83.

63. In 2003 researchers put artificial synapses on a silicon chip. "Spare Parts for
the Brain," *The Economist Technology Quarterly,* June 21, 2003, 22. The
possibilities for the chip have not nearly been exhausted. According to
Nathan Myhrvold, in the year 2010 computers will require thirty seconds
to perform a task that a 1970s computer would require a million years to
do. Frank Schirrmacher, "Wake-Up Call for Europe Tech," July 10, 2000,
available online at www.edge.org/3rd_culture/schirrmacher/schirrmacher
_index.html.

64. Robert E. Rubin and Jacob Weisberg, *In an Uncertain World: Tough
Choices from Wall Street to Washington* (New York: Random House, 2003),
71, 75.

65. Ibid., 99.

66. Energy research will head in unpredictable directions: solar arrays might be
placed in space; carbon dioxide could be scrubbed from the air and
processed into artificial gasoline; wind turbines could be built at sea.
Kenneth Chang, "As Earth Warms, the Hottest Issue Is Energy," *New
York Times,* Nov. 4, 2003.

67. Whether good fiscal-monetary policy can be good politics is a perennial question for elected officials. An emphasis on the culture of entrepreneurship, however, is intrinsically popular with most voters, because it aligns with the interests of citizens.

68. See generally Kai Bird and Martin J. Sherwin, *American Prometheus: The Triumph and Tragedy of J. Robert Oppenheimer* (New York: Knopf, 2005).

69. All quotations from Marc Andreessen in this section come from a personal interview with the author in 2004.

70. Personal interview with the author, 2004.

71. All quotations from and biographical data about John Doerr in this section come from a personal interview with the author in 2004.

72. That credence fueled his successful effort in 2004 to persuade California voters to spend $3 billion on stem cell research. "California Gives Go-Ahead to Stem Cell Research," *MSNBC.com*, Nov. 3, 2004, at http://www.msnbc.msn.com/id/6384390.

73. Personal conversation, 2004.

74. Trust, scientists discovered in 2005, is based on increased blood flow to a specific portion of the brain as trusting experiences occurred. Henry Fountain, "Study of Social Interactions Starts with a Test of Trust," *New York Times,* Apr. 1, 2005. Perhaps the zest for entrepreneurship was cultivated by cultural feedback that strengthened some part of the brain.

75. On global warming, see Steve Connor, "Global Warming: Past the Point of No Return," *The Independent,* Sept. 18, 2005. The Arctic's ice may all melt within a century. Even if carbon emissions were curtailed, in the future, entrepreneurs will need to convey all that H_2O to the world's deserts, shrinking seas, and disappearing aquifers. On global poverty, see Jeffrey D. Sachs, *The End of Poverty: Economic Possibilities for Our Time* (New York: Penguin, 2005). See also "Worldly Wealth," *Prospect Magazine,* July 2004, available online at http://www.prospect-magazine.co.uk/ArticleView.asp?link=yes&P_Article=12702. According to this article, "there may be political or social barriers to achieving a rich world. But there seems to be no insuperable physical or ecological reason why 9 billion people should not achieve something like the lifestyle of today's rich." Leading the world's population to this condition is within the power of America, as the world's hotbed of entrepreneurship.

76. Robert Reich called for "positive economic nationalism, in which each nation's citizens take primary responsibility for enhancing the capacities of their countrymen for full and productive lives, but who also work with other nations to ensure that these improvements do not come at others' expense." Reich, *The Work of Nations: Preparing Ourselves for Twenty-first-Century Capitalism* (New York: Knopf, 1991), 311. Reich's prescient book did not foretell the Golden 90s as much as it did the worried 00s.

77. Michael Porter argued against the backdrop of the Japanese challenge in the 1980s that "what is in many ways most necessary in the United States is a . . . return to some neglected historical values, of individual initiative,

education, competition, long-term investment, tough regulation, and free trade." Porter, *The Competitive Advantage of Nations* (New York: Free Press, 1990), 733. This, or any, American culture would have to compete for supremacy, because "dominant nations . . . export their culture and character to other nations." Ibid., 736.

78. Schein rightly states that "firms are created by entrepreneurs who have a vision of how the concerted effort of the right group of people can create a new product or service in the marketplace." Edgar H. Schein, *Organizational Culture and Leadership* (San Francisco: Jossey-Bass, 1991), 210. Those inclined toward entrepreneurship will more likely take a chance, more likely succeed, when part of a culture that encourages them. Legal reformers should focus on that cultural outcome. Jerry Yang said, "In truth, the entrepreneurial bug is probably in all of us and it's the environment that brings it out." Steven Ferry, "An Interview with the Chief Yahoo," *Visions,* Feb. 1999. What he called environment is what this book calls "culture."

CHAPTER 5 : America the Hopeful

1. Personal conversation, 2003.
2. Entrepreneurship perhaps cannot be taught, but entrepreneurs do learn how to convene.
3. David Hayden, "Leadership in the E-Commerce Revolution," speech presented at the World Bank Government Borrower's Forum, Rome, Apr. 20, 2000, available online at http://terrypearce.com/art-d-hayden-speech.htm.
4. Critical Path (what an aspirational name!) saw its stock rise to $116 a share by March 2000. "Ex-Critical Path Exec Gets Prison Time," *CNET News .com,* Sept. 11, 2002, at http://news.com.com/2100-1033-957592.html. With that stock, the company bought other companies in numbers that amounted to more than a billion dollars. See Carrie Kirby, *San Francisco Chronicle,* "Critical Condition: David Hayden Hopes to Revive Ailing Critical Path," Apr. 6, 2001.
5. F. Scott Fitzgerald, *The Great Gatsby* (New York: Collier, 1986), 182.
6. These possessions belonged to, respectively, Scott McNealy, Sun CEO (who allegedly played 300 rounds of golf a year and had a handicap of less than one); Larry Ellison, Oracle CEO; and Jim Clark. For information on Clark, see Michael E. Lewis, *The New New Thing: A Silicon Valley Story* (New York: Penguin, 2000).
7. According to Marty Kaplan, director of the foundation that Lear eventually created to further this end, Lear had met Hayden and "thought he was like-minded about patriotic themes and had deployable assets." Personal conversation, 2003.
8. Phil Hirschkorn, "Norman Lear Plans Traveling Show for U.S. Declaration of Independence," *CNN.com,* June 30, 2000, at http://archives.cnn.com/2000/STYLE/arts/06/30/declaration.02/.
9. Paul Berman, *A Tale of Two Utopias: The Political Journey of the Generation*

of 1968 (New York: W. W. Norton, 1997), 121 ("the main consequence of the '68 uprisings . . . was a new kind of individualism").

10. For the technical discussion of the seven laws, go to Cameron's Web site, www.identityblog.com.

11. See Kim Cameron's Identity Weblog, "What Is a Digital Identity?" Mar. 7, 2005, at http://www.identityblog.com/2005/03/07.html (italics omitted).

12. Lawrence Lessig has written that the "rough divide between the free and the controlled has now been erased. . . . We are less and less a free culture, more and more a permission culture." Lessig, *Free Culture: How Big Media Uses Technology and the Law to Lock Down Culture and Control Creativity* (New York: Penguin, 2004), 8. That is one of the results of the identity process of the physical world.

13. Orhan Parmuk, *Snow,* trans. Maureen Freely (New York: Knopf, 2004), 275 (internal quotation marks omitted).

14. Ben Feller, "90 Percent of Kids Use Computers," *Boston Globe,* Oct. 29, 2003.

15. John G. Palfrey, Jr., and John Henry Clippenger, "A Proposal for an Open P2P Browser/Platform for Digital Rule Making and Self-Governance," draft, Berkman Center for Internet and Society, Harvard Law School, June 21, 2004, 3.

16. Malcolm Gladwell argued that "the best way to understand . . . any number of the . . . mysterious changes that mark everyday life is to think of them as epidemics." Gladwell, *The Tipping Point: How Little Things Can Make a Big Difference* (Boston: Little, Brown, 2000), 7. Gladwell was tempted toward technological determinism as the explanation but ended by describing various forms of human action ("Connectors" and "Mavens" and "Salesmen," 265) as the causal agents of such cultural change. He was testifying for the architecture of leadership.

17. Everett Ehrlich, "Q: What Will Happen When a National Political Machine Can Fit on a Laptop? A: See Below," *Washington Post,* Dec. 14, 2003.

18. E-mail to Reed Hundt from Peter M. Shane, Jan. 16, 2005.

19. Yochai Benkler, "Freedom in the Commons: Towards a Political Economy of Information," *Duke Law Journal* 52 (2003), 1245, 1247 (discussing "nonmarket and decentralized production"). MIT Sloan School professor Eric Von Hippel contended that users on the edge of distribution networks play an active role in altering goods and services. Because of their activity, the producers alter their output to fit the modifications they observe. In effect, marketplace interactions set standards, not legal institutions. The power to alter legal, technological, and historical architectures shifts away from the stewards of the architectures themselves (judges, engineers, masters of historical events) to the people who are the advocates, believers, and critics of the culture that the architectures sustain. Informed and able people become the heroes of their own lives. See Von Hippel, "Innovation

by User Communities: Learning from Open Source Software," *MIT Sloan Management Review* (Summer 2001).

20. Mancur Olson, *The Logic of Collective Action: Public Goods and the Theory of Groups* (Cambridge, Mass.: Harvard University Press, 1971), 2, 15, 35 (italics omitted).

21. Yochai Benkler, *Coase's Penguin, or Linux and the Nature of the Firm,* abstract, *Yale Law Journal* 112 (2002), 369.

22. Moynihan quoted in Samuel P. Huntington, "Cultures Count," in *Culture Matters: How Values Shape Human Progress,* ed. Lawrence E. Harrison and Samuel P. Huntington (New York: Basic, 2000), xiv.

23. Benvenuto Cellini, *Autobiography,* trans. George Bull (London: Penguin, 1999), 264.

24. Henry Adams, *The Education of Henry Adams* (New York: Oxford World Classics, 1999), 414. ("No scheme could be suggested to the new American . . . but the next great influx of new forces seemed near at hand, and its style of education promised to be violently coercive. . . . Thus far, since five or ten thousand years, the mind has successfully reacted, and nothing yet proved that it would fail to react—but it would need to jump.")

INDEX

Academe: absence of debate in, 83–86; conservatives in, 84; financial concerns of, 85; foreign students in, 85; Internet underrated in, 72; patriotism lacking in, 85–86; professions and, 84–85; as unprepared for new technology, 76

Accountability, in government, 111, 113

Adams, Henry, 185n24

Africa, markets in, 100

All in the Family (TV), 118

Amazon.com, 66, 76, 78, 121

AMD, 37

American Creed, 152n91

American Dream, 1, 2; challenges to, 26, 55–56; as entrepreneurship, 9, 38, 47, 58–59, 76; of heaven on earth, 133; immigration and, 47–48; values in, 48; of wealth, 13

Andreessen, Marc, 31, 37, 65, 77, 116; and the browser, 71–76; on entrepreneurial leadership, 114

Antitrust law, 82, 95–98

AOL, 61–71; business model of, 67, 71; and changing architecture, 67–68, 70–71; creation of, 61–66; in foreign markets, 36; as leader in technology, 23, 95; merger with Time Warner, 71

Apple Computer, 43, 64, 71

Architectures: communication within, 33; creation of, 159n9; entrepreneurs of, 150n82; functions of, 8, 25–26, 82; group classifications in, 125; impact of, 31–34; remaking, 26, 29–32, 77–80, 89. *See also* Law; Leadership; Technology

Asia: consumers in, 18, 36, 100; entrepreneurship in, 19–20; immigrants from, 52; outsourcing jobs to, 5, 39; reform in, 58. *See also specific nations*

Assurance contracts, 130

AT&T: breakup of, 79, 159n13; cable companies acquired by, 78; market capitalization of, 37; monopoly of, 67, 79; phone lines of, 65, 73

Atari, 63

Auto industry: assembly line of, 108; competition in, 14–15; in Detroit, 44

Barksdale, Jim, 48

Barlow, John Perry, 69

Barrett, Craig, 48, 115

Basu, Kaushik, 171n27

Baumol, William, 39

Bell companies, 65, 68, 73, 74, 95

Bell Labs, 118

Benkler, Yochai, 130

Berlikom, 44

Berners-Lee, Tim, 31, 72

Bezos, Jeff, 76

Bhagwati, Jagdish, 161n21

Big Bang, 113

Bismarck, Otto von, 32

Blockbuster Video, 72

Blogging, 127

Bohr, Niels, 109

Bono, 132

Boolean algebra, 30

Brazil Telecom, 44

Brin, Serge, 90

Britain: decline from world dominance, 9; in global competition, 42; as a nation of shopkeepers, 60

British Telecom, 44

Broadband, 70–71, 103

Browsers, 65, 71–76

Bush, George W., 122, 123

Bush administration: antitrust law abandoned by, 82, 95–98; big business as beneficiary of, 86–87; as blind to global competition, 81–82; distrust of, 53, 83; and the economy, 38, 54; and education, 81, 94; and elections, 122; enemies of reform in, 80–83; entrepreneurship discouraged by, 82; and free trade, 99; group classification by, 124; income inequality increased in, 54–56, 82–83; lack of funding for programs in, 81, 82, 94; media as tool of, 128; pensions disappearing in, 82; political base of, 52; secrecy in, 83; and war on terror, 122–23

Business schools: competition for graduates of, 37; enrollments in, 93; limited contributions of, 84–85; U.S.-Chinese partnerships of, 24

Cable television: fiber optics in, 73; universal service policy in, 70

CAFTA (Central American Free Trade Agreement), 99

Cameron, Kim, 124, 125–26

Cantillon, Richard, 19

Capitalism: in China, 2, 12–13, 14; opening new markets to, 42, 170n24

Carnegie, Andrew, 38, 47, 48

Case, Steve, 61–67, 70–71, 76, 77, 114–15, 116

Cato Institute, 59

Cellini, Benvenuto, 132

Cell phones, 36

Central American Free Trade Agreement (CAFTA), 99

CERN, 72

Cervantes, Miguel de, 4

Chambers, John, 46

Chen Tianqiao, 179n49

Chile–United States Free Trade Agreement (2003), 99

China: ancient civilizations of, 12; business skills imported by, 23–24; capitalists in, 2, 12–13, 14; Communist Party in, 2, 13, 15–20, 24–25, 111; consumerism in, 14, 15, 17–18; developing world markets, 100–101; domestic markets in, 2, 12–13, 14, 17–18, 23; economic growth in, 16, 24–25, 26; education in, 3, 17; and energy sources, 162–63n32; engineers in, 4–5; entrepreneurship in, 2, 4, 9, 15–16, 19–20, 81, 143–44n44; environmental pollution in, 22; exports of, 14; foreign investment in, 12, 14, 18, 24; as foremost nation in new age, 10; free speech in, 142n37; in global competition,

1–3, 5, 9, 15, 23, 41–44, 58, 81–82, 123, 161n25; government control in, 2, 13–14, 143n38, 146–47n65; hiring in, 42, 60; intellectual property rights disregarded in, 3, 49; Internet's disruptive influence in, 13, 142–43n38; labor cost advantage in, 3, 15, 48; mercantilist strategy of, 177n42; middle class in, 4, 16–17, 18; new culture of, 25, 26; one–child policy in, 17, 26; outsourcing and off-shoring jobs to, 5, 15, 39, 42, 45; overseas communities of, 25; per capita income in, 16; political instability in, 13; population shifts in, 13; poverty in, 13, 16; privatization in, 16; standard of living in, 16–17; state-owned businesses in, 2, 16; superrich in, 13; technical education in, 3; technology in, 2, 14, 15, 16, 20–24, 25, 40, 143n38, 146–47n65; Third World markets for, 15; Tiananmen Square massacre (1989) in, 13, 19–20, 143n44; in transition period, 15–16; urbanization in, 17; violent history of, 12; wealth creation in, 2; Western influence on, 13; Western perceptions of, 11–15, 18–19
Chinese language, 59–60
Chip. See Integrated circuit
Chua, Amy, 178n43
Cisco Systems, Inc., 43, 46, 90
Citibank, 65
Clark, Jim, 72, 74–75
Clinton, Bill, 122, 123; centrism of, 124; on dissent in China, 139n15; and the economy, 34
Clinton administration: balanced budgets of, 3, 34; and culture of

entrepreneurship, 34–35, 124; end of, 53; and the Internet, 69, 77; liberal thinking in, 84
Codex (Leonardo), 119
Cold war: communism in, 15, 45; end of, 34; militarism of, 122–23, 124
Collaboration, 132, 133
Columbus, Christopher, 11
Communication of ideas, 117–33; in culture of entrepreneurship, 131–32; Declaration of Independence and, 118–22; and digital identity, 124–30; by generation of '68, 122–25; by group classification, 124–25; and group rights, 132–33; in groups of scale, 130–31; media in, 119–23, 128; militaristic, 122–23; power of ideas in, 65–66, 117–22
Communications: bankrupt companies in, 107; borderless, 45; Chinese government control of, 2, 13–14, 143n38, 146–47n65; competition in, 35, 86; ideas in (see Communication of ideas); and international law, 49; satellite, 79; technology of, 18, 35–36, 62–71, 179n48
Communist Party: in China, 2, 13, 15–20, 24–25, 111; in cold war, 15, 45; entrepreneurs as members of, 20; state corporatism of, 15–20; as workers' party, 20
Community: self-contained, 132; separateness from, 46
Competition: and antitrust law, 95–97; business strategy to meet, 3; in deregulated industries, 34; essential traits of, 28; expanding process of, 61, 78; global (see

Competition (continued)
Global competition); market share
increased in, 159n9; risk taking in,
28, 37; rule of law controlling,
102; in technology boom, 78–80,
109; within China, 2
CompuServe, 61, 64, 65
Computer architecture, 30–31
Computers: productivity gains via,
66, 116; telephone connections
of, 67–68
Confucian philosophy, 25
Congress, U.S.: and antitrust law, 98;
benefits to big business from, 86;
and Internet, 69; and labor unions,
44; and media conglomerates, 82;
and trade treaties, 52
Connectivity, 67, 79, 119
Consensus, building, 133
Consolidation, in Bush administration, 82, 95
Consumption: in Asia, 18, 36, 100;
in China, 14, 15, 17–18; global,
100; and standard of living, 13,
15, 16–17, 39, 48, 60, 101, 106;
in U.S., 14, 35, 42, 47
Control Video Corporation (CVC),
63, 64
Corning Glass Company, 73
Corporations: competition from start-
ups, 60, 78–80, 95, 102, 154n106;
employee benefits cut by, 106,
180n54; executive compensation
in, 53; executives as world citizens,
159–60n15; failure rates of, 107;
information gathering in, 179n47;
international focus of, 51–52,
178n44; Internet underrated by,
73–74; purposes of, 46; rising
profits of, 4; in social context, 87;
taxation and, 86

Corruption, and lack of accountability, 111, 113
Creative destruction: of market hierarchies, 40; 1990s culture of, 38;
and rule of law, 70; in Schumpeterian entrepreneurship, 6, 19,
33, 37; in start-ups, 7, 115; in
technology, 107, 115
Critical Path, 119, 121
Cultural Revolution, 16, 17
Culture: architectures in creation
of, 25–26, 29, 82; beliefs and
values in, 25; broad definition
of, 26; in competitive survival,
27–28, 64; as control mechanism,
26; corporate, 45–46; economic,
152n93; ideas as instruments
of change, 121; impact of local
businesses on, 44; international,
45–46; as learned product of
group experience, 151n90; role
of leadership in alteration of,
31–32, 58; and rule of law,
44–45, 150n86; as social convention, 150–51n87; transient, 45
Culture of entrepreneurship, 27–34;
architectures in formation of,
31–34, 58; creation of, 25; expansion of, 131–32; feeding on itself,
66; immigrants drawn to, 33–34;
leadership in, 77; 1990s golden
age of, 6, 38; quantum paths in,
109–10; risk taking in, 37, 109,
114–15; stock market crash and,
77–80; technological principles
applied to, 108–10; values in, 27,
143n43

Declaration of Independence, U.S.,
118–22
Del Toro, Benicio, 121

Democracy: direct, 129–30; factionalism in, 18, 53; U.S. as embodi-
ment of, 178n44; waning influ-
ence of, 101
Democratic Party: lack of ideas in,
81; and loss of jobs, 53
Deng Xiaoping, 13, 17, 26
Diamond, Jared, 152n94
Digital identity, 124–30; assurance
contracts in, 130; in groups of
scale, 130–31; political market for,
128–30; seven essential laws of,
122, 126–27; youth market for,
127
Diller, Barry, 74
Direct democracy, 129–30
Disney Company, 74
Distribution channels, disruption of,
78–79
Dobbs, Lou, 39
Doerr, John, 37–38, 77, 115–16
Dong, D. F., 145n58
Douglas, Michael, 121
Drudge, Matt, 132

Easterbrook, Gregg, 166–67n52
eBay, 75, 121; and changing architecture, 70; creation of, 76; e-mail
as springboard of, 66, 67, 79; as
leader in technology, 23
E-commerce business model, 75
Economic culture, 152n93
Economies of scale, 2, 14, 22, 42,
60, 78
Education: business focus on, 48;
business schools, 24, 37, 84–85,
93; charitable contributions for,
48; college dropouts, 164–65n40;
cooperative, 130; costs of, 81, 93,
94; culture of belief in, 92–93;
declining enrollments in, 91;

diminishing quality of, 55, 86;
of engineers, 37, 42, 91, 93; of
entrepreneurs, 24, 116; e-rate program in, 112–13; importance of,
92–95; of international students,
48, 85; of leaders, 111; lifelong
learning, 93; and national economy,
17, 53; of older populations, 50; in
other nations, 48; private funding
for, 175–76n126; public spending
on, 81, 94, 106, 173n8; technical,
3, 48; technology in, 112–13; unsound methods in, 94–95
Ehrlich, Everett, 129
"Eight Bigs," 14
Einstein, Albert, 109
Eisner, Michael, 74
Ellison, Larry, 38
E-mail: and AOL, 61–71; network
effects of, 79
Employees. *See* Workers
Energy law, 83
Energy research, 181n66
Engineering: in China, 4–5; education for, 37, 42, 91, 93; new elite
in, 54
Enron Corporation, 54, 85
Entrepreneurship: American Creed
in, 152n91; as American Dream, 9,
38, 47, 58–59, 76; in China, 2, 4,
9, 15–16, 19–20, 81, 143–44n44;
coining of word, 19; as coming
from the people, 170n24; competition in, 2, 5, 19, 36, 53, 54n106;
creative destruction via, 6, 7, 19,
33, 37, 38, 40, 70, 107, 115; culture of (*see* Culture of entrepreneurship); different meanings of,
19; economic growth through,
26, 50; education for, 24, 116;
as effect, 137n13; enhanced, 7;

Entrepreneurship (continued)
   individual identity in, 124; joint
   ownership in, 19, 109, 110; leaders in, 15–16, 110–16; 1990s
   golden age of, 6, 32, 34–38; in
   the Renaissance, 132; research and
   development as basis of, 90–92;
   and return on investment, 36, 42;
   risk taking in, 28, 37, 59, 64, 80,
   105, 109, 110–15, 116; rule of
   law changed to discourage, 82;
   rule of law to support, 35, 67–70;
   Schumpeterian, 6, 19, 33, 37;
   start-up (*see* Start-up businesses);
   in technology start-ups, 6, 30–31,
   35, 76 (*see also* Internet); theory
   of, 136n11; visionaries in, 116;
   and wealth creation, 25; in youth
   culture, 114
E-rate program, 112–13
Ethics, 9
European Community, 34
European Reconstruction Development Bank (ERDB), 47
European Union, research and development in, 91
Executives: compensation of, 53; as
   world citizens, 159–60n15
Export: and currency manipulation,
   14; and efficiencies in manufacturing, 14; of jobs (*see* Jobs); treaties
   to support, 81
Export-Import Bank, 47

Federal Communications Commission
   (FCC), 67–69, 82, 86, 95, 112
Federal Trade Commission (FTC), 95
Fiber optics, 49, 67, 73, 99
Filo, Dave, 75
Financial sector, in start-ups, 77
Ford, Henry, 38

Fox, 74
Franklin, Benjamin, 148n69
Free choice, restriction of, 125
Freedom, individual, 132
Free markets, 1, 45
Free trade, media support of, 52
Free trade agreements, 99
Friedman, Tom, 39, 170n24

Gates, Bill, 38, 48, 93, 115, 119
Gates Foundation, 175–76n26
Generation of '68, 122–25
Gibson, Mel, 121
Gingrich, Newt, 62
Gini coefficient, 166n46
Global competition: antitrust law
   and, 97–98; Bush administration
   and, 81–82; changes in law to
   meet, 3, 5, 24, 26, 29–30, 35,
   80–83, 89–107; Clinton administration and, 34–35; impact of,
   1–3, 5, 9–10, 14–15, 39, 41;
   in information technology, 3, 6,
   22–24, 36, 41–44; local costs and
   benefits vs., 46, 53; teamwork for,
   132; U.S.-China, 1–3, 5, 15, 23,
   41–44, 58, 81–82, 123, 161n25;
   U.S.-Japan, 3, 14–15, 123; U.S.
   relinquishing its leadership position in, 50; on wages, 53
Globalization, victims of, 52–53
Global markets, 2, 3, 15, 36, 40,
   41–44
Global output, and national productivity, 7
Global population, 9–10
Global warming, 182n75
Goldberg, Whoopi, 121
Gomory, Ralph, 39
Google, 23, 90, 116, 130
Gordon, Robert, 92

Gore, Al, 16, 38, 73, 77

Government: big business as beneficiary of, 82, 86–87; distrust of,
53, 83; fundamentalist Christians
in, 85–86; indifference to entrepreneurship in, 77; laissez-faire,
45; purchasing power of, 104;
secrecy in, 83; upper-income control of, 55; uprooting corruption
in, 111–13. See also Bush administration; Clinton administration

Government contracts, 86

Great Leap Forward, 16

Greenspan, Alan, 110–11, 113

Group classifications, 124, 125; and
collective good, 130–31; individual choice of, 132

Group definition, 125

Group rights, 125, 132–33

Grove, Andy, 33, 66, 97, 108, 109,
115

Grove's Law, 33

H1-B visa program, 37

Hanks, Tom, 66

Hayden, David, 119–22

Hayek, Friedrich A., 178–79n46

Health care, 38, 86, 105, 107, 131

Health insurance, 106

Hong Kong: business experiences
learned from, 25; democracy in, 18

Household income, falling, 4

Huawhei, 43–44

Hu Jintao, 14, 142n37

ICANN, 172n44

Ideas: communication of (see Communication of ideas); power of,
65–66, 117–22

Identity: digital, 124–30; search for,
123–24

Immigration, 33–34, 35; and American Dream, 47–48; business grievances about, 86; of Latin American
workers, 98–99; laws of, 52; political attention to, 52; reverse,
47–50; and technology, 37, 80,
154n104; wage competition from,
39, 53, 55

Imports: and balance of power, 47;
and competition, 20; of skilled
workers, 23–24, 37, 48; of technology, 21–22, 36

Income. See Wages

Income inequality: middle class and,
4, 38, 53–54, 123; in U.S., 4, 5,
38, 53–56, 82–83, 101, 106, 123

Increasing returns, 22

India: consumers in, 18; technological workers in, 80

Indian Institutes of Technology,
154n104

Industrial revolutions, 12, 27,
153n95

Information age, beginning of, 53

Information highway, 73–75, 103

Information technology: Chinese
market for, 14, 20–24, 25; global
competition in, 3, 6, 22–24, 36,
41–44; trends in, 6, 35, 59. See
also Internet

Insurance: against risk, 105; health,
106; livelihood, 105

Integrated circuit: in culture of entrepreneurship, 108–9; quantum
mechanics behind, 109; technology of, 108–9

Intel Corporation, 115; influence of,
44, 67; Israeli production facility
for, 21–22; as leader in technology, 23, 53; scholarships offered
by, 48

Intellectual property: Chinese disregard for rights of, 3, 49; international creation of, 49–50; and technological development, 36; in U.S., 3, 50

International Monetary Fund (IMF), 47

Internet: addressing system of, 172n44; and AOL, 61–71; and architecture of law, 29–30, 35, 62, 67–70; and architecture of technology, 130–32; assurance contracts on, 130; barriers lowered by, 13, 25, 67–68; browsers, 65, 71–76; business challenges of, 76; buying and selling via, 49, 118–22; children's use of, 127; collaboration on, 130–31; communication of ideas via, 65–66, 118–22, 123–33; digital identity via, 124–30; disinformation distributed on, 128, 137n1; as disruptive influence in China, 13, 142–43n38; educational uses of, 112–13; English as lingua franca of, 29; entrepreneurial development of, 6, 29; global distribution of, 36, 69, 128; individual identity sought via, 123–24; leaders of, 76–77; market-driven environment of, 69, 104; music on, 80; new culture created via, 9, 35, 128; open architecture of, 31, 67, 71, 95; as outside the rule of law, 69; politics conducted on, 128–30; public good of, 102–3, 130–31; social idealism of, 80, 126–33; as social network, 127–28; technological architecture of, 30–31, 132; universality of, 128, 131; Web sites on, 72

Interstate highway system, 102

Inventions, in technology, 113

Israel, technology imported by, 21–22

Japan: auto industry in, 14–15; competition from, 3, 14–15, 123; consumers in, 18; economic slump of, 3; efficiencies in manufacturing in, 14; exports of, 14; information technology in, 36; military protection for, 15; mom-and-pop stores in, 60; optical cables connecting U.S. and, 99

Jefferson, Thomas, 118, 148n69

Jiang Zemin, 14, 26

Jobs: creation of, 6–7, 27, 57–59, 61, 135–36n5, 174n15; entrepreneurial, 156n117; global competition for, 2, 21–22; loss of, 52–53, 54, 55; mobility in, 7; outsourcing and offshoring of, 5, 6, 15, 36, 39, 42, 45–47, 52

Judicial review, 18

Judiciary, right-wing ideology in, 84

Jupiter, 37

Justice Department, U.S., 95, 96–98

Kaplan, Marty, 118–21

Keynes, John Maynard, 83

Kilby, Jack, 108

Kingsbury Commitment, 67

Kissinger, Henry A., 12

Knight Ridder, 65

Kondratiev, Nikolai, 152–53n95

Kondratiev wave, 34, 37

Korea, in global competition, 42

Krugman, Paul, 162n27

Kuhn, Thomas, 150n87

Labor: costs of, 3, 15, 42, 48; global competition for, 1, 4–5; global differentials in, 21. See also Workers

Labor unions: corporate escape from, 44; and loss of jobs, 52–53; and rule of law, 44–45; and technology, 159n13

Laissez-faire government, 45

Latin America: consumers in, 100; ties to, 98–99

Law: absence of, 25; architecture of, 8, 25–26, 29–30, 49, 82; Bush administration direction of, 82–83, 86; buying, 83; changes in, to meet global competition, 3, 5, 24, 26, 29–30, 35, 80–83, 89–107; communications networks opened by, 179n48; and cost of public goods, 101–3; and culture, 44–45, 150n86; and economics, 148n73; effects on technology of, 33, 35, 62, 67–70, 124, 179n48; group classifications in, 125; of immigration, 52; importance of technology vs., 148n69; judicial review, 18; legislative process, 18; and political reform, 90; in restricting competition, 161n25; and risk reduction, 105; as source of freedom, 143n38; spending money to make money, 90–92; unforeseeable effects of, 149–50n81; upper-income influence on, 54–55; use of term, 172n1

Law schools, diminished role of, 84

Leadership: allocation of authority by, 112; architecture of, 8, 25–26, 31–32, 82; culture altered by, 31–32, 58; distrust of, 54, 56; elections of, 18; by entrepreneurs, 15–16, 110–16; future, 123–24, 133; in global competition, 23, 50; ideas as tool of, 118–22; illogical and unrealistic, 84; managing change via, 149n76; market, 28; open access to, 77; overwhelming challenges to, 111; reform in, 114–16; and risk taking, 110–14, 133; in technology fields, 77; training for, 111; uncertainty handled by, 40, 110–11, 133; unexpected sources of, 132; visionary, 116

Lear, Norman, 118–22

Lehrman, Lew, 120

Leonardo da Vinci, 119

Levin, Jerry, 71, 73

Lieberman, Joseph, 144n51

Linux, 31

Lip-Bu Tan, 19

Macintosh computer, 64

Magellan, 119

Maginot Line, 41

Malone, John, 73–74

Manufacturing, 14, 144n50, 168n5

Maoism, 25

Mao Zedong, death of, 2, 13

Markey, Ed, 66

Marxism, 26

MCI, 65, 73, 75

McKinsey & Company, 37, 140n24

McKinsey Global Institute, 39

McLuhan, Marshall, 66

Media: Chinese government control of, 2; communication of ideas via, 119–23, 128; conglomerates of, 82; and Internet, 72–76; mainstream views of, 52, 125; movies on demand, 73–74; universal service policy in, 70. *See also* Internet

Medicare and Medicaid, 50, 105

Mergers: and antitrust law, 96–97; and 10x change, 97

Microsoft Corporation: competition of, 31, 64, 75, 96; digital identity and, 124; in global markets, 43; Justice Department lawsuit against, 95, 96; as leader in technology, 23; market capitalization of, 36; new markets for, 78; in Seattle, 44; technology for its own sake in, 65
Middle class: in China, 4, 16–17, 18; and income inequality, 4, 38, 53–54, 123; shrinking, 165n44
Milken, Michael, 73
MMORG market, 179n49
Moore, Gordon, 108, 115
Moore's Law, 78, 100, 108, 110, 181n61
Morgan, J. P., 126
Mosaic, 72–73, 75
Moulitsas Zúniga, Markos (Daily Kos), 132

NAFTA (North American Free Trade Agreement), 99
Napoleon Bonaparte, 119
Napster, 80
Narrowband access, 70
NASDAQ-100 list, 59
National Medal of Technology, 77
National Recovery Administration (NRA), 95
National Science Foundation (NSF), 71
Natural resources, Chinese market for, 20
Netscape, 37, 75, 95, 116
Networked industries, 45–46, 95
Network effects, 22, 43, 64, 70
Neumann, John Von, 30
New Deal, 4, 95, 105
Nintendo, 74

Nixon, Richard M., 12
No Child Left Behind, 94
Norms, three types of, 171n27
North American Free Trade Agreement (NAFTA), 99
North Korea, U.S. concerns about, 15
Noyce, Robert, 108, 115

Offshoring: of jobs (see Jobs); of productivity, 50, 51–52; virtual benefits of, 52
Oil industry, 83
Oligopoly, 131
Olson, Mancur, 130
Omidyar, Pierre, 76
Open access, 31, 67–70, 71, 95
Oppenheimer, J. Robert, 113–14
Optical fiber technology, 49, 67, 73, 99
Outsourcing, of jobs. See Jobs

Page, Larry, 90
Palm Corporation, 37
Paramount Pictures, 74
Paranoia, tech-driven, 108–9
Parks, Rosa, 33
Patent system: taking the initiative in, 50; in U.S., 50, 91
Pearl Harbor, 3
Perlstein, Rick, 146n64
Pizza Hut, 62–63
Planck, Max, 109
Politics: decentralization in, 129; of the Internet, 129–30. See also Government
Polo, Marco, 11, 13
Population growth, 98–101
Porter, Michael, 35, 36, 60, 182–83n77
Postmodernism, 84, 125

Poverty: in China, 13, 16; in U.S., 4, 38; world, 47

Power, decentralization of, 130

Prestowitz, Clyde, 82

Privacy, invasion of, 126

Probabilities, 111, 133

Procter and Gamble, 62

Prodigy, 61, 64, 65

Productivity: broadband-driven, 103; computer-driven, 66, 116; offshoring and outsourcing, 50, 51–52; of U.S. workers, 7, 15, 36, 50, 92; and wages, 50

Prospect theory, 107

"Psychologist's fallacy," 143n39

Public goods, 50, 55, 101–3, 106, 131

Pudong, China, 20

Purchasing power, 17–18

Qualcomm, 36

Quantum mechanics, 109–10, 133

Rachleff, Andy, 116

Reagan, Ronald, 118

Real estate, lower prices sought in, 44

Redstone, Sumner, 72, 73

Reform: in Asian culture, 58; limited support for, 86–87; political, 90; three architectures of, 82; in U.S. leadership, 26–27, 80–83, 114–16

Regulations, avoidance of, 44

Reich, Robert, 182n76

Renaissance, 132

Republican Party: as opposed to entrepreneurship, 80, 82; political base of, 52, 53

Research and development: establishment in, 115; funding of, 34, 90–92; investment in, 90–92; location of, 49

Retirement, individual savings for, 106

Retirement pensions, 82, 105, 107

Ricardo, David, 16

Risk taking: in entrepreneurship, 28, 37, 59, 64, 80, 105, 109, 110–15, 116; insurance against, 105; leadership in, 110–14, 133; in start-ups, 37, 105–7, 109

Roosevelt, Franklin D., 95

Rostelcom, 44

Rubin, Robert, 110–11, 113

Ryan, Meg, 66

Ryder, Winona, 121

Safety net: Bush administration threats to, 82; government insurance as, 105–7; retirement pensions, 82, 105, 107; retirement savings, 106

Samuelson, Paul, 40

San Disk, 37

Satellite communications, 79

Say, Jean-Baptiste, 19

Schumpeter, Joseph, 19, 153n95

Schumpeterian entrepreneurship, 6, 19, 33, 37

Sen, Abhijit, 146n62

Seniority systems, 79–80

Sequoia, 75

Shanda, 179n49

Shane, Peter, 129

Shareholders: foreigners as, 51; goals of, 51, 163n32; increasing numbers of, 51; patriotism unknown to, 51–52; return on investment to, 36, 38, 51, 67; in start-up firms, 78; and stock market crash, 38, 53, 54, 77; value maximization for, 51

Shenzhen, China, 20

Shiller, Robert, 105
Silicon Graphics (SGI), 72
Silicon Valley, 37, 44, 61, 65, 77, 79
Skype, 130
Smith, Ray, 74
Social convention, role of, 150–51n87
Social Security, 50, 56, 105
Solow, Robert, 145n55
Sotheby's, 118–21
South Sea Bubble, 19
Soviet Union: in cold war, 45; collapse of, 34, 42, 46, 122
Spacey, Kevin, 121
Spanish language, 60
Spence, Jonathan, 14
Sperling, Gene, 106
Standard of living: in China, 16–17; improvements in, 106; in U.S., 13, 15, 39, 48, 60, 78, 101; worldwide, 101
Start-up businesses: basic research behind, 90; in China, 2; in competition with large, established firms, 60, 78–80, 95, 102, 154n106; in grass-roots politics, 129; investment in, 35; job creation in, 7, 58, 135–36n5; key assets for, 72; motivations for, 75; new markets created by, 7; partnerships in, 109; profitability of, 102; risk taking in, 37, 105–7, 109; uncertain paths of, 109, 110; value creation in, 61; venture capitalists and, 19, 37–38, 61, 74, 75, 77, 78, 79, 80, 90, 104, 115, 136n5
Stem cell research, 33
Stock market crash, 38, 53, 54, 77–80
Stock options, 36, 53
Sunnyvale, California, 37
Switched video network, 73

Taiping Rebellion (1850–64), 12
Taiwan: business experiences learned from, 25; democracy in, 18
Tariffs, 53
Taxation: benefiting big business, 86; benefiting upper-income population, 53, 55; of estates, 106; global, 159n14; and income inequality, 82–83; of international communications, 49; targets for, 105
Taxonomy, individual identities subsumed by, 125
TCI, 73
TechFaith, 145n58
Technology: architecture of, 8, 25–26, 30–31, 76, 82, 130–32; bankrupt companies in, 107; Chinese competition in, 3, 5, 40; Chinese government control of, 143n38, 146–47n65; Chinese market for, 2, 14, 15, 20–24; common standards in, 24; of communication, 18, 35–36, 62–71, 179n48; competition for skilled workers in, 37, 48; competition in production sparked by, 109; complexity managed via, 149n76; of computers, 30, 35; in culture of entrepreneurship, 108–10; decentralized, 129; digital identity in, 124–30 (see also Internet); in education, 112–13; effects of law on, 33, 35, 62, 67–70, 124, 179n48; entrepreneurship stimulated by, 76; global markets for, 36, 41–44, 161n25; importance of law vs., 148n69; and intellectual property, 3, 36; invention in, 28; labor unions displaced by, 159n13; leadership in, 77; Moore's Law in, 78,

100, 108, 110, 181n61; new product creation, 108–9; 1990s boom in, 77–80; rate of change in, 28, 59; in Silicon Valley, 37, 44, 61, 65, 77, 79; start-ups in, 6, 30–31, 35, 58, 76, 78–80, 115; unforeseeable effects of, 149–50n81; U.S. proprietary techniques in, 3

Telecommunications Act (1996), 69, 86, 112

Telephone service, 36–37; and AOL, 65, 67–68; cellular, 49, 70, 78; competition for, 68–69, 86; connectivity in, 67–68, 79; costs of, 153–54n101; fiber optics in, 73; international, 49; and Kingsbury Commitment, 67; universal service policy, 70, 95

Television: broadcast, 118, 122, 128, 131; cable, 70, 73; communication of ideas via, 121–22, 128; and group classifications, 125; interactive, 62; universal service policy in, 70

Think tanks, 84

Third World: markets in, 15, 100; ruling elites in, 58

Tian, Edward, 16

Tiananmen Square massacre (1989), 13, 19–20, 143n44

Time Warner, 62, 71, 73, 74, 95

Tocqueville, Alexis de, 147n66

Toffler, Alvin, 62

Tonkin Gulf, 3

Transistor, development of, 118

Treaties: and antitrust policy, 97–98; rejected by Bush administration, 81; trade, 52, 81, 99

Trust, 182n74

Twain, Mark, 164n38

Uncertainty: leadership and, 40, 110–11, 133; in quantum paths, 109–10, 133

United Nations Millennium Goal, 47

United States: agrarian interests voted in, 52; balanced budget in, 3, 34; China in competition with, 1–3, 5, 15, 23, 41–44, 58, 81–82, 123, 161n25; consumer markets in, 14, 35, 42, 47; corporate profits in, 4; culture of entrepreneurship in, 28–34; debt of, 47; domestic markets of, 46; economic slowdown in, 50; fiscal and monetary policy in, 110–11; foreign investments by, 12; foreign investments in, 34–35, 50; in global competition, 1–3, 14–15, 47; government inattention to business in, 47; imports of, 47; income inequality in, 4, 5, 38, 53–56, 82–83, 101, 106, 123; international image of, 178n44, 179–80n50; job creation in, 6, 57–59, 61; middle class in, 4, 53–54, 82–83, 123; political center absent in, 122–23; population growth in, 98–101; poverty in, 4, 38; presidential elections in, 121–22; productivity of, 7, 15, 36, 50, 92; reform needed in, 26–27, 80–83, 114–16; shrinking market of, 47; slow-growing market in, 42; social problems in, 39; standard of living in, 13, 15, 39, 48, 60, 78, 101; stock market crash in, 38, 53, 54, 77–80; technology in, 23, 35; waning influence of, 47, 101; in war on terror, 46–47, 53, 122–23